Maine

Charles C. Calhoun
Photography by Thomas Mark Szelog

COMPASS AMERICAN GUIDES
An Imprint of Fodor's Travel Publications, Inc.

Maine

Copyright © 1994 Fodor's Travel Publications, Inc.
Maps Copyright © 1994 Fodor's Travel Publications, Inc.

LIBRARY OF CONGRESS CATALOGING-IN-PUBLICATION DATA
Calhoun, Charles C.
Maine/Charles C. Calhoun: photography by Thomas Mark Szelog.
   p.   cm. —(Compass American Guides)
   Includes bibliographical references and index
   ISBN 1-878867-52-0 (hard) $24.95; ISBN 1-878867-51-2 (paper) $16.95
   1. Maine—Guidebooks. I. Title II. Series: Compass American Guides (Series)
F17.3.C34   1994   93-49545
917.4104'43—dc20   CIP

Editors: Julia Dillon, Barry Parr

Managing Editor: Kit Duane
Photo Editor: Christopher Burt

Designers: Christopher Burt,
Candace Compton-Pappas
Map Design: Eureka Cartography

Compass American Guides, Inc., 6051 Margarido Drive, Oakland, CA 94618
Production House: Twin Age Ltd., Hong Kong   Printed in China
10 9 8 7 6 5 4 3 2 1

The Publisher gratefully acknowledges the following institutions and individuals for the use of their photographs and/or illustrations on the following pages: Abbe Museum, Bar Harbor, pp. 164, 165; Abbie Sewall, for permission to use photographs by Emma D. Sewall, pp. 19, 22, 36, 44, 73, 129, 190; Bowdoin College Museum of Art, gift of Mr. Harold L. Berry, p. 94; Brian Vanden Brink, pp. 24, 39, 42, 53, 61, 70, 71, 103, 119, 126, 127, 131, 138, 160, 192, 216, 217; The Claremont Hotel, p. 169; Colby College Museum of Art, Waterville, pp. 28, 49, 115, 120, 122, 123, 177; Concord Free Public Library, p. 223; Farnsworth Art Museum, Rockland, pp. 25, 56, 66, 107, 134, 148-149, 219, 235, 254-255; L. L. Bean Co., p. 85; Library of Congress, pp. 59, 63, 72, 92, 96, 100, 161; Maine Maritime Museum, Bath, p. 110-111; Maine State Museum, p. 118; Musee d'Orsay, Art Resource, p. 60; Nordica Museum, Farmington, p. 205; The Peary-MacMillan Arctic Museum, Bowdoin College, p. 93; Thomaston Historical Society, pp. 132, 133; Underwood Photo Archives, pp. 183, 201; The Wilhelm Reich Museum, p. 197.

Many thanks to: Rebecca Cole-Will at Abbe Museum for her piece on Maine's Paleo-Indians; John Fuhrman for his piece on fishing in Maine; John McChesney for his piece on Thomaston Pond; Jessica Fisher for the index; reader William Jordan; and artist Candace Compton-Pappas.

*To the Estys: Don and Mae, Bob and Karen, Kristen and Laura,
and in memory of Donald — C. C.*

*To my wife, Lee Ann Szelog,
the heart and inspiration of these photographs — T. M. S.*

ACKNOWLEDGMENTS

If I have succeeded in conveying Maine's true spirit, it is due to the help and encouragement of people too numerous to name here. But there are several who contributed so directly to this book, let me try to list them: Mark Cutler (who introduced me to Maine and who has been a source of trenchant commentary on the place ever since), Jason Moore, Ruth Peck, Sally W. Rand, the Esty family of the dedication, Vicki Bonebakker and the Maine Collaborative, and the staff of Hawthorne-Longfellow Library at Bowdoin College, especially Judy Montgomery. I am also grateful to the staff of the Maine Humanities Council, the Maine Historical Society, the Portland Room of the Portland Public Library, the Pejepscot Historical Society in Brunswick, the Maine State Library, and Curtis Memorial Library in Brunswick.

Professor William B. Jordan Jr. of Westbrook College vetted the text for historical accuracy with his accustomed skill and good humor, and any errors that remain are, alas, mine. It was a special pleasure to work with editors as patient, knowledgeable, and imaginative as Julia Dillon and Kit Duane at Compass American Guides.

C O N T E N T S

Maps

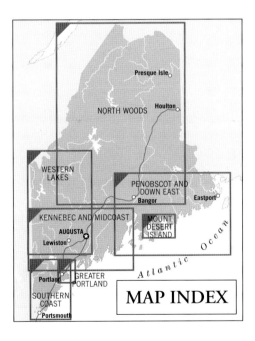

FACTS ABOUT MAINE

The Pine Tree State

CAPITAL: Augusta
STATE FLOWER: White Pine Cone and Tassel

Chickadee

White Pine Cone

STATE BIRD: Chickadee
STATE TREE: Eastern White Pine
ENTERED UNION: March 15, 1820
STATE ANIMAL: Moose

POPULATION (1991): 1,234,602

White	98.4%
Black	.4%
Hispanic*	.6%
Asian/Pacific	.5%
American Indian	.4%

*Population of Hispanic origin is an ethnic grouping and not additive to the population racial groupings.

FIVE LARGEST CITIES:

Portland (metro)	152,478
Lewiston	39,757
Bangor	33,181
Biddeford	21,900
Augusta	21,400

Moose

*E*astern White Pine

ECONOMY:

Principal industries:
manufacturing, services, trade,
government, finance, insurance,
real estate, construction

Principal manufactured goods:
paper and wood products,
leather products

International airports at:
Portland, Bangor

Per capita income (1991): $17,306

Sales Tax: 6%

GEOGRAPHY:

Size: 33,265 sq. miles

Highest point: 5,267 feet Mount Katahdin, Piscataquis County

Lowest point: Atlantic Ocean sea level

CLIMATE:

Highest temperature recorded: 107°F (42°C) at North Bridgton on July 10, 1911

Lowest temperature recorded: -48°F (-42°C) at Van Buren on January 19, 1925

Wettest Place:
50.68 inches annual rainfall at Bar Harbor in Hancock County

Driest Place:
32.72 inches annual rainfall at Upper Dam in Oxford County

FAMOUS MAINERS:

L. L. Bean ♦ Joan Benoit ♦ James G. Blaine ♦ Stephen King
Hannibal Hamlin ♦ Marsden Hartley ♦ Henry Wadsworth Longfellow
Edna St. Vincent Millay ♦ Kate Douglas Wiggin

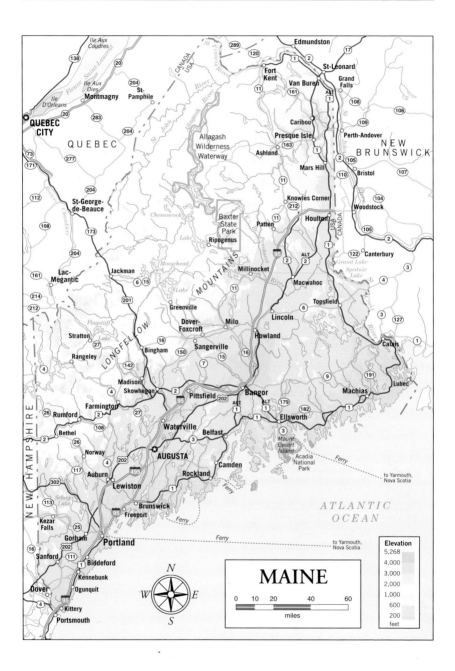

INTRODUCTION

A VISITOR RECENTLY REMARKED TO A REPORTER for the weekly *Maine Times* how disappointed she was on her bus tour to shop-filled Bar Harbor, "I thought we were going to see quaint little villages and fishing boats along the coast." She was, of course, a 15- or 20-minute ride from places where she could have seen all that and more; if she'd only had the opportunity to set out on her own, she might have experienced the Maine she had envisioned.

This book is written for travelers of an independent frame of mind, who are willing to take an occasional risk and stray from the beaten paths—and in midsummer Maine, some of them can be very well beaten indeed. If your time is very limited, it may make sense to take a package tour or hit the obvious spots. But if there is even one day to spare, I hope to lure you away from the U.S. Route 1 and I-95 corridor and the overcrowded resorts—one almost indistinguishable now from another—and to introduce you to a state many of whose most interesting features are barely known to the tourist industry.

The basic framework of this book harks back to the WPA guides of the 1930s: a series of itineraries reflecting the shape of the land. In the case of Maine, then and now, the best way to perceive this land is not as a coastal strip edging a huge, unexplored backcountry, but as a series of great river valleys reaching into the heart of the Northland, connecting the interior and the sea. This is the way the early French and British explorers saw the country, and the route the earliest settlers took in search of timber and farmland. The Piscataqua, the Androscoggin, the Kennebec, the Penobscot, and the St. Croix rivers flow through the forests and mountains of western and northern Maine, then meet the Atlantic along the state's legendary rocky shore. These are not simply rivers of great beauty but keys to understanding the land and people of Maine.

LEARNING MAINE

■ THE FOUR SEASONS

WINTER

Maine is in the kingdom of the cold. Aside from skiers headed for the resorts in the western mountains, few people visit Maine by choice between the first heavy frosts of November and the leafing out of the trees in May. Yet winter, more than any other season in this far corner of New England, has shaped the look of Maine's townscape and the character of its people as fundamentally as the last retreating glaciers of the Ice Age sculpted the hills and valleys of the state, some 18,000 years ago. So much that seems quintessentially "Mainer"—the low-key personalities, the ability to spend long periods of time alone, the warmth and loyalty demonstrated once a friendship has been established, the willingness to make do with what is at hand—so much of this can be explained by the fact of winter.

It is a glorious season. The snow comes in dramatic bursts. Anyone who can possibly avoid traveling stays close to home. But once the storm passes, the landscape comes alive: children learning to skate or slide, older kids playing hockey on the frozen pond, ice fishermen socializing in their little huts, the most intrepid birdwatchers up early in search of tree sparrows, cedar waxwings, hawk owls. The harbors—full of mallards, harlequin ducks, and eiders amid the lobster boats—never completely freeze. In the distance, clouds of sea smoke wrap themselves around the islands. Cross-country skiers, noisy snowmobiles, and daring youths who slide their four-wheel-drive trucks in circles on the ice now animate the winter woods, where Currier & Ives scenes of horse-drawn sleds have yet to fade from living memory.

At night the quiet returns. Dark comes by 4 P.M. Now and then icy slush cascades off the roof. On the very coldest nights, when the countryside seems of an unearthly quiet, the bare trees make cracking noises in the dark. In the clear air the Milky Way turns out to have so many stars that it really *does* look like spilled milk. On certain auspicious nights, the aurora borealis flickers so coolly and elusively across the sky, you wonder if you are really seeing it. Back indoors, you read the seed catalogues around the wood stove and await the next season.

SPRING

Everything conspires to make you believe that it cannot happen. At some point in January comes a sudden thaw, perhaps leaving the ground bare of snow for several weeks. There will be another false start in February, and several more in March, just as your neighbors are returning with their indecent tans from a week of winter break in Florida. The daylight hours will lengthen, but the trees remain stubbornly bare and the turf, soggy by day, freezes crisp after dark. Sand off the roads blows in your eyes. What elsewhere might promise to be a spring shower turns into more snow. Brought indoors, the pussy willow will open, and at night the mating raccoons screech. By day the only sign that nature is stirring is the excitement of the herring gulls dining at the town landfill.

Then two things happen. Sometime in April, you will hear the ice crack. The breaking up of river or creek ice is a more certain sign of spring than any daffodil. As the surface crust breaks up, and the snow in the distant hills begins to melt, modest streams become torrents. In the old days—but again within memory—the spring freshet marked the beginning of the season when logs crowded the rivers. After a winter of cutting in the forest, during spring the new timber would have been floated downriver, collected in huge booms where the white water had ceased and the rivers widened, then parceled out to the sawmills. Almost all of this is mechanized now, and the heroic age of forestry replaced by a more corporate endeavor. But in the mind's eye of everyone who knows Maine's story is the image, when the waters churn over the falls again, of a forest economy feeding into the rivers.

Then one day in May, depending how far you are from the moderating touch of the sea, color washes over the drab countryside. Actually, the transformation takes a week or two, perhaps more in truculent years, but it always *seems* an overnight sensation. A few warmish days will bring out the maples and birches, then the oaks, as a band of color marches up the brown and gray hillsides in a reverse image of fall. It is still sweater weather—and on the coast may remain so, at least after dark, all summer long—but the population will slowly emerge from its cocoon of Gore-Tex and wool, exposing pale skin to the thin springtime light.

(following pages) A cold, still winter night makes for a quintessential Maine scene.

SUMMER

"Where are you are going this summer?" someone will inevitably ask.

"Who wants to go anywhere?" is the triumphal reply. "We're in Maine!" Suddenly the long wait proves to have been worth it. Forgotten are the chilblains, the fuel bills, the cars skidding on black ice. It is time to sit in the sun and smell the balsam sap rise from the woods or the sweet stench of the rockweed the tide has left exposed on the shore. The fiddleheads of June give way to the peas and raspberries of July, and then to the tiny wild blueberries of August. At night, while most of the rest of the country swelters or turns up the air-conditioning, it's time to build a log fire. The cool breeze off the ocean or out of the hills lets you wear wool and go barefoot at the same time. True, summer has its tiresome spots—an exasperating array of flying insects (some too small to see, some almost too large to swat), sudden thunderstorms inland, and days when it seems the fog will never lift along the shore. But the intense sweetness of the very best days is all the more valued by a people who know that winter will return.

For about 150 years now, a good number of outlanders have also come to enjoy Maine's summer climate and scenery. In fact, this seasonal migration of summer visitors can be traced back many thousands of years; at least some of the indigenous peoples of the Maine forests came downriver by canoe each summer and lived for the warmest months on the shore, leaving shellheaps and other reminders. (Their distant descendants, selling sweetgrass baskets and other crafts they had made to supplement a meager income, were still a familiar sight in summer resort towns as late as the 1940s.) Modern tourism, however, began with the arrival of a group of painters—including Thomas Cole, Frederick Church, and above all Fitz Hugh Lane—in the two decades before the Civil War. Their romantic depictions of Maine's harbors and most especially of Mount Desert Island's rocky shores inspired a first wave of "rusticators"—well-to-do families seeking an escape from urban Boston, New York, and Philadelphia in the 1870s. Some built huge summer "cottages," rustic or palatial, in a string of fashionable resort towns along the Maine coast, Bar Harbor being the most famous. Other waves of summer visitors headed for the woods and lakes, where weary businessmen sought to restore their health and their sense of manliness by close encounters with bear, moose, and trout.

Some of the descendants of these late nineteenth- and early twentieth-century summer people still spend Fourth of July through Labor Day in their great-grandparents' cottages; a few have even settled in the state year round. Some of the patterns of modern Maine tourism reflect the earlier models, though on a vastly different scale. The state today accommodates a mass migration of admirers in July and August, many of whom do not stray very far from the U.S. 1 coastal strip. Given that many year-round residents choose to go off to their "camps" (the local name for any kind of house on a lake) in the same months, the brief tourist high season puts a strain on some of the state's resources, not least its sense of calm, slow-moving, rather sparsely settled rusticity. (No wonder some Mainers hate the "VACATIONLAND" label on their license plates!) Mercifully or not, the season is brief, and the roads soon empty.

"The Cottage Door," a summer scene photographed by Emma D. Sewall at the turn of the century. (Courtesy Abbie Sewall)

FALL

September is the ideal month to visit Maine. The summer crowds have thinned dramatically, yet the weather will remain near-perfect through early October. Seacoast towns that were uncomfortably crowded at the height of the season seem suddenly manageable again after Labor Day. Although some attractions close once the public schools are back in session, there is a growing awareness of a fall visitor season, one that has less to do with the foliage—which, incidentally, is as splendid in the hills of Maine as anything to be seen in Vermont or New Hampshire—than with an informed search for the qualities that made Maine desirable to start with: its remoteness, its unspoiled scenery, its moments of solitude, its timelessness.

On the coast, the light begins to do remarkable things. In the early morning fog, the trunks of the paper birches, normally white or gray, appear a yellow-green, and distant objects turn insubstantial. The sound of a boat's horn seems more palpable than the fuzzy rocks on the shore. By midmorning, however, the sun has burned through the fog, and that Fairfield Porter look of vacation weather has returned: flawless blue skies, shimmering water, dark green spruces and firs. In late afternoon, Fitz Hugh Lane returns to his easel. The low golden light, the mood of utter stillness, the feeling of ripeness that fills his views of Somes Sound or Camden Harbor is repeated at a hundred coves and inlets from Kittery to Calais.

Inland has its autumn charms, too, especially in a state with 2,200 lakes. But the mood is sharper. On the coast, you can lull yourself into feeling that October will last forever. Away from the sea, however, by late August there are already signs of approaching winter. It is more a matter of fading light than cooler weather, but the note of warning is unmistakable. By September the nights are decidedly nippier. By October there is a smell of Arctic air pushing down from Canada. But what a show the land makes. There is no putting it in words. It must have been one of the most remarkable sights to confront the earliest settlers, accustomed to the brownness of the European autumn. Whether you are a "leaf peeper" on a chartered bus tour or a child running and leaping into a pile of leaves, the setting, for a few short weeks, is the stuff of alchemy. And then, with one strong storm, it is all gone. The hills are left bare, and everyone goes inside again.

Fall arrives in Maine in early to mid-September, turning
the maple leaves into a riot of fiery color.

SUMMER SWIM

*A*s children, our play followed a rather fixed pattern through the year. In March we would take advantage of the high winds and fly homemade kites; in April we cut poles and built stilts so that we could walk high above the muddy roads; in May we played marbles, jumped rope, and rolled hoops which usually were the cast-off iron rims of old wagon wheels.

All summer we went swimming in the Mill Cove, which had sedge and cut-grass along its sides and mud in its bottom. On afternoon high tides, when the wind was southwest—as it usually was in fair summer weather—fifteen or twenty of us would show up for a swim. On these afternoons, the water was warm. All morning the sun had been pouring down on the mudflats, warming the slowly incoming water to about 70 degrees, and we were all there to enjoy it. We had no bathing suits. Some of the boys wore no underclothes in summer. Speed in getting undressed was somehow regarded as a great virtue. To shame the slow members of our gang, someone would shout, "Last one undressed got to f—— a leaf!" Although some of us were too young to understand what this desperate punishment meant, the threat would put speed into us and we would literally tear our clothes off to avoid the penalty.

—Wilbert Snow, *Codline's Child*, 1968

"Blueberry Pickers" by Emma D. Sewall. (Courtesy of Abbie Sewall)

■ LEARNING THE LAND

Maine covers almost as much of the northeastern corner of the United States as the five other New England states combined, though relatively few visitors see more than about 10 percent of it—the coastal strip bounded on one side by U.S. 1, and on the other by the Atlantic. What immediately strikes visitors from more thickly settled parts of the country is how green most of the state is. Sparsely populated overall, none of its cities is too far removed from the countryside. Maine seems to many people "from away" a land that the second half of the twentieth century and its bulldozers have yet to touch.

Maine is actually greener today than it was a century ago. After the Civil War, the state's agriculture went into gradual decline as the soil, thin to start with, was exhausted, and as Maine's more ambitious youths moved west in search of better farmland or more prosperous economies. Much of the land that was cleared for farming in the nineteenth century reverted to forest in the twentieth. The sight of a stone wall in the woods, or of a cellar hole surrounded by the hardy lilac bushes someone planted in the days before the young men marched off to Bull Run and Antietam—all these are reminders of a land on which the human touch proved transitory. Even in the great North Woods, where, when seen from the air, the spruce and hemlock and white pines seem to stretch forever, the timber companies long ago cut down most of the virgin forests. What is left—save for a few inaccessible pockets, or those preserved on purpose as "forever wild"—is a sort of industrial forest, regularly denuded of its trees by clear cutting for the paper industry.

In order to understand this land, it helps to know two events in geological history. Some 350 to 400 million years ago, molten rock from deep inside the earth was pushed up by heat and pressure and, intruding through the layers of bedrock that covered the eastern United States, formed ranges of mountains. The results of this complex upheaval can be seen all over the state alongside road cuts or at the falls of rivers where layers of rock suddenly point skyward, or where dikes of different colored rock have flowed. Perhaps the most striking evidence of this great upheaval is to be seen on Mount Desert Island, where the famous pink granite—the color of poached salmon—has been exposed everywhere the older surface rock has been eroded away. About a million years ago, glaciers began to push their way south as far as Long Island, New York, in nine long cycles of advance and withdrawal, the last glacier beginning to recede around 18,000 years ago. At their coldest moment, ice about a mile thick—four times the height of Acadia National Park's

This German Lutheran Church in Waldoboro was established in the mid-eighteenth century by Germans who immigrated here with the promise and expectation of finding a prosperous city, instead of which they found wilderness. (Brian Vanden Brink)

Cadillac Mountain—covered New England, compressing the land. Every Maine riverbed and lake, gravel pit and sand deposit, glacial erratic and smooth-faced shelf of rock bears witness to the coming and going of the ice. There are mountaintops where the scratches and grooves look so sharp, they seem new—which, by a geological reckoning of time, they are indeed.

Maine's political geography has been somewhat more tenuous: there are several points in its history when the story might have taken a different turn. Had eighteenth-century diplomacy between England and France taken a slightly different path, French might be spoken today up and down the Kennebec. Had Massachusetts not been willing to give up its appendage in 1820, the District of Maine might still be paying its taxes to Boston. The long disputed boundary with Canada was not settled until the 1840s, and even today there are towns in northern Maine where the local economy seems to straddle the border. Sometimes "Maine" seems to exist as a well-defined entity more in the minds of people from outside the state than among its own intensely local citizens, whose strongest loyalties often are to their own town and their own kin.

■ LEARNING THE SEA

The Maine poet Robert P. Tristram Coffin (1892–1955) once wrote of two distinct Maines: one of "woods and lakes and mountains," and another of "woods and mountains and sea." He identified with the latter, as do most of the people who come each summer to eat lobster, watch the gulls, and stare into the eastern horizon. In truth, except perhaps in the potato fields of Aroostook County (something of a world of its own), much of the state is oriented toward the sea. This is more than a matter of romantic notions about sea captains and clipper ships. It is rather a tribal memory of the days before the railroad and the interstate, when water carried commerce and ideas, when Maine timber floated downstream to the mills, and when Maine families traveled upstream from the seaports in search of rich valley land. However landlocked they might seem, both Augusta (the state capital) on the Kennebec and Bangor on the Penobscot are still accessible from the sea.

And while there is much of interest and beauty inland, and while I suppose a clever publicist for the state could do wonders with lumberjacks or snowshoes or moose, it is the legendary rocky coast of Maine which draws visitors summer after summer, and it is the coastal mystique—part lobster bake, part spiritual retreat—which sets the state apart from the other 49. What other state would run a tourist promotion campaign that features its boyish-looking governor waving two crustaceans in the air?

Painter Fitz Hugh Lane's Shipping in Down East Waters *was part of the body of work which inspired the first wave of "rusticators," who came to Maine to escape the urban pressures of Boston, New York, and Philadelphia in the 1870s. (Farnsworth Art Museum, Rockland)*

The coast has many attractions. For one thing, there is so much of it. Although only about 250 miles separate Kittery on the New Hampshire border from the West Quoddy Head Light on the Canadian, it would take you some 3,000 miles to trace the convolutions of the shore that were created at the end of the Ice Age, when the sea rushed into the sunken valleys that emerged from under the glaciers. (This would not include the shorelines of Maine's thousands of islands or the waterfront of Maine's 2,200 freshwater lakes and ponds.) As you travel "Down East"—that is, northeast along the coast—the beauty of this shoreline grows wilder. And while there may be a very real problem of public access in many areas, at least the shoreline *looks* expansive in all but the most crowded parts of the state. (And *looking* is quite enough for many people; the ocean water is very cold.) Despite some very scenic roads and overlooks, the visitor who does not go directly out on the water, even if only in the local mail boat or inter-island ferry, really has not seen Maine. It is the view of the land from the sea—of dark fir trees against the sky, of safe little harbors, of surf crashing on the ledges—that meant "Maine" to the first three centuries' worth of European arrivals, and that still draws their American descendants today.

■ LEARNING THE ARCHITECTURE

Maine has one of the greatest assemblages of distinctively American architecture to have survived from the nineteenth century. Because of the state's economic decline after the Civil War, there are many towns that have retained their pre-modern streetscapes, with houses ranging from simple late eighteenth-century Capes (one and a half-story cottages) to stately Federal and Greek Revival homes to Victorian fantasies where woodcarvers went on a spree. It is a tribute to the skill with which these houses were built—and the sense of pride in place which so many Mainers exhibit—that such a large number of these 100- to 250-year-old structures still function successfully as houses, quite often inhabited by descendants of their original owners.

As we travel around the state, this guide will pay particular attention to some of the structures most characteristic of this Maine architecture, including both vernacular (or everyday) examples and a few high-style marvels that appear in architectural history books. The aim of such a tour is not to enjoy buildings simply for their aesthetic value, but rather to use them as a way of understanding the people who erected them—and who choose to live in them still. And there's an added benefit—in every Maine town some of the grandest houses are inevitably now bed-and-breakfasts, waiting to welcome the curious traveler for the same price you would pay at a good but flavorless motel.

SOUTHERN COAST
A N D Y O R K C O U N T Y

What happens to me when I cross the Piscataqua and plunge rapidly into Maine at a cost of 75 cents in tolls? I cannot describe it. I do not ordinarily spy a partridge in a pear tree, or three French hens, but I do have the sensation of having received a gift from a true love.

—E. B. White, "Home-Coming," *The Essays of E. B. White,* 1955

The bridge no longer exacts a toll—though the Turnpike more than makes up for it—but many travelers still experience that slight lift of the spirit as they leave the outskirts of Portsmouth and the enclosed feeling of New Hampshire, soar high over the industrial-looking river, and reach the wooded shore of what for many Americans is a very different place from wherever they came from.

This immediate sense of being in "a place apart" was probably more striking to travelers of White's generation. They could make a leisurely journey by car through a series of landscapes of saltwater farms and slightly dusty villages that the twentieth century seemed to have overlooked, as they followed U.S. Route 1A—an old colonial post road—on its meanderings along the coast northward from York. Today, much of Kittery—the town that announces Maine to the northbound traveler—is still a charming place, but many tourists might come expressly for a partridge at Kittery's upscale discount outlet mall. The state tourist bureau's most recent promotional campaign lists outlet shopping third, after fall color and spectacular seacoast, among the most compelling reasons to visit Maine.

The notion of anyone making a trip to Maine to shop tickles an older generation of residents—people who are more likely to seek out hunter's orange blaze or Arctic-weight underwear at Reny's in downtown Bath or Wiley's in Ellsworth than to try on button-downs at Brooks Brothers in Kittery. And it horrifies those who've moved to the state in the past twenty-odd years to escape such a consumer-dominated culture. Here lies the question facing anyone planning to visit York and Cumberland counties, Maine's densely populated southwestern corner: Is this *really* Maine?

Well, yes and no. If your vision of Maine involves surf crashing on pink granite cliffs or loons bassooning on lonely lakes, you will be largely disappointed. Most of the landscape is a continuation of the coastal plain that runs from Cape Cod almost all the way to Portland and Casco Bay. It is broken by the mouths of several slow-moving rivers, softened by long stretches of salt marshes thick with birdlife and shellfish, and enriched by miles of magnificent dunes and beaches. Sections of this coastal corridor are also packed with condominiums, shopping malls, motels, fast-food joints, and midsummer traffic jams. A remarkable number of people there commute, year-round or seasonally, to Boston, an hour or so away; their number will increase when train travel, now in the works, is once again a reality in Maine.

The perfect symbol of this side of York County is Ogunquit's famous Perkins Cove. Not too long ago a quaint, even seedy, collection of wharves and fishermen's shacks, much painted and sketched by the summer's artists, today it is a tightly packed cluster of condos and motels, boutiques and seafood restaurants, yachts and excursion boats—a sort of nautical theme park, where the smell of auto fumes mixes with that of lobster butter and bayberry candles. While most of the coastal corridor is intensely commercial, many of the farms further inland, carved out in

The Cove *by Maurice B. Prendergast. (Colby College Museum of Art, Waterville)*

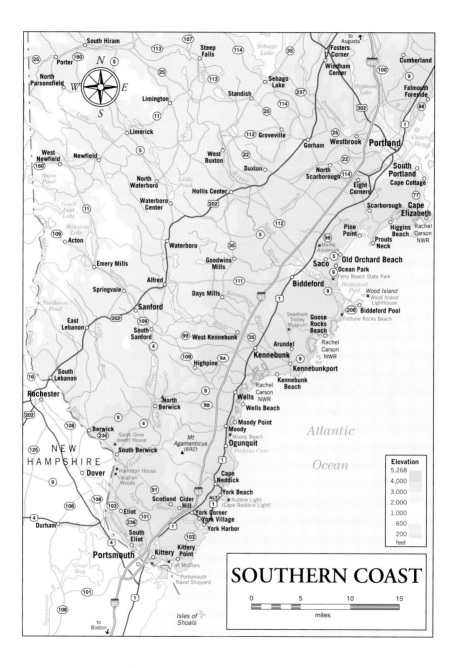

SOUTHERN COAST

0   5   10   15

miles

Elevation
5,268
4,000
3,000
2,000
1,000
600
200
feet

the past two centuries, have since reverted to fields and woodland. In recent years this part of Southern Maine has become the site of a new exurbia—moderate to expensive houses on big lots in what, before 1980, would have seemed the middle of nowhere.

■ SOUTHERN PISCATAQUA

The southern part of the Piscataqua Valley, one hundred years ago, was the epicenter of a different exurban phenomenon: the invention of Colonial Revival America. For reasons commendable (the country was becoming too ugly) and deplorable (immigrants were "ruining" New England), a good number of prosperous and well-educated people in and around Boston in the last decades of the nineteenth century decided that they preferred to live in a place that at least looked like the America of their eighteenth-century ancestors. Since much of Massachusetts was already beyond saving, they looked farther afield and discovered to their delight, among other places, the sleepy backwaters of Portsmouth, Kittery, the Yorks, and the Berwicks.

This region had been anything but sleepy in the eighteenth century, when a thriving lumber business brought prosperity to the Piscataqua and when the merchant-princes of Portsmouth built splendid Georgian houses from the profits of sugar, slaves, timber, and rum.

■ KITTERY

On the Maine side of the river, at Kittery Point, **Lady Pepperrell's mansion** of 1760—the finest Palladian house in the Piscataqua Valley—still stands on a hillside that once overlooked a river filled with tall-masted ships and flat-bottomed gundalows. (To get there follow Route 103 just past Fort McClary.) Sir William Pepperrell, the richest landowner in early eighteenth-century Maine, led the combined British and Colonial forces that successfully besieged the French fortress of Louisburg, in Canada, in 1745—a military exploit that led to his becoming the first American baronet (a hereditary knighthood) and that helped persuade his Massachusetts militiamen that they could take on a professional European army, a lesson not forgotten in 1776. The year after his death, Lady Pepperrell (who, even after the Revolution, insisted on keeping her British title) built the imposing house, which has many stylistic similarities with Longfellow's Craigie House in Cambridge, Massachusetts. (The house, privately owned, is opened a few days of the year; inquire locally. The 1730 meeting house across Route 103 is also worth seeing. In its Old Burial Ground is the grave of Celia Thaxter's husband, with an epitaph by Robert Browning.)

In the nineteenth century, Kittery was best known for its Navy Yard (today, the Portsmouth Naval Shipyard), where in 1815 was launched the 74-gun ship *Washington* and, during the Civil War, the *Kearsage,* which sank the Confederate raider *Alabama.* The Treaty of Portsmouth ending the Russo-Japanese War in 1905 was signed in the naval administration building.

■ THE ISLES OF SHOALS AND CELIA THAXTER

If there is any one spot where Maine can be said to have begun, it is on a cluster of granite outcroppings, battered by the sea, some eight miles off Portsmouth, New Hampshire, near the mouth of the Piscataqua River. Virginia's Capt. John Smith, who landed there in 1614, wanted these islets named after himself and referred to them as "Smyths Iles." But apparently the islands' granite ledges made more of an impression than Smith did on the cod fishermen and the occasional pirate who frequented the place throughout the seventeenth and eighteenth centuries. They opted for a far more descriptive name, the Isles of Shoals. The nine small islands—four of them now in Maine, the others in New Hampshire—were inhabited by Europeans long before the nearby coast was, the distinction between the isles and "the mayne," or mainland, possibly having been the source of the future state's name. Nobody really knows.

Salting cod for distant markets gave way to tourism as early as the 1840s, when, for bored city dwellers, the notion of a rocky island far out at sea began to seem less fraught with peril and more wildly romantic. A small hotel industry flourished, attracting both the well-to-do and the creative—among the latter Nathaniel Hawthorne, Mark Twain, Sarah Orne Jewett, Edwin Booth, Edward MacDowell, and Paderewski. But the isles would probably have been as little remembered as other vanished resorts, once the hotels went out of fashion early in

OF all the wonderful things in the wonderful universe of God, nothing seems to me more surprising than the planting of a seed in the blank earth and the result thereof. Take a Poppy seed, for instance: it lies in your palm, the merest atom of matter, hardly visible, a speck, a pin's point in bulk, but within it is imprisoned a spirit of beauty ineffable, which will break its bonds and emerge from the dark ground and blossom in a splendor so dazzling as to baffle all powers of description.

The Genie in the Arabian tale is not half so astonishing. In this tiny casket lie folded roots, stalks, leaves, buds, flowers, seed-vessels,— surpassing color and beautiful form, all that goes to make up a plant which is as gigantic in proportion to the bounds that confine it as the Oak is to the acorn. You may watch this marvel from beginning to end in a few weeks' time, and if you realize how great a marvel it is, you can but be lost in "wonder, love, and praise."

this century, had it not been for the happy collaboration of a woman of letters and America's leading Impressionist painter.

Celia Thaxter (1835–1894) was the daughter of a disappointed politician turned lighthouse keeper who had opened the Appledore House, one of the first of New England's great wooden seaside hotels, in 1848. The solitude of an island childhood enabled her to cultivate many artistic skills, one of which—writing popular verse—was to place her among the best-known writers of her day. In the 1860s, a Boston publisher turned down Emily Dickinson's work because he already had one female poet, Thaxter, on his list. Her childhood and her visits each summer back to Appledore inspired the essays, published as *Among the Isles of Shoals* (1873), in which she described both the pastoral side of the island life and the poverty and drunkenness of its long-time inhabitants. Even better known today is *An Island Garden*, written in 1893 and recently republished with its original illustrations. The book is anything but genteel; it is one of the grittiest garden books of its day, full of struggle against slugs, gulls, thin soil, and ceaseless wind.

Thaxter—once dubbed "Miranda of the Isles" by Hawthorne—found a way to bring the world to her. Each summer she conducted on Appledore a salon that attracted much of the New England intelligentsia. Among the artists, musicians, and writers there in the 1890s was a young painter who had recently seen in France the liberating effect *plein air* had had on the Impressionists. A splendid subject was at hand: Thaxter's flower beds. In the spirit of the Colonial Revival, she had attempted to replicate an old-fashioned English cottage garden of hollyhocks, poppies, dahlias, wallflowers, calendulas, nicotiana, sunflowers, and asters—all the more brilliant in their colors against the blue of the sea. The 400 or so paintings and drawings that Childe Hassam produced on his visits to Appledore, including the watercolors which illustrate *An Island Garden*, are among his best work.

Visiting the Isles of Shoals today is a bit more of a project than it was in Thaxter's time. Unless you are attending a conference at the religious center on Star Island, there is not much chance to stay overnight (the Appledore burned in 1914.) But there are day excursions—combined with whale watching—in summer and fall out of Portsmouth. Appledore Island is now the home of Cornell University's Shoals Marine Laboratory. The garden has been partially restored and can be visited by arrangement with the laboratory.

(left) A page from Celia Thaxter's An Island Garden *with illumination by Childe Hassam.*

■ SOUTH BERWICK AND SARAH ORNE JEWETT

The winding coastal Route 103, probably the oldest road in Maine, passes many interesting old houses and Fort McClary (1812), between Kittery and York, but the traveler who wants to understand the region's importance in the American imagination ought to detour upriver about 20 miles to South Berwick. It was the site in 1631 of the first permanent European settlement in what was to become Maine. It is a town that has experienced since then several waves of modest prosperity—as a shipbuilding center, an early mill town, and more recently home of a defense industry—but its fate is to be remembered more for its years of decline than for its successes, perhaps in part because author Sarah Orne Jewett (1849–1909) was its elegist:

> *I* am proud to have been made of Berwick dust; and a little of it is apt to fly in my eyes and make them blur whenever I tell the old stories of bravery, of fine ambition, of good manners, and the love of friend for friend and the kindness of neighbor to neighbor in this beloved town. Her children and the flock of her old academy are scattered everywhere. They can almost hear each other's voices round the world, like the English drumbeat. They have started many a Western town; they are buried

Hamilton House in South Berwick has long been considered one of the most beautiful houses in Maine and was a favorite excursion spot for Sarah Orne Jewett.

Gravestones of Captain Frisbee and his family in the graveyard of Kittery's First Baptist Church.

in Southern graves for their country's sake; they are lost in far northern seas. They sigh for the greenness of Old Fields and Pound Hill, for Blackberry Hill and Cranberry Meadow, from among the brick walls of many a crowded city; but some of the best have always stayed at home, and loved the rivers and the hills as their fathers and mothers did before them. They keep to the old ambitions, they mean to carry the flag of their town and state as high and free as they can! There is no town that has done its duty better than old Berwick, in war or in peace, in poverty or pride, in the days of her plain, hard-fighting youth, or the serenity of her comfortable prime.

Photographer Emma D. Sewall's classic portrait of spinsterhood, "When The Day's Work Is Done" fits the sentiments of Sarah Orne Jewett's writings. (Courtesy of Abbie Sewall)

In this passage from "The Old Town of Berwick," Jewett's nostalgia for her old New England heritage reaches near-epic proportions; her sentiments also reveal the motive of the Colonial Revival—to reassert Protestant New England's role in defining what it meant to be American. While other writers and artists were busy searching barns and attics for discarded eighteenth-century paneling or collecting blue-and-white china, Jewett was busy transforming the human remnants of an earlier prosperity—the elderly sea captains, the village spinsters, the impoverished widows clinging to gentility—into a series of stories depicting Maine as a place where history stood still and the descendants of America's heroes lived dignified, hard-working lives. Her most famous locale—the Dunnet Landing of *The Country of the Pointed Firs* (1896)—is an imaginary place farther Down East (somewhere between Boothbay and Tenants harbors, she once said), but it was in the South Berwick of her childhood that she learned to listen to the quietness of Maine. It found its way into her sketches and stories, just as it did in so many twentieth-century depictions of Maine, literary and visual, all the way up to, say, Berenice Abbott's 1968 photographs of a state just on the verge of modernity.

There are two places to experience the world of Sarah Orne Jewett. The most elucidating is her family's house in South Berwick, the **Sarah Orne Jewett House** at 5 Portland Street, now owned by the Society for the Preservation of New England Antiquities (SPNEA) and open in the summer. Despite its location at a busy crossroads, flanked by two pizza parlors, the 1774 white clapboard building has enormous dignity behind its picket fence. The house is an excellent example of how a Georgian house could be gently transformed into a comfortable, Victorian-era home (although the Arts and Crafts wallpaper in the hall was, for its day, an adventurous touch). Jewett's bedroom-study remains more or less as she left it. As an adult, she spent most of her life in Boston, but she returned each summer to this house in her beloved, if sleepy, town.

In her own day, Jewett was best known for her skill as a regional colorist, someone who could write charming and humorous stories about country folk, quoting them in their own dialect. Today, her reputation is based more on the fact that she gave voice to the women of her time, both the village women who seem to make up most of the population of her fiction and the sensitive, upper-middle-class female summer visitors who, with great respect for local ways, serve as her narrators and observers. Aside from her father, a country doctor, Jewett's own closest emotional involvements were with other women, and she spent much of her life in what used to be called a "Boston marriage"—a shared domestic arrangement—with Annie Fields, the widow of Hawthorne's publisher.

She also had a large circle of friends who shared her passion for the Piscataqua region's past, among them Emily Tyson and her stepdaughter Elise, who were responsible for preserving one of the most beautiful houses in Maine—**Hamilton House** (1787, renovated 1899), on a bluff overlooking the Salmon Falls River just outside of town, at the end of Old South Road. For many years the home had been a favorite excursion spot for Jewett, who in her story "River Driftwood" called it the last of "the stately old colonial mansions that used to stand beside the river" and made it famous as the setting of her novel *The Tory Lover* (1901), a tale of the conflicting loyalties created by the Revolution. The house was in great disrepair, but Jewett eventually brought it to the attention of the Tysons, Bostonians with enough money to turn the property into a showplace of the Colonial Revival. In its original state, the house had overlooked warehouses and wharves, the source of the builder's fortune. Today, the river is pleasantly quiet; one looks up the bank, through tall grass, toward the handsome Georgian facade, the entire setting a romantic re-creation that tidies up the past. The house is also owned now by SPNEA and open in summer, and its Colonial Revival garden is an idyllic spot for weddings. The nearby **Vaughan Woods,** part of the original estate, offers some wooded riverside trails.

The other major feature of interest in town is **Berwick Academy** (1791), the oldest secondary school in the state. In the nineteenth century, every Maine town of any significance had such an academy, a sort of finishing school in which students whose parents could afford to give them more than a district-school education could prepare for college (or, in the case of females, learn enough to be literate wives and mothers). Those, like Berwick, with some private endowment have survived as day or boarding schools; others have kept their historic names but have become part of the public system; many others have disappeared. The campus, like its surrounding neighborhood, includes several attractive historic homes, some of them open for house tours in summer.

From the Berwicks—North and South—the traveler can continue north into the western mountains of Maine or return toward York and the Turnpike, either by way of the pleasant old town of South Eliot or the more rural State Route 91, which offers vistas of the marshy York River.

(right) Old York has managed to preserve more than 50 buildings from the late seventeenth and eighteenth century. (Brian Vanden Brink)

■ OLD YORK

York and Kittery Point vie for the distinction of being the oldest settlement in what became, first, the Province and later, the District of Maine—both claim their earliest settlers arrived in 1623—but York has certainly managed to preserve itself as a "historic" environment in a way no other Maine town can rival. Much of this was the work of Colonial Revivalists who not only rescued and "restored" a number of important eighteenth-century buildings but also did their best, in the days when zoning was unknown, to keep visual reminders of the early twentieth century

out of the center of town. The result today is an environment which seems slightly contrived but which is certainly a pleasure to stroll through. There are enough sites open to the public to call for at least a day's visit. York, as the highway signs remind you, is actually "the Yorks," the town's 66 square miles being comprised of four distinct communities: York Village, York Harbor, York Beach, and Cape Neddick. First-time visitors may want to start with the historic Village, to keep their sense of chronology, then move northward toward the more lighthearted diversions offered in late twentieth-century Ogunquit.

The area of **York Village** was first identified as Agamenticus, the Abnaki Indian name for the river that creates York's harbor. An English speculator with the sumptuous name of Sir Ferdinando Gorges was granted a charter by James II in 1635 to create a "Province of Mayne" and chose this fishing village as his capital, chartering the town in 1640 under the name of Gorgeana (said to be the first such charter of an English town in the New World). His ambitious plans for laying out a great city in the wilderness were abandoned in 1652, however, when Puritan Massachusetts got control of the province, which was to remain part of Massachusetts until its statehood in 1820. Renamed York after one of Cromwell's victories, the town was an important shipbuilding center and fishing port for a century or more, then was rescued from its post-Civil War decline by the arrival of summer residents and tourists.

Today, more than 50 buildings of the late seventeenth and eighteenth centuries remain. A distinctive colonial building style in southern Maine and New Hampshire —the so-called "logg garrison" house, with its overhanging upper floor—was associated early on with York. According to legend, when the Indians or the French attacked, while the men fired their muskets, the women could pour boiling water from the projecting floor onto the enemy below. In truth, overhanging stories are a traditional European building style brought to America and adapted to log construction. But like the "borning rooms" (which were simply extra chambers) or "Indian shutters" (which were to preserve heat and privacy, not fend off arrows and tomahawks), "garrison houses" have entered architectural folklore. The style reappears, vestigially, in late twentieth-century tract houses all across New England. (The threat from Indians, on the other hand, was quite real until the eighteenth century. York still "remembers" the Candlemas Day massacre of 1692. Colonial depredations against the "savages" were comparably barbaric.) The Old York Historical Society will welcome you at the **Jefferds Tavern** (ca. 1750), the center of a well-maintained complex along Lindsay and York streets of pre-Revolutionary structures, each with explanatory exhibits. These include the **Old School House** (1745), the **Emerson-Wilcox House** (period rooms, 1750–1850), the **Old Gaol Museum** (which housed prisoners from 1719 until 1860), the **John Hancock Warehouse** (once owned by the famous patriot), and the **George Marshall Store** (which houses a genealogical library).

But perhaps the most important place, for anyone seeking to understand the Colonial Revival is the **Elizabeth Perkins House,** located across the river where Bartlett Road ends. In 1898, when Elizabeth Bishop Perkins and her mother decided to buy a picturesque old house as a retreat from New York City summers, they could have joined their fashionable friends on the ocean at York Harbor. Instead they chose a decaying property on the bucolic York River. Over the next 37 years, the younger Perkins turned a rather simple mid-eighteenth-century house into a showplace of the Colonial Revival, a process that involved many more disguised alterations (including a servants' wing and a garage) than the Tysons had found necessary at Hamilton House. But the final product—including a supposedly seventeenth-century dining room, stripped down to expose its beams and timbers—looked exactly the way genteel house restorers thought the setting for domestic life in pre-Revolutionary New England should look. Despite its backwater location, the Perkins House became a social center for the York summer colony, a status enhanced in 1905 when its owners had the delegates from the Portsmouth Treaty negotiations to tea. And the style Elizabeth Perkins had helped set spread rapidly through the summer community and beyond, for both Henry Sleeper's fantastical Beauport on Cape Ann in Massachusetts and Henry DuPont's vast Winterthur in Delaware echo a fascination with an idealized colonial America that the historic preservationists of Old York did much to popularize.

SPNEA tactfully declined Elizabeth Perkins's offer of the house (on the grounds that it had been altered too much) but did accept in 1977 another famous York dwelling, the **Sayward-Wheeler House** (ca. 1720), a house which had survived largely because of family pride and which had welcomed respectful tourists since the 1860s. The white clapboard building at 79 Barrell Lane is quirky and of no great stylistic importance, but its riverfront setting and its mementos of the town's leading pre-Revolutionary family (including loot from the capture of Louisburg) make it one of the most interesting historic houses to visit in Maine. Jonathan Sayward, rich from the West Indies trade, lived there from 1735 until 1797—his reputation in the community being secure enough to protect him despite his Loyalist sympathies during the Revolution. His grandson, Jonathan Sayward Barrell, continued

The Old York Gaol housed prisoners from 1719 until 1860.
(Brian Vanden Brink)

the family business but, like many New England merchants, was almost ruined by President Jefferson's Embargo of 1807. His unmarried daughters, like characters in a Sarah Orne Jewett short story, remained in the house, living in genteel poverty yet keeping their ancestral possessions in place. In 1901, the house was bought by more prosperous relations, the Wheelers, who made minor improvements but also sought to keep the contents intact in honor of the family. The parlor in particular, with its ancestral portraits and Chippendale chairs against the wall just where the Saywards placed them, evokes the life of a rich provincial merchant's family on the eve of the Revolution. The room is low-ceilinged and cramped, but the furnishings are almost luxurious, suggesting that juxtaposition of comfort and crudity in which prosperous Americans of the eighteenth century lived. The ambience is much less graceful and stylish than the Colonial Revivalists insisted upon, and all the more authentic for that.

The Sayward-Wheeler House is one reminder of the Piscataqua Valley's many literary associations, for Sayward's granddaughter—born in the house in 1759— was Sally Sayward Barrell Keating Wood (known in her day as Madam Wood), Maine's first successful popular writer, remembered now for her Gothic novel *Julia and the Illuminated Baron* (1800). Years later, one of York's early parsons inspired another Gothic story: Hawthorne's "The Minister's Black Veil." Today a mix of posh summer homes, hotels, and bed-and-breakfasts, York Harbor was a fashionable literary neighborhood a century ago, attracting writers as varied as Mark Twain and Thomas Nelson Page; Kittery Point was the summer home of Boston's William Dean Howells (1837–1920). On the New Hampshire side of the river is the birthplace of Thomas Bailey Aldrich (1836–1907), whose *Story of a Bad Boy* recalls his Portsmouth childhood.

An older generation of guidebooks described **York Beach** as a touch of liveliness between the "serenity" of York Harbor and of Cape Neddick. Summer colonists a century ago found it a touch too lively, for the trains brought "the unwashed," presumably to wash on the splendid sand beach, and the genteel feared they might spill over into their neighborhoods. Today there is still a distinct change in population density (and traffic) between the communities, but York Beach has an attractively retro quality of its own, compared to the glitzier resorts farther along the coast. Two landmarks appear on the northern side of the town of York: to the inland rises **Mount Agamenticus,** only 692 feet tall but a traditional navigational aid on this flat coastline. From the summit there are memorable views of the White Mountains and the Atlantic. On a little island just offshore stands the much-photographed **Nubble Light,** also known as Cape Neddick Light.

Nubble Light on Cape Neddick.

A CHILDHOOD IN OGUNQUIT

*O*gunquit was a magic place for me as a child, when every summer beginning in 1917 for about ten years Lucy Stanton lent us her studio for one month. We ate at the old High Rock Hotel, so it was a real holiday for my mother. Both she and my father loved to swim, and we used to walk along the Marginal Way to one of the rocky coves, the charm being those jagged rocks standing up from soft white sand. I know of no other place that combines the two. I haunted the local library and gradually borrowed and read through all the Waverly novels, taking them out one by one in a closely-printed edition with a musty smell, usually climbing up a pine tree and sitting there most uncomfortably. I wonder why reading in a tree is such a pleasure! There must be something atavistic about it—I can still smell the pine gum and feel its stickiness on my fingers. It is all so present to me that it is quite a shock to find old photographs and realize, looking at my father's stiff white collars and my mother's big hats, and her bathing costume which included long black stockings, how long ago it really was.

—May Sarton, *The House by the Sea*, 1977

"He Cometh Not" by Emma D. Sewall. (Courtesy of Abbie Sewall)

■ OGUNQUIT

Ogunquit is about as distinctive as any other resort town between the Gulf of Mexico and the Gulf of Maine, for those who do not stray from U.S. Route 1. But much can be forgiven when you see the three miles of beach—a broad, firm expanse of sand extending even farther if you add **Moody Beach** in adjacent Wells. There is nothing else quite like it north of Cape Cod. The town has managed to protect most of it from development. Thanks to an intercoastal river, several strategically placed parking lots, and the local trolleys (named, a bit too cutely, Daisy, Tulip, Petunia, and Daffodil), the beach itself is one of two places where you can escape from the sight, sound, and smell of the automobile. The other is the mile-long **Marginal Way,** an oceanfront path along the more dramatic part of Ogunquit's shorefront. The developer of the property in the 1920s, concerned about complaints that summer people were buying up all the ocean frontage and blocking the public's view of the water, laid out a right of way between the house lots and the rocky shore and deeded it to the town.

Since the 1890s, Ogunquit has been known as an art center, attracting such major figures as Elihu Vedder (1836–1923), Walt Kuhn (1877–1949), and Yasuo Kuniyoshi (1893–1953) as well as lesser lights who produced studies of lobster traps and beached dories for the tourist trade. The **Ogunquit Art Association** was formed in 1928 in Charles H. Woodbury's studio, and the town continues to support several galleries, a picturesquely sited **Museum of Art** (the gift of Henry Strater), whose glass walls provide a vista out to sea, and a well-regarded summer playhouse. But the cultural side of Ogunquit tends to be swallowed up now in the sheer mass of summer visitors, catered to by elbow-to-elbow motels and inns and boutiques—as does the fact that since World War II Ogunquit has been the leading gay resort north of Provincetown.

■ WELLS

Ogunquit's neighbor, Wells, dates from the 1640s—Gorges named it for the English cathedral town—but strip development along U.S. 1 has obliterated any sense of age to the place. What gives Wells some interest, geographically speaking, is the broad tidal marsh that separates the busy commercial area from its beach. Visiting the beach, the nineteenth-century travel writer Samuel Adams Drake noted its hard, firm sand—and its surprising ability to shift. He wrote in *Nooks and Corners of the New England Coast* (1875):

> *M*any years ago, while sauntering along the beach, I came across the timbers of a stranded vessel. So deeply were they embedded in the sand, that they had the appearance rather of formidable rows of teeth belonging to some antique sea-monster than of the work of human hands. How long the wreck had lain there no one could say; but at intervals it disappeared beneath the sands, to come to the surface again . . . like a grave that would not remain closed.

Like barrier beach communities up and down the Atlantic coast, Wells today faces the problem of whether to maintain its protective jetties with sand dredged from its harbor, or to allow the free-roaming sea to wash against the beach, naturally eroding and replenishing the sands (which would erode many beachfront properties). The scale is small, but the problem of just how much development the beaches can tolerate is as real in southern Maine as it is on Long Island or the Jersey shore. Wells is a town with an environmental consciousness, thanks in part to programs at its wildlife preserves, and its sense of the past lives on at its historical society and in some of the best antique shops and antiquarian bookstores in the state.

Travelers in search of sandy beaches can find more at Kennebunk Beach, Biddeford Pool, and Old Orchard Beach, but the public beaches in season will be very crowded, with limited parking. Thanks to a recent court case involving Wells's Moody Beach, private beachfront is virtually off limits to the public, even between the high and low tide marks. If going to the beach is what you really came to Maine for, it might be advisable to invest in a short-term shorefront rental or a room at a motel with access to the water.

■ RACHEL CARSON NATIONAL WILDLIFE REFUGE

As the stretches of uninterrupted countryside grow fewer in crowded southern Maine, to find a beautiful estuary preserved as a refuge for migratory birds (and for us, too) only a few minutes' drive from the clogged streets of Kennebunkport is a particular pleasure. The Rachel Carson National Wildlife Refuge in Wells is hardly wilderness—you can glimpse houses along the edge, and the distant roar of

(right) Rachel Carson National Wildlife Refuge near Wells.

the surf has to compete with the traffic on busy Route 9. But it is a fitting memorial to perhaps the most influential writer on ecology in our time, a biologist whose early works *Under the Sea Wind* and *The Sea Around Us* reflected her summers on the Maine coast, and whose *Silent Spring* in 1962 awakened the nation to the dangers of DDT and other pesticides.

The Wells site is one of nine saltwater marshes between Kittery and Cape Elizabeth that make up the refuge. These tidal estuaries and their upland "edge habitats" of woods and fields form a chain along some 45 miles of coast that offers migrating birds a place to feed, rest, and rear their young. Threatened by development in the 1950s and '60s, this stretch of coastal wetlands was saved, at least in part, by the federal government's purchase of some 4,000 acres (eventually, about 7,000 acres more will be included).

For the moment, the Wells site is the most accessible for the general public (other parts of the refuge can be seen from the road or hiked), thanks to a well-explained trail laid out by the U.S. Fish and Wildlife Service. While the marsh itself is too fragile for human traffic, it can be admired from several vista points along the one-mile trail. Perhaps at their tawny best on a sunny fall day, the tall marsh grass—saltwater cordgrass *(Spartina alterniflora)*—and the shorter salt hay *(Spartina patens)* form what is one of the most productive ecosystems in the temperate world. Migratory birds stopping here in the spring and fall include black ducks, black-bellied plover, and thousands of other shorebirds. Visitors can also spot scoters, mergansers, and eiders seeking winter protection in the marshes, followed in summer by egrets and herons.

Travelers who want to know more about this environment should also visit the nearby **Wells National Estuarine Research Reserve,** at Laudholm Farm (a historic saltwater farm accessible from U.S. 1 in Wells, on 1,600 acres of woods, wetland, and meadow). A full calendar of nature programs and bird walks for children and adults is offered year round. (**Please note:** Anyone walking in the country in southern coastal Maine should take precautions against the ticks which carry Lyme disease. Wear long pants and sleeves, use insect repellent, and stay on the trails.)

(right) Sunny Beach, Ogunquit *by Gertrude Fiske presents a nostalgic view of the area's now sometimes-overcrowded summer beach resorts. (Colby College Museum of Art, Waterville)*

■ KENNEBUNKPORT AND KENNEBUNK BEACH

Kennebunkport was so much in the news through the 1980s, thanks to George Bush and his family, that it is hard to realize now how much it owes its national profile to an earlier celebrity—the historic novelist Kenneth Roberts (1885–1957). His intensely factual tales of colonial America were so well regarded that the village of North Kennebunk changed its name to one of his titles, and appears on today's maps as **Arundel.** Today's televised historical "docudramas" garner high ratings, but in Roberts's day such novels as *Rabble in Arms, Northwest Passage, Oliver Wiswell,* and *Arundel* were not only hugely popular—earning Roberts a fortune—but were a source of information about colonial America that reached a large audience in ways no contemporary writer has matched. A native of nearby Kennebunk with a strong affinity for local history, Roberts might have remained a journalist had he not befriended in the 1920s a well-established fellow writer who summered in Kennebunkport, Booth Tarkington. Roberts had little natural gift for narrative, but by reading his manuscripts aloud to the nearly blind older man, and working

out the problems of plot and characterization with him—while Roberts's wife Anna stood by to type the final draft—he produced a series of widely read books. Roberts used the history of his region and of his own ancestors to follow up the success of *Arundel* in 1930 with three other novels in four years, to comprise what he called "The Chronicles of Arundel," which traced the fate of his characters from the French and Indian War through the Revolution.

In his later years, Roberts cultivated a reputation as a crusty curmudgeon. His house at Kennebunk Beach did not shelter him sufficiently from the "twittery idle people" who wanted to meet the famous writer, or from the noise of modern resort life. His chronicle of peeves included "lawn mowers, golfers, crying children, gabbling old women, squawking automobile horns, mentally deficient chauffeurs," later adding telephones, airplanes (he is said once to have fired a shotgun at a passing plane) and chirping birds. The financial success of *Northwest Passage* in 1936 enabled him to build a more secluded retreat. His much publicized ability to throw a fit had some positive results, however: he was a pioneer in the eventually successful campaign to ban billboards from Maine's highways.

It would be interesting to know what a man who so loathed hearing Maine called "Vacationland" would make of his beloved Kennebunkport today. Many of the old sea captains' and shipbuilders' houses still stand on its shaded streets—a good number of them expensive bed-and-breakfasts—and the proximity along Ocean Avenue of the Bushes' ancestral Walker's Point, the little Gothic Episcopal St. Ann's Church on the sea (where the former president has so often been photographed), the Arundel Yacht Club, and the Kennebunk River Club might indicate that this was a last outpost of the Protestant Ascendency. But in the center of town, **Dock Square** and its neighboring streets are, all summer and on fall weekends, as packed and as democratized as any suburban mall. Few people would want to revive the Kennebunks' air of WASP exclusivity—the barriers now are mostly economic—but Kennebunkport itself, like Boothbay Harbor and Bar Harbor farther "down east," seems at times to be about to sink under the weight of its touristic success.

The family of George Bush was already well established at Walker's Point in Kenneth Roberts's day. As the historian Joyce Butler relates, efforts at the turn of the century by the Kennebunkport Sea Shore Company to turn the local shorefront into a fashionable summer resort—a rival to Newport and Bar Harbor—quickly showed signs of succeeding. The Village Improvement Society, packed with more summer people than year-round residents, had seen to it that the village had well-kept fences and hedges, clean streets and docks, neat iron railings, road-side landscaping, and an "entire absence" of rubbish or unsightly advertising. The area's natural and man-made beauty was enhanced, in the eyes of its promoters, by the summer colony's busy round of teas, dances, regattas, fairs, and literary events. The arrival of electric lights and long-distance telephone service in 1902 meant one could rusticate with a new degree of comfort and convenience. The villagers were startled, however, to learn that same summer of the purchase of a Cape Arundel peninsula called variously Damon's Park, Flying Point ("Flyin' P'int" as the old-timers pronounced it), and Point Vesuvius by the Walker family of St. Louis. As Butler writes, "there was more than rocks on the 11-acre point of land that jutted out into the ocean. Picnickers had long been attracted . . . by picturesque coves on either side of the approach from the mainland; wandering, well-worn, woodland paths; a small pond; fragrant juniper and sun-warmed blueberries; and unsurpassed views in both directions." The lonely domain of a few fishermen or the occasional hunter would soon be thoroughly civilized.

The Walker family was well known in town, for they had been summering there for some 20 years, either staying in one of the large wooden hotels that char-acterized the first stage of the summer people's arrival or renting a cottage. It was G. H. Walker who purchased Damon's Park from the Sea Shore Company, reput-edly for $20,000, and during the winter of 1902–03 the local newspaper reported the arrival of 17 railroad cars of lumber for the two houses his family was building on the point. Nineteen carpenters worked through the winter, and by July one "cottage" was ready to be occupied, with the other completed by the end of summer. In 1903, the local summer newspaper *The Wave* published photos of Walker's son's cottage, comfortably stuffed with wicker furniture, oriental rugs, flowers, books, family photos, bibelots, and a Tiffany lamp. As Butler concludes, "The Walkers had found their Eden, although the people of the Kennebunks had lost part of theirs."

There was nothing particularly unusual about this; the history of what soon was called Walker's Point is a familiar story on the Maine coast. From Kittery to Mount Desert Island, many vacant shorefront plots that were regarded locally as common property were bought up and divided into building lots for rich people "from away." But this story did take an uncommon turn. In recent times, most of the point has been owned by Walker's daughter, Dorothy Walker Bush, and her son, George Herbert Walker Bush, the forty-first president, who now divides his

Frank Boring in a patriotic display during a Fourth of July parade.

year between Kennebunkport and Houston, Texas. Since the 1992 election, Ocean Avenue is no longer so abuzz with Secret Service details, reporters, cameramen, White House aides, and foreign dignitaries, but the tourists still stop at a lookout point across the inlet to stare—longingly, or simply curiously—at the famous family's summer retreat.

■ KENNEBUNK

The fascination some people felt for colonial America found many outlets in York County earlier in this century, but it is the early 1800s that intrigue many of us in Maine today. These were the founding years of the modern state, and much of Maine's towns, industries, educational system, religious beliefs, and ways of everyday life took shape in the decades from 1790 to 1860. There are two places any traveler who shares this curiosity ought to visit in southernmost Maine.

Kennebunk, a few miles inland from the more famous port, is by comparison an oasis of quiet. The meandering Kennebunk River, which seems hardly more than a stream, was in fact in the early nineteenth century a busy shipbuilding center, bringing a degree of prosperity still reflected in the handsome Federal houses that line Route 35. The most spectacular of these is the famous **Wedding Cake House** (private), once a rather chaste Federal mansion of about 1825. In the

1850s, owner George Bourne encased his dwelling and barn with exuberantly Gothic filigree woodwork. The effect is difficult to convey in words, other than to say that the house in no way resembles a wedding cake. It is a fantasy—half ecclesiastical, half Sir Walter Scott. There is reason to believe that its creator—an otherwise conventional shipbuilder—found in its architectural details an escape from his problems, personal and professional. His once-booming shipyard of Bourne & Kingsbury, down the bluff behind the house, started to decline in the 1840s, launching its last vessel in 1852; Bourne was soon to experience a series of family tragedies, and in his final years he busied himself with his Gothic pinnacles, arches, and tracery, his crockets and quatrefoils and cusps, doing much of the intricate

The Wedding Cake House in Kennebunk. (Brian Vanden Brink)

woodcarving with his own hands. The work was completed in the summer of 1856. By December, he was dead of typhoid fever. Subsequent owners have treasured his handiwork, on what must now be the most photographed house in the state.

At 117 Main Street in town is another local treasure, the **Brick Store Museum**, housed in an 1825 store but cleverly linking three other period buildings in a way that maintains the nineteenth-century street front and provides a series of intimate exhibition spaces and an attractive gift shop. The museum is noted for its furniture and portraits of the Federal period—the era of the town's great prosperity—and for rotating exhibits on local neighborhoods, writers like Roberts and Tarkington, and life in general in the Early Republic. It offers an exemplary lesson in how a small, local museum can maintain scholarly standards and conservation practices while appealing to a wide public. The museum also offers walking tours of local architecture, including the nearby **Storer House** (1758), where Roberts was born and where Lafayette was entertained on his American tour in 1825.

■ SACO AND BIDDEFORD

Saco and its neighbor Biddeford are distinctly different communities. The former is a "classic" New England town of old white houses, shaded streets, and the **Thornton Academy**. The latter is a red-brick mill town with one of the state's largest concentrations of citizens of French Canadian descent. In the mid-eighteenth century, however, both towns were centers for the lucrative Saco River lumber trade. Portraits and possessions of two families that grew rich in that trade—those of Thomas Cutts and Daniel Cleaves—can be seen today at the **York Institute** (371 Main St.; Saco), another small museum of very high quality. Named for York County (somewhat to the confusion of people who go searching for it in the town of that name), the York Institute is housed in a Colonial Revival building (1926) by the Portland architect John Calvin Stevens and features changing exhibits on local architecture, the lumber industry, Maine archaeology, and the like. The two rooms devoted to the decorative arts of the Federal period—some of it locally made—are a reminder of the degree of luxury and sophistication that rich New Englanders enjoyed at home in the Early Republic.

In the basement is a re-creation of a "Colonial" kitchen, as typically interpreted by house restorers and museum curators of the Colonial Revival—an appropriate place to end this tour of York County's history. The kitchen as symbol of hearth, home, and family was an important and reassuring part of the Colonial Revival ideology, reinforced by such props as the musket over the mantel, the herbs hanging from the beams, the pewter mugs, the inevitable spinning wheel, and the crib close to the fire. It was a version of the past that glorified pre-industrial domesticity —and ignored the danger of flying sparks—and conveyed a romantic longing for the "good old days" when life seemed simpler. Unfortunately, inventories of actual colonial households do not suggest anything so cozy; an eighteenth-century kitchen was hot, dirty, smoky, and on occasion dangerous to those who had to labor there. A more realistic view of life in early Maine will emerge as we travel through the state.

■ OLD ORCHARD BEACH

A popular, traditional warm-water port for French-speaking Canadians, Old Orchard Beach lies northeast of Saco on Route 98 off U.S. 1. In addition to a glistening crescent of sand, Old Orchard is a museum of architectural styles. There are vestiges of its days as a fashionable Victorian summer resort as well as the more modest, almost toylike dwellings in Ocean Park, where many religious camp meetings and conferences took place starting in the 1880s. Much of the crowded beach area itself, with its fried dough stands, has a 1950s resort feel to it. In winter, when the pier-side carnival rides are covered with snow, the look is almost surreal, and at night strangely melancholy. Despite the high human density of the beachfront, and evidently in the absence of much in the way of zoning, all sorts of high-rise condos and motels have been squeezed into the "strip" (although some of them were ripped untimely from their developers' womb when the recession hit). Old Orchard Beach in summer is a suburb of Quebec. As many visitors have noted with amusement, beguilement, or alarm, the skimpiness of the bathing suits, male and female, is a more immediate sign than the French being spoken that you have left the Anglo-Saxon world, at least for the time being.

P O R T L A N D
A N D   E N V I R O N S

CONTINUING NORTH FROM OLD ORCHARD BEACH and across the Scarborough River, you leave behind the overpopulated resorts of southern Maine, and enter the more "year-rounder" townships of Scarborough and Cape Elizabeth. As almost every municipal sign will tell you, Scarborough was established in 1657, and the cape in 1765. The hamlets were largely ignored until the 1970s and '80s, when Portland's economy took off: condos and short blocks of two-bedroom homes sprang up in meadows and fields, accommodating commuters—especially young couples with families—to the re-energized city. Fortunately, development slowed down before any great damage to landscape or historic architecture was done. Fields and ponds—many of them owned by the same family for generations—remain plentiful today, and the occasional early nineteenth-century connected

A view of Portland from Baxter Boulevard as painted by Josiah Thomas Tubby in 1933. (Farnsworth Art Museum, Rockland)

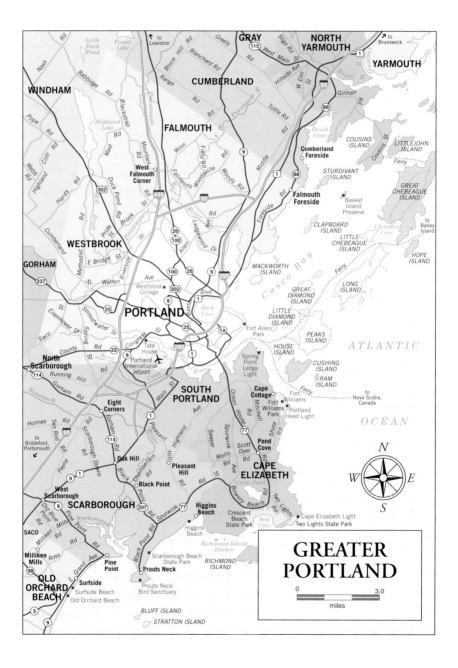

GREATER
PORTLAND

0   3.0
miles

farm building, covered in faded yellow or gray clapboard, still stands solemn on its modest acreage. A few old pocket neighborhoods can be found along quiet streets, but most of the larger Shingle-style and Colonial homes are visible only from the ocean, standing on points or near the beaches in between. But although much of the land and many of the beaches are privately owned, there are some public beaches and parks tucked away which are well worth a visit.

■ WINSLOW HOMER AT PROUTS NECK

In the southeastern corner of Scarborough is Prouts Neck, a triangular outcropping of land with wide sandy beaches on its eastern side. The beauty of this shore was immortalized by the artist Winslow Homer (1836–1910), who spent many years in his salt-stained, shingled home painting the stormy seas, as well as the Mainers and summer colonists he saw on the neck. Returning to New York from Europe in 1882, Winslow Homer found himself at a crossroads in his career. His early work—as a Civil War illustrator and skillful watercolorist of outdoor scenes—had given little indication that he would become, relatively late in life, one of the greatest American painters of the century. But his two years in England, where he had studied the lives of fishermen in the North Sea port of Tynemouth, had revealed to him what would be his most powerful subject: the struggle of men and women with the brute force of the sea.

As early as 1875, Homer had visited Prouts Neck, the small point of land protruding into Saco Bay about 12 miles south of Portland. In 1883, he and his brother decided to move there, in hopes of bringing the whole family, including their parents, to summer on the point—and eventually of subdividing their property to sell to other cottagers. The plan worked perfectly, and today Prouts Neck manages to be two things at once: a very comfortable summer colony of large houses and a cultural symbol of the wildness, the terror, the implacability of the sea.

How the former happened is a familiar story on the Maine coast: a scenic locale attracted a few summer visitors who boarded in local houses or in quickly constructed wooden hotels; some of them returned to buy property and erect Shingle-style or Colonial Revival summer "cottages" in which they and succeeding generations of their families could enjoy the clean air and unspoiled ocean view while not really abandoning the comforts of urban life. Since the Homer family had bought up almost the whole Neck, they could be very choosy about whom they allowed to build.

Winslow Homer preferred to have few neighbors, for he enjoyed being left alone, either in the studio he built in the former stable of his family house, "The Ark," or during his long walks along the craggy shore. He also liked to be there well into autumn, weeks after the "season" had ended, for as winter approached the North Atlantic pounded the rocks with 30- or 40-foot waves, sending "mare's tails" of salt spray into the air. Like Turner roped to the mast of a ship in order to study a storm at sea, Homer sat on the rocks, fascinated by the violence of nature. He also had an opportunity to observe more of the actual lives of seafaring people, for there was still a local fishing fleet in the area. In his walks around the Neck, Homer studied at different times of day and in varying weather the visual effects of waves as they struck the ledges and cliffs. Previously working in watercolor, Homer turned to oil paints in 1884. Among the results was what is regarded as his first masterpiece, *The Life-Line,* in which a woman is being rescued from a wrecked ship—both she and her rescuer suspended from a rope over a foaming sea. Through the late 1880s and 1890s he went on to produce paintings such as *The Fog Warning* and *Artist's Studio in an Afternoon Fog* which made his international reputation.

Homer found many other subjects as well, notably the lives of hunters and fishermen in the Adirondacks and of the people of the Bahamas and the

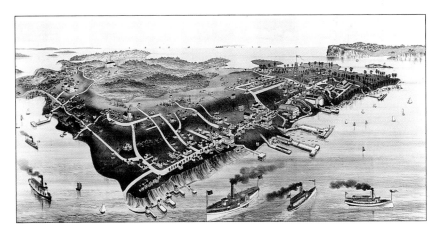

An old lithograph takes a bird's-eye view of Peak's Island in Portland Harbor. (Library of Congress)

Winslow Homer's A Summer Night *depicts his family and friends dancing on a moonlit evening in Prouts Neck. (Musee d'Orsay, Art Resource)*

Caribbean. But he always returned to Prouts Neck and the lessons of nature he had learned there. In 1909, the last oil painting he completed before putting away his palette for good was *Driftwood,* a scene of a fisherman in oilskins trying to salvage a huge log from the wave-beaten rocks. The setting, according to Winslow Homer scholar Philip C. Beam, is Kettle Cove, where 34 years earlier Homer had made his first drawing at Prouts Neck.

■ PROUTS NECK TODAY

Prouts Neck now is the site of a private beach club, where access to the wide white sands is limited to the folks who rent or own homes in the immediate neighborhood and are therefore entitled to membership in the "P.N.A." (Prouts Neck Association). Temporary membership is available to visitors to the **Black Point Inn,** a rambling, shingled house on a hill just past the entrance gate to the beach. Here, you can feast on an elegant if pricy buffet lunch by the inn's saltwater pool (the inn wisely provides uniformed waiters to carry your lobster-laden lunch tray around the pool), but most members and guests prefer the tuna sandwiches and hot dogs sold at the beach's concession-cafe. For a quick, free stint on a similar beach, further up the neck is the public **Scarborough Beach**, northeast on Route 207. Just past the beach's entrance is the red-painted Len Libby's candy store: pick up some of the almond crunch and head for the beach, strolling between the cattails to the powdery sand and calm surf. You might notice that nothing prevents the sunbathers here from walking onto Prouts Neck territory, but they seem to recognize that Scarborough is every bit as beautiful and prefer to stay where they are. A livelier beach, on the other hand, can be found farther northeast along Spurwink (Route 77) at **Higgin's.**

The porch of a private home commands an inspiring view of sand and sea. (Brian Vanden Brink)

■ CAPE ELIZABETH

North of Scarborough is Cape Elizabeth, site of another public beach, **Crescent Beach State Park,** a scenic, sandy expanse along Route 77. Cape Elizabeth is also home to several of the state's most photographed lighthouses. Two of them can be found near Crescent Beach at **Two Lights State Park,** where you'll find Cape Elizabeth Light—which functions—as well as its defunct twin. Those young at heart—both literally and figuratively—should climb the old army look-out tower for a view of the Atlantic. Afterward, a stop by the **Lobster Shack** will provide you with more fried clams than you'll want to eat—but the seagulls circling outside the restaurant will help you get rid of them. On foggy days, be forewarned that the foghorn's blare is enough to discourage even the hardiest lobster-roll fan. Instead, try **Dick's** lobster pound—turn left off Two Lights Road on your way out then left on Richmond Terrace—for take-out crustaceans and deadpan commentary from Dick himself.

Maine's most photographed lighthouse is probably **Portland Head Light** (north on Route 77, turn right onto Shore Road) located at Fort Williams Park. Commissioned by George Washington in 1791, the lighthouse has appeared on everything from U.S. postage stamps to cereal commercials. Gazing down at the crashing surf upon the rocky crags, today's visitors can only imagine the fear Maine's jagged coastline must have instilled in ship captains. On an ominous ledge nearby, white lettering tells the story of the Christmas Eve wreck of the *Annie C. Maguire* in 1886.

From Fort Williams, it's a short jaunt into **South Portland** via Shore Road, which turns into Cottage Road, onto the **South Portland Bridge** to Portland. From this angle, the Victorian townhouses of the Western Promenade stand atop a hill straight ahead and to the left; behind them, the Gothic Revival redbrick towers of St. Dominic's rise elegantly over the gray rooftops. You'll have little choice but to follow York Street to the right into town.

■ PORTLAND

Portland is by national standards a small city—but in a state of not much more than a million people, its approximately 65,000 residents form the largest group of humans to be found in any one place. Portland has been Maine's most populous community since the eighteenth century. Although only briefly the state's capital (1820–1836), it has dominated the state's economic and cultural life almost from the beginning. One way to look at Maine politics is as an on-going debate between this metropolitan center—which today tends to be a good deal more liberal, socially and politically, than the rest of the state—and the scattered towns and villages and smaller urban centers (such as Lewiston and Bangor) over how the state should run.

Also an extremely attractive place to live, this small city inevitably appears on most of those "the nation's most liveable communities" lists. In part this is a tribute to its location—only two hours from Boston and much closer to some of the most beautiful scenery in New England—and its geography, a combination of hills, bays, and islands. But it is also a tribute to Portland's revitalization of itself over the past 20 years, from a pleasant but somewhat run-down city living on the glory of its maritime past to a much livelier and more prosperous-looking community, enriched in both senses of the word by an influx of young, well-educated, civic-minded residents in the 1970s and '80s.

In their headier moments, the city's promoters like to compare the place to San Francisco. There are some parallels: the views of deep blue water

Looking east along Middle Street in Portland, 1863, three years prior to a great fire which destroyed most of the downtown area. (Library of Congress)

from steep streets, the rows of wood-frame Victorian houses, the abundance of restaurants, the active cultural life, the interesting mix of an Old Guard Yankee society with a less conventional arts community, even a politically active gay and lesbian presence. All these might suggest a San Francisco East, but the comparison is exaggerated. In truth, Portland is its own place, a thriving harbor town with an interesting past and a lot of rough edges beneath its veneer of sophistication. What it lacks in charm it makes up in character.

■ FINDING YOUR WAY

There are two ways to orient yourself. One way is to climb the early nineteenth-century signal tower, the **Portland Observatory,** on **Munjoy Hill.** Standing where anxious shipowners peered at the horizon 150 years ago in search of familiar sails, you can take in a panoramic view of the city, its hundreds of neighboring islands, and its hinterland, with the White Mountains of New Hampshire far to the west. The center of Portland is a long, rather narrow peninsula, surrounded on three

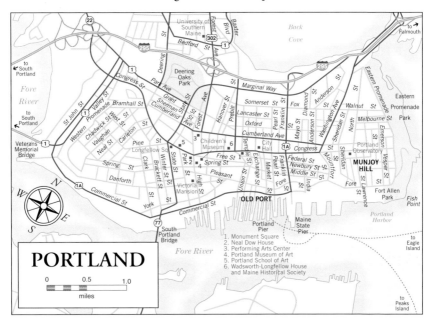

PORTLAND

0   0.5   1.0

miles

1. Monument Square
2. Neal Dow House
3. Performing Arts Center
4. Portland Museum of Art
5. Portland School of Art
6. Wadsworth-Longfellow House and Maine Historical Society

sides by **Back Cove, Casco Bay,** and the **Fore River.** From Munjoy Hill on the east to **Bramhall Hill** on the west, the city's main thoroughfare, **Congress Street,** follows a ridge between those two hills, with the rest of the city spilling down on either side from it. In modern times, the city has spread far westward, but the peninsula continues to define the identity of Longfellow's "city by the sea." Where other cities have pigeons, downtown Portland has seagulls.

The other orientation technique would be to drive around the perimeter of this peninsula, perhaps starting at **Deering Oaks Park,** the wooded edge of the old city celebrated in Longfellow's poem "My Lost Youth." In the late nineteenth century, landscape architect Frederick Law Olmsted was commissioned to design a greenbelt of sorts around downtown Portland, and the most important elements survive. These include, in addition to the park, **Baxter Boulevard** around the tidal flats of the Back Cove and the Eastern and Western Promenades. The Eastern Prom forms much of Munjoy Hill's Casco Bay frontage, and it is a curious twist of urban geography that this unfashionable part of town got by far the best view. Munjoy Hill was farmland in the eighteenth century, with a tiny settlement of free blacks; it became heavily Irish in the immigration of the 1840s and 1850s, with various other ethnic groups arriving as soon as local industries needed their labor and skills. Today it is still largely a working-class neighborhood, with the sort of interesting Victorian row houses that in San Francisco, say, would long ago have been gentrified. Portland's rich traditionally lived in the western part of town, with its inferior view; today, the Western Prom overlooks the rather industrial Fore River.

There are four other older parts of the city worth examining. To the south is the **harbor,** still a vital part of the region's economy for both its fishing and shipping industries. In the eighteenth and nineteenth centuries, lumber piled on these wharves went to Boston or the West Indies; today it goes to timber-poor countries like China and Turkey. The waterfront has also become a residential and tourist center, amid much controversy between condominium developers and those people who want to guarantee its survival as a working harbor.

Across busy Commercial Street, in what 20 years ago was a semi-derelict warehouse district, is the bustling **Old Port,** some eight or ten city blocks of late Victorian commercial buildings converted to restaurants, offices, apartments, and boutiques. Although the recession has taken its toll on many small businesses in the area, the Old Port (particularly Exchange Street) continues to be the city's leading tourist attraction, the sort of place in which visitors—particularly visitors who

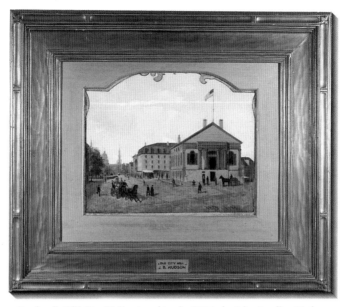

Portland's Old City Hall painted in the 1890s by John Bradley Hudson. (Farnsworth Art Museum, Rockland)

like to shop—can be turned loose for an afternoon. The area's eclectic architecture is notable not so much for any particular building, but for its very pleasing mix of revival styles in brick, terra-cotta, and granite.

Somewhat more "real" (in the sense that more Portlanders spend their days there) is the traditional downtown along **Congress Street,** with its center running from the ornate Beaux-Arts City Hall past **Monument Square** up to **Longfellow Square.** In a pattern repeated in many Maine downtowns, this once-thriving center lost much of its liveliness when suburban malls in the 1970s began drawing retail business out of downtown (only to find, in the 1990s, that huge discount warehouses would do the same thing to the malls). Despite the presence of much of Maine's legal and banking community at one end of Congress Street and its leading medical center at the other, the traditional downtown grew decidedly seedy at a time when the Old Port was being rediscovered. In the 1990s, Congress Street is perking up as the culture industry—an expanded **Maine Historical Society,** the **Portland Museum of Art,** the **Children's Museum,** the **Portland School of Art** (which has just moved into what used to be the street's largest department store), the **Portland Stage Company,** the

Portland Symphony, various dance companies—gives new life to the notion that cities need centers.

The fourth neighborhood is less easily defined by streets than by chronology: it is residential Portland of the early nineteenth century. A good many blocks of it survive, scattered on the western side of town along such streets as Spring, Danforth, High, State, and Park. This is an area to stroll through at leisure; for a more authoritative introduction, Greater Portland Landmarks, the city's leading preservation group, offers frequent walking tours of these and other parts of town. Portland has its share of traffic and parking problems, but it is still a city in which one can work downtown, lunch in an interesting restaurant in the Old Port, see a film, eat a lobster dinner on the waterfront, and go home to a handsome nineteenth-century row house—without ever having to drive.

■ HISTORY ON THE HARBOR

There are any number of pleasant spots from which to watch modern Portland pass by—**Green Mountain Coffee** on Temple Street, for example, or the sidewalk of **Raffles Bookstore Cafe** (a revamped shoe store) on Congress, or the park beneath the huge *trompe-l'oeil* mural in the center of the Old Port. But you might stroll down to the harbor, where some of today's city folks ferry from their island homes to the mainland, passing among the ghosts of Portland's founding fathers, as well as its first enemies.

Lacking a boat yourself, you can at least take one of the ferries from Commercial Street to the various islands in **Casco Bay** whose residents commute by water to work in Portland. Several of Casco Bay's islands are home to thriving communities, though others are little more than ledges. Even on the bay, however, it is difficult after a little reading, or a visit to the Maine Historical Society, not to think of history—especially that of the city's beginnings. After all, the bay's islands were named the Calendar Islands by seventeenth-century explorer John Smith, who claimed there were 365 of them. Though realistically numbering between 130 and 220, Casco Bay's islands are replete with legend, much of it involving pirates (like Captain Kidd), privateers, and islanders of varying degrees of respectability. Take Captain Keiff of Crotch Island. During stormy weather he would tie a lantern from his horse's neck and ride up and down the shore in hopes of luring a passing vessel onto the rocks, after which he would salvage the wreck.

It was on another island that Christopher Levett, seeking to promote New England back home among his countrymen, built a house in 1624, before returning to England to write an account of his voyage lavishly praising the potential of Maine. Over the next century a trickle of English colonists joined the handful of fishermen already in Casco Bay, but early attempts at permanent settlement were thwarted by the series of "wars" with the French and their Indian allies. Indeed, the first of the three great disasters to befall the future city of Portland took shape in the spring of 1690 on the islands of Casco Bay. By that time some 40 families had settled around the Back Cove of what was called "the Neck" (the Portland peninsula). Sailing from their hiding places on the islands, the French and Indians ambushed a company of soldiers on Munjoy Hill, burned all the houses in town, and laid siege to the garrison at Fort Loyall (at the foot of modern India Street) into which the terrified settlers had fled. Tricked into surrender by promises of safe passage, almost all of the English population was massacred on the spot.

"The Neck" remained uninhabited for another 26 years, but as the eighteenth century progressed what was then called Falmouth slowly grew into an important market and courthouse town, the center of commerce for a rapidly developing interior. (The French problem had disappeared in 1763 when the British won Canada; the Native Americans in southern Maine were slowly being eliminated, thanks in part to a large bounty offered for the scalp of any male Indian over the age of 12.) Enthusiasm for the American Revolution was much less intense on "the Neck," which depended heavily on maritime trade, than in the more radical backcountry. Many of the more respectable citizens of Falmouth, for example, were horrified in the spring of 1775 to learn that the fire-breathing Colonel Samuel Thompson of Brunswick had captured the captain of a British sloop of war, the *Canceau,* that was protecting a Loyalist shipbuilder in Casco Bay. Captain Mowatt was eventually released, at the insistence of the townspeople, but he left furious at his humiliation, and he and the *Canceau* were back in the harbor with other warships by October. According to legend, he was determined to teach the rebels a lesson; recent scholarship suggests that his mission in fact was to lay waste to all the coastal towns, and Falmouth simply happened to be, thanks to the wind and tide, the easiest to reach. In any case, he gave the townspeople a few hours to evacuate their goods before his guns leveled the town and his marines landed to set fire to the ruins. It is some indication of the confusion in which the American Revolution was fought that whatever Falmouth property the British had left behind, the militiamen from nearby Gorham soon looted.

■ RESURGAM

When Mowatt sailed away, more than 400 buildings on "the Neck" lay in ruins. The destruction turned more Mainers against the British, and after the war Falmouth—renamed Portland—quickly recovered. The Embargo of 1807 was a disaster—grass grew on the wharves, vessels rotted—but again the economy picked up, especially after the arrival of the railroads. There was some hope that Portland might even surpass Boston as a major Atlantic port, thanks to its rail connections with Canada, but this never happened, partly because of Maine's smaller population, partly because Boston still exerted a good deal of control over Maine's economy (a situation which continues today, especially in banking).

The next great disaster was homemade. During the especially festive Fourth of July celebrations in 1866 marking the end of "the War of the Rebellion," someone threw a firecracker into a boatbuilder's yard on Commercial Street. Wood shavings caught fire, the wind was blowing hard, the water supply proved inadequate, and by the next morning 10,000 people were homeless. The fire, one of the worst in the country to that date, destroyed much of the eastern half of Portland. Longfellow, who happened to be visiting, said it reminded him of Pompeii. The uniformity of style that redbrick and granite gives to so much of the Old Port today is due to the rapid rebuilding of the city in the 1870s and 1880s. After this disaster, the city adopted as its motto *Resurgam* ("I shall rise")—a slogan it had more than once lived up to.

■ HISTORIC HOMES

The eighteenth and nineteenth centuries brought to Portland a cast of characters who shaped the city into a center for commerce and art. For an understanding of Portland's development, architecture may offer the most accessible clue. There are four house museums in Portland of considerable interest, each representing a specific period of the city's development. In the little neighborhood of Stroudwater —a survivor of the eighteenth century incongruously close to Portland's busy airport—you will find, for example, the **Tate House** (1755) at 1270 Westbrook Street. In the days of sail when Britain ruled the waves, the Royal Navy had to make sure it had a reliable supply of tall, straight pines to provide masts and spars for its ships. When the traditional sources in the Baltic were depleted in the early eighteenth century, New England—particularly sparsely settled Maine—became the major source. A great deal of unpleasantness resulted when agents of the Crown started marking trees with the "King's arrow" and telling the colonials, who thought they owned this valuable timber, not to cut them. In the middle of this business, on the shores of Casco Bay, was George Tate, the mast agent; he obviously did well, for his house in Stroudwater, with its unusual stepped gambrel roof, is a luxurious dwelling (now maintained by the Colonial Dames) for the time and place—another glimpse of what a distance separated the elite and the common folk in pre-Revolutionary America.

Much of the elite that owed its prosperity and status to its ties with the royal government had to flee New England early on during the Revolution, and the post-war period enabled a new set of people—many of them lawyers whose fathers had been prosperous farmers—to rise to the top. Maine, and Portland in particular, was an especially promising place in the 1790s, when trade boomed and a flood of new settlers poured into the backcountry. A fine example of the fruits of this prosperity is the **Wadsworth-Longfellow House** (1785) at 487 Congress Street, the first brick house in Portland, built by the poet's grandfather, Gen. Peleg Wadsworth, and

Interior of the Wadsworth-Longfellow House, built in 1785, and the first brick house in Portland. (Brian Vanden Brink)

The Victoria Mansion has one of America's best-preserved high-style interiors of the late 1850s. (Brian Vanden Brink)

maintained much as it was during the tenure of the general's son-in-law, the lawyer and Federalist politician Stephen Longfellow. The house, now part of the Maine Historical Society complex, is filled with mementos of Henry Wadsworth Longfellow's childhood, and serves as a reminder that Portland had a lively literary culture in the early decades of the nineteenth century, including the lawyer-novelist John Neal and the satirist Seba Smith (whose "Jack Downing" sketches in back country dialect were the origin of later Down East humorous writing.)

Neal Dow, temperance reformer and Portland mayor. (Library of Congress)

The pre-Civil War generation in Portland is represented by two very different houses, a few blocks from each other. Along with the Longfellow House, one of the few other remaining early nineteenth-century dwellings from Congress Street's residential days is the Greek Revival **Neal Dow House** (714 Congress), maintained—appropriately enough—by the Women's Christian Temperance Union. Dow, a controversial Portland mayor and Civil War general, was the force behind the much debated Maine Law, passed in 1850 and not rescinded until 1934, which was the country's first large-scale experiment with prohibition. Dow was reviled by some—John Neal complained that the state motto *Dirigo* ("I direct") ought to have been changed to "Water, water, everywhere, but not a drop to drink"—and honored by others; today his house sits quietly, little visited, its dark Victorian library apparently ready for his return any moment from one of his many reformist campaigns.

Of a very different nature is the **Victoria Mansion** at 109 Danforth Street, an imposing Italianate pile clad in brownstone (shipped from Portland, *Connecticut*). The rather severe exterior conceals a dramatic surprise, one of the best-preserved high-style interiors of the late 1850s in the country, a lush collage of stained glass,

THE VILLAGE BLACKSMITH

*U*nder a spreading chestnut-tree
    The village smithy stands;
The smith, a mighty man is he,
    With large and sinewy hands;
And the muscles of his brawny arms
    Are strong as iron bands.

His hair is crisp, and black, and long,
    His face is like the tan;
His brow is wet with honest sweat,
    He earns whate'er he can,
And looks the whole world in the face,
    For he owes not any man.

Week in, week out, from morn till night,
    You can hear his bellows blow;
You can hear him swing his heavy sledge
    With measured beat and slow,
Like a sexton ringing the village bell,
    When the evening sun is low.

And children coming home from school
    Look in at the open door;
They love to see the flaming forge,
    And hear the bellows roar,
And catch the burning sparks that fly
    Like chaff from a threshing-floor. . . .

—Henry Wadsworth Longfellow, 1841

A village blacksmith photographed by Emma D. Sewall.
(Courtesy of Abbie Sewall)

gilt, satin, walnut, mahogany, marble, and velvet, filled with Herter Brothers furniture and *trompe-l'oeil* murals. Named for a later owner's museum dedicated to the British monarch, the house was built between 1858 and 1860 for a Maine native, Ruggles S. Morse, who had made a fortune in the hotel business. Designed by Henry Austin, the house does suggest something of a luxury hotel of the Civil War era—in its sky-lighted central hall, its massive gas chandelier, its grand stairway, its stately public rooms, and its state-of-the-art plumbing. Morse had many commercial ties with New Orleans; on the landing is a stained glass window in which you will find the state seals of Maine (the sailor and farmer) and of Louisiana (the pelican). Like many Mainers with shipping and other business interests in the South, he was less than enthusiastic about the Civil War—which he spent in New Orleans. His house, the grandest in Portland in its day and intended only for summer use, remains in such a remarkable state of preservation because it has had so few changes of owners.

■ MODERN PORTLAND

The city adopted its motto *Resurgam* as a tribute to its resolve in the face of earlier adversity, but it's also not a bad description of the city's renaissance in the 1980s. As in so many other Maine communities, the economic slump of the early 1990s is giving Portlanders a chance to catch their breath and reassess exactly what kind of city they want. The quality of life in Portland long suffered for lack of a good college or university in town (an attempt in the 1790s to build Bowdoin College on Bramhall Hill lost out, for political reasons, to Brunswick, half an hour to the north). This is changing with the growth in the past decade of the **University of Southern Maine.** The new campus library, recycled from an old landmark bakery, can be seen from I-295; USM's other features, such as the splendid Osher-Smith map collection and the distinctive New England Studies Program, are putting it on the national map.

The Portland Museum of Art is a well-established institution in new quarters downtown. The postmodern building, designed by Henry Cobb of the I. M. Pei architectural firm, with its echoes of Sir John Soane's house and his Dulwich Art Gallery in London, and its free use on the facade of highly stylized Renaissance forms, is one of the few contemporary buildings of any note in the state. The

(right) Along the waterfront in today's Portland.

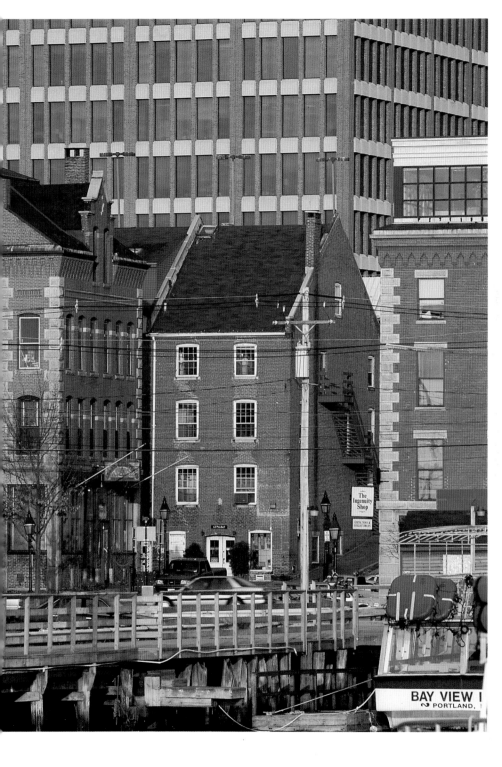

museum, however, seemed at first more building than collection; the gift of the Payson family's fine Impressionist and Post-Impressionist works now joins the museum's important State of Maine collection.

Another major development stands to have some even stronger ramifications on life in Portland. There is serious talk of rebuilding a train station on the site of old Union Station, a châteauesque granite pile that used to sit where there is now a little shopping center off Congress Street. (It was pulled down in the early 1960s, an act of civic vandalism that gave rise to Portland's now quite influential historic preservation movement.) This possibility of a quick, safe, and comfortable (though probably not inexpensive) ride to and from New England's largest city suggests that for at least some people, Portland could become, like Salem and Marblehead, a place to live if you work in Boston.

■ ON THE TOWN

Portland has by far the greatest number of restaurants in the state—and the greatest variety, ranging from Middle Eastern (the **Afghan Restaurant,** on Exchange Street) to American Southern (**Uncle Billy's Bar-B-Que,** across the bridge in South Portland.) The city's most sophisticated cooking can probably be found at the **Back Bay Grill** (on Portland Street, near the main post office), where a recent menu offered, for example, risotto with lobster, and venison in a peppercorn sauce. Also of interest at the ambitious end of the scale is the new **Cafe Brix,** near the airport.

Restaurants of varying quality—and unpredictable longevity—are found scattered throughout the Old Port in particular; and just beyond its limits, across Franklin on Middle, is a sort of restaurant row, from **Hugo's Portland Bistro** to the intimate **Cafe Always** and including the very popular **Pepperclub,** with its innovative and largely vegetarian menu. The most successful "serious" restaurants in Portland seem to be those that manage to combine the new interest in relatively unadorned, almost home-style cooking with seasonal ingredients and considerable technical skill (often showing Tex-Mex or Cajun influence): the best examples being **Alberta's** on Pleasant Street and **Katahdin** on Spring Street (near the Museum of Art), both of them with notably funky decor, and including the smaller **West Side Cafe** (a neighborhood hangout on Pine Street), the **Madd Apple Cafe** (next to the Portland Stage Company), and **Walter's Cafe** (Exchange Street). The **Victory Deli**

NEW MAINE COOKING

When journalist Robert Carter and his friends were cruising down the Maine coast in the summer of 1858, one day they caught more fish than they could salt and store. So they asked their pilot to make a chowder. "He went to work, and as we had salt pork, potatoes, and onions on board, and plenty of 'hard tack,' or crackers, in less than an hour we were sitting in front of as fine a chowder as one could wish to eat." It was a scene that catches the essence of traditional, unadorned Maine cooking—making do with whatever ingredients from land or sea are at hand, relying on pork or bacon for some flavor, and filling the stomach with potatoes and bread. Such food could be wonderfully restorative, especially in cold or wet weather, and variations on this chowder theme in particular can still be found in restaurants all along the coast.

Otherwise, traditional Maine cooking is hard for the traveler to discover today, except perhaps at church suppers, grange hall events, and the more rural local fairs. Traditional Franco-American cuisine survives in the *tourtières,* or pork pies, found in supermarkets, but Yankee and Franco-American culinary traditions alike have dwindled in an age of fast, heat-and-serve food. New England bean-hole suppers and clam bakes survive, but only as self-conscious rituals that preserve the memory of simpler days. If a vote were held today, pizza would probably be elected the state dish.

What has happened, however, is the emergence over the past 20 years of a new style of Maine cooking, one that takes advantage of some very traditional ingredients (as well as some startling new ones) and applies to them techniques of cooking from other traditions, notably Mediterranean and Asian cuisines. While only a few restaurants, comparatively speaking, experiment in this new style, the idea has caught on in enough private kitchens to suggest that it is not a passing fad.

Take fiddleheads, for example. They are the young, tightly furled shoots of the common cinnamon fern *(Osmunda cinnamomea),* found in moist, shaded places throughout the state. In an age when people had to get through winter on whatever they could salt, pickle, or store in a root cellar, the sight of the first fresh green fiddleheads in early spring must have been a delightful one. The traditional method was to boil them like any vegetable and serve them with butter. (They can also be canned, but their vernal charm is lost.) Today, fiddleheads are cooked as briefly as possible, preferably in a steamer, and make an appearance in June in any number of "new" dishes, including risottos, pastas, and soups. Their flavor is subtle—slightly asparagus-like, but more tart and grassy—and they look wonderful, like little question marks.

Their use is testimony to a renewed belief in the importance of seasonal foods, not only for their freshness but as a way of reattaching one's life to the cycle of the year.

Seafood is the largest field of experimentation. At a time when some popular species are being overfished, it is good news that species like monkfish are now being sold rather than thrown overboard. A few years ago, only a seagull would have eaten a Maine sea urchin. Today they are gathered by divers and sent by the ton to Japan (alas, at the risk of being depleted), and a few Americans are discovering what the French have known for centuries—that the orange roe of the sea urchin offers one of the most delectable tastes of the sea. Similarly, there is a new market for mussels, which, like Maine oysters and salmon, are proving a seafood that can be successfully "farmed." And dare one admit it—that boiled lobster (however delicious) is something of a cliché, and not Maine's only *fruit de mer?* Equally flavorful are Maine crab meat (claw meat, preferably) and Maine scallops. Both achieve a tender sweetness in Maine's cold waters that is unsurpassed.

From the back-to-the-earth movement of the 1970s have emerged several small cottage industries around the state, producing tangy Maine goat cheeses, fresh herbs, superb honeys and preserves, organic lamb and beef, peasant-style breads, and smoked seafood. Gathering wild mushrooms, once a hobby, now is a small-scale business in a few communities. A new appreciation of some very traditional foods—venison, for example—has led to its appearance on more and more restaurant menus.

The popularity of farmers' markets in summer and fall in so many Maine towns is further evidence of an awakened appreciation of freshness and taste. While rarely a bargain, they are often a visual delight and a welcomed alternative to the wooden produce in the supermarkets. Here you can find a dozen varieties of old-fashioned apples, as many kinds of peppers and squash, freshly picked berries, vegetables with the dew still on the leaf. These outdoor markets, like the new cooking, are evidence that tradition and innovation can sometimes find common ground.

Whether traditional or "new" Maine cooking, lobster is still the star ingredient.

Dale Roberts and friend stroll past a mural on the wall of the Bath Iron Works' Portland facility.

(two locations: at Monument Square and across from USM's library) remains a favorite for breakfast; **Ruby's Choice** (Free Street) makes the best burgers in town; tiny **Silly's** (on the Munjoy Hill end of Cumberland Avenue) has the best Jamaican jerk chicken, and **Street & Company** (Wharf Street) is the place for seafood beyond the boiled lobster level. For Asian food, **Hu Shang** (Exchange Street) is a local institution, though it now has a number of Thai and Vietnamese rivals.

For picnic food, try **Micucci's** (an old-fashioned Italian deli) or **Foodworks**, both on India Street, or such Old Port shops as the **Whip & Spoon** (which is also the state's best kitchen goods store), **Fresh Market Pasta,** and the **Portland Greengrocer.** For a bowl of chowder to go, or just to look at the catch of the day on its bed of seaweed and ice, the **Harbor Fish Market** on Custom House Wharf offers both a picturesque locale and a wide selection of fresh and smoked seafood. For the same fare fried or broiled, try the nearby **Porthole** or **J's Oyster** or **Cap'n Jim's,** all of them intensely local eateries in a rapidly gentrifying neighborhood.

Neal Dow must be quivering in his grave, but central Portland today also offers the state's largest concentration of places to have a drink. In fact, the Old Port on warm nights can turn a bit rowdy, though compared to most other American cities Portland is still a relatively safe place to be after dark. An Irish-style pub called **Brian Boru's** (near the Civic Center) is the current favorite, rivaled by two Free Street landmarks, **Three-Dollar Dewey's** (good chili) and **Gritty McDuff's**, a pub that is a local pioneer in micro-brewing (made only 30 feet from the tap, as the owner likes to point out, are its Best Bitter, Portland Head Light Pale Ale, Black Fly Stout, and Sebago Light Ale, with various seasonal additions, such as Christmas Ale). The other local product to taste in Portland pubs is the widely distributed Geary's beer.

Although most Portlanders now shop at the huge Maine Mall and its imitators, the center of town has lots of interesting specialty stores. Stylish Maine-made crafts, including jewelry and pottery, can be found in such places as the **Nancy Margolis Gallery, Abacus,** and the **Maine Potters Market,** all in the Old Port. Portland's best bookstores include **Bookland** (off Monument Square and at other locations) and **Books Etc.** (Exchange Street), but the real treasure-troves are in its second-hand and antiquarian stores, notably those of **Douglas N. Harding** (in a landmark Congress Street building near the Museum of Art), **Carlson-Turner** (on Congress, near the historic Eastern Cemetery), and **Allen Scott** (a cozy, rambling Exchange Street shop that looks exactly the way a bookstore of character ought to look). And Maine's dean of antiquarian bookmen, **Francis O'Brien,** is still going strong on High Street.

A century ago, Portland's best known product was its pressed glass (an ornate sampling of which is on display at the Museum of Art); today it is the Shaker-influenced furniture designed and made by **Thos. Moser Cabinetmaker,** whose handsome building can be visited on Cumberland Avenue. Portland's lively art gallery scene slowed down in the late 1980s, but has since bounced back. The market for antiques remains stable, if not strong, and can be sampled at the auction house of **F. O. Bailey** or, for smaller items like estate jewelry, at **Geraldine Wolf's,** both in the Old Port.

After dark the best places to stay in Portland are not new buildings but well-rehabilitated old ones: the poshest hotel in town is the **Regency,** which occupies a medieval-looking, red-brick former armory in the Old Port; the best-known hotel is the **Sonesta,** convenient to "museum row"; the most talked-about bed-and-breakfast is the **Pomegranate Inn** on Neal Street. Nighttime entertainment can range from a rock concert or a Portland Pirates' hockey game at the **Civic Center** to the Comedy Connection at the **Baker's Table** or shows at the newly restored **State Theater** (which is somewhat between a dinner theater and a cabaret/concert hall). The liveliest places after dark are **Raoul's, Granny Killam's,** and **Zootz's,** all offering progressive music and crowded dance floors to a youngish clientele. For more laid-back activity, a few rather upscale pool halls can be found above the storefronts in and around the Old Port; try **Old Port Billards** on Fore Street. Bargain entertainment after dark can be found at **The Movies** on Exchange Street (adventurous selections of foreign, vintage, and non-commercial films) and the price-cutting **Nickelodeon Cinema,** at Temple and Middle, facing the lobsterman statue.

As you leave Portland going north on I-95, you'll get a splendid view of the city behind you: a few miles north of the city, look across the tidal flats near the mouth of the Presumpscot River. In the distance, above the waters of Casco Bay, the eastern end of the city of Portland on a sunny day literally shimmers on its hilltop. You are soon traveling on one of the most beautiful sections of the interstate in Maine. Across the Presumpscot estuary you'll see 60-acre **Gilsland Farm,** a "gentleman farm" within sight of downtown Portland that is now headquarters of the Maine Audubon Society. One of 15 Audubon sanctuaries in the state, the farm offers two miles of nature trails and one of Maine's best museum-style gift shops.

ANDROSCOGGIN RIVER

As you leave Portland and head north along Casco Bay, you leave behind the towns first settled as outskirts to "Falmouth" (including present-day Falmouth), and arrive at towns established around the Falls of the Androscoggin River. While initially Brunswick (settled in 1628, incorporated in 1738) was this area's financial and cultural center, most of today's Maine visitors would consider the town of Freeport (incorporated in 1789), with its countless discount shops and outlets, the area's major draw.

■ FREEPORT AND L. L. BEAN'S

For anyone attending a New England college in the 1960s and 1970s, the midnight trip to L. L. Bean's was a familiar ritual. You bought beer, jumped in the car, drove however many hours it took, looked for the big statue of the Indian chief on U.S. 1 just outside of Freeport, and arrived at the famous sporting goods store at some odd hour of the morning, where you mingled with the hunters (in fall) or the fishermen (in spring) until it was time to begin a groggy drive back to the dorm. At the time the journey mattered more than the purchases; nonetheless, by dressing in the L. L. Bean style—which seemed almost no style at all—you pledged your allegiance to everything Maine stood for. The heavy blue sweaters, leather-topped rubber-soled boots, khaki trousers, and plaid flannel shirts proclaimed that you were ready for the woods and the rugged shores of Maine, even if you were spending most of your time in Cambridge or New Haven.

■ BEAN'S BEGINNINGS

Born in Greenwood in Oxford County in 1872, Leon Leonwood "L. L." Bean grew up in a culture in which hunting, fishing, and trapping were not simply a pastime but a way of putting food on the table. He was good at it and, as he recalled in his memoirs, by age 13 or 14 had sold his first buck for $12 to a pair of unsuccessful hunters. Orphaned at an early age, he was sent to work on a farm, paid his way through Kent's Hill School in Readfield by selling soap, worked in a

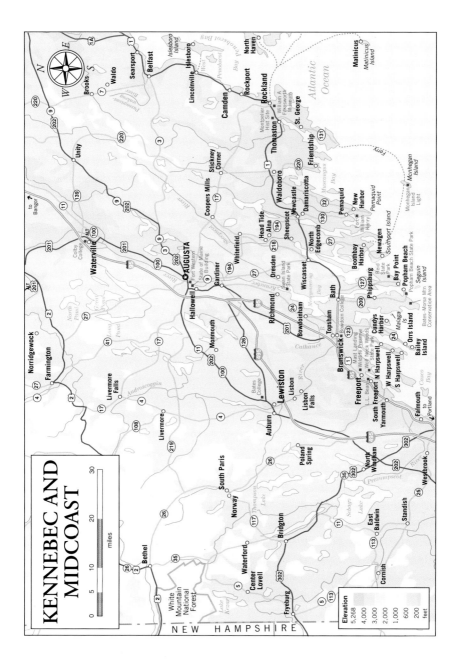

KENNEBEC AND MIDCOAST

shoe store, married a Freeport woman, and in 1905 founded Bean Brothers, a Freeport clothing store, with his brother. His would have been an unremarkable story had it not been for a pet peeve: when out hunting in the woods, his feet always got wet. An avid outdoorsman, Leon had trouble finding a comfortable hunting shoe that was both light and waterproof. So in 1911 he took a pair of rubber shoe bottoms from his store and asked a local shoe maker—Freeport's leading industry at that time—to stitch on a leather top. The idea seemed to work, but the first large batch was a disaster. The rubber was too flimsy to hold the stitching, and Bean had to take back 90 of the 100 he had sold. Undeterred, he borrowed $400 from his brother and convinced a Boston manufacturer to produce a light but sturdy rubber shoe with a heel low enough to attach a soft leather top.

From the start, he grasped two principles of successful marketing. First, money was to be made in a national mail order business (his first mailing in 1912 went to holders of nonresident hunting licenses). Second, Bean insisted on a notably generous attitude toward the return of goods, a policy which continues today. What came to be known as "the Bean boot" remained the company's best known product, but Bean took advantage of the new and highly mobile leisure culture of the 1920s to offer a range of hunting, fishing, and camping products. When Freeport's most famous son, explorer Donald B. MacMillan, outfitted an Arctic expedition in 1923, for example, he came to Bean's for footwear. In 1925 Bean introduced the trademark chamois shirt; in 1944, he added the popular canvas tote bag (known originally as the "Canvas Ice Carrier"). *LIFE* magazine ran a feature on the store in 1941, and during World War II, the company advised the U.S. Armed Forces on cold weather gear. In the meantime, the famous L. L. Bean's catalogue, with its nostalgic cover (probably a major source of Maine's image as an outdoor paradise in the American mind) and homespun prose, carried the store's name across the country.

While mail order remained the core of the business—the original store was on the second and third floors above Freeport's post office, with a mail chute going directly down—more and more customers took to dropping by to chat with L. L. Bean, who by the 1950s had become a popular Maine landmark himself. According to company legend, the store began staying open all night in 1951 because Bean was tired of sportsmen rapping on his window before dawn. Until his death in 1967, he could be found advising sportsmen on trout flies or duck calls and the like.

Then in the late 1970s, something unexpected happened. Already well known in hunting and fishing circles and frequented by old-time New Englanders, Bean's found a huge new market and a swarm of imitators as a result of the craze for "preppy" clothing. The preppy look—a remarkably long-lived, aggressively casual style—developed in East Coast boarding (or "prep") schools after World War II and by the 1960s became the official leisure-time costume of upper-middle-class America. By the late '70s, the preppy look was adopted far and wide. The requirements of the style—the slightly rumpled, well-worn feel, the use of conservatively colored natural fabrics, the suggestion that the wearer was socially secure enough to dress down—were all met with Bean's comfortable, traditional, and occasionally even frumpy clothing. The Bean "look" has since become a much-emulated American

L. L. Bean models his hunting safety coat for a 1940s
company catalog. (Courtesy of L. L. Bean Co.)

mode of dress: when the Pacific Rim leaders met at Seattle for a summit in November of 1993, most of them followed President Clinton's informal lead in adopting what the *New York Times* called "today's L. L. Bean diplomatic dress code."

To this day, L. L. Bean's remains a place you have to visit if you want to understand Maine. The company is still owned by Bean's descendants; meanwhile the store continues to expand far beyond its founder's dreams: since 1976 the store has had its own ZIP code—04033—and since the construction of the sprawling current store in 1984, its own indoor trout pond. Nonetheless, the store still sells well-made, sensibly priced merchandise for use in the Great Outdoors. Despite the international scale of its operations and the immense size of its floor space since a 1989 remodeling, its signature product continues to be versions of that 1911 hunting boot. Much of what the store sells has not changed in half a century: fishing rods and flies, shotguns, canoes, and outdoor gear. And Bean's runs a public "Outdoor Discovery" program, which offers lectures and workshops on everything from bow-and-arrow hunting to trail bike maintenance to sea kayaking.

Jennie Harrington stitching one of L. L. Bean's famous Maine Hunting Boots.

■ RETAIL CENTRAL

The success of L. L. Bean's brought on an onslaught of retailers to Freeport, Maine. While Bean's folksy store had long been a landmark, the real business had always been in mail order sales. But in the 1970s, I-95 made Freeport seem even closer to Boston, and the crowds in the store grew larger. Savvy marketers began to wonder: if people detour from the interstate to shop at Bean's, would they linger if Freeport had something else to offer? The chance arose in 1982 when fire destroyed a commercial building across the street from Bean's. A Dansk "factory outlet store" was built in its place. The rest, as they say, is retailing history. In 1981 the town had 55 retail businesses; in 1990, there were more than 150.

Today, an alien from another planet arriving in Freeport with a credit card could, in a matter of hours, outfit itself as a very upscale earthling. Clothing from Benetton, Calvin Klein, Donna Karan, Laura Ashley, Brooks Brothers, J. Crew, Ralph Lauren, Banana Republic; shoes from Cole-Haan, Bass, and Reebok; leather goods from Dooney & Bourke and Coach; household goods from Mikasa and Corning-Revere—these are only a few of the name-brands whose outlets line Main Street and spill down the hill (where Bean's itself has a factory outlet). Most of the stores are concentrated within easy walking distance of downtown. Even the local historical society has gone retail, at its Harrington House, packed with gift items and reproduction antiques. Only yesterday, it seems, Freeport was a sleepy town, where most people worked in the local shoe factories; today, with an estimated 4 million visitors a year, it has probably surpassed Acadia National Park as the state's leading tourist attraction.

■ BEYOND SHOPPING

Whether people see Freeport as a destination or simply stop there on their way to some less commercial spot remains a matter of debate among Maine's tourism promoters. But the town is worth the short detour from the interstate. For one thing, local preservationists have tried to maintain some village flavor despite the boom (which, incidentally, local taxpayers are finding less of a windfall than was promised). One result is that Freeport must have the only Greek Revival McDonald's in the country: when the town refused to allow a nineteenth-century house to be demolished, the fast-food franchise did an adaptive re-use of the property. And any serious traveler will be intrigued by the **DeLorme Map Store,** near the center of town; the firm makes by far the best maps of Maine and offers a wide selection of others, including topographical ones.

If trying on all those sweaters and shoes has given you an appetite, you're actually lucky to find yourself in downtown Freeport. Two blocks from L. L. Bean's, the dining room of the **Harraseeket Inn,** at 162 Main, is presided over by the most widely praised chef in the state, Sam Hayward. Hayward is especially noted for his devotion to the best local and seasonal produce: Pemaquid oysters from Damariscotta, wild mushrooms from Mount Vernon, game birds from Warren, raspberries from Bowdoinham, organic herbs and greens from Lisbon. Fall is said to be Hayward's favorite season—according to the rather chatty menu notes, it begins for him "sometime after the emergence of chanterelles and blackberries in August"—and a typical autumn dinner at the Harraseeket might include a sophisticated salad of cool-weather field greens and toasted Maine chevre as well as a very traditional quahog chowder and a chop of farm-raised venison. As that menu suggests, Hayward is one of the neo-traditionalists among Maine chefs: he subtly adapts the sort of cooking you might find at a Grange hall in a small Maine town. Visitors with a leisurely schedule might want to watch for the inn's wine-tasting weekends and seasonal festivals; the **Broad Arrow Tavern** in the basement offers lighter meals; the popular Sunday brunch, quite lavish ones.

Freeport, for all its crowds, is still a fairly intimate place, as some very scenic countryside is only a few minutes' drive from downtown. Before the Civil War, this was an agricultural area, with some shipbuilding. Many of its early nineteenth-century houses survive along the inlets of Casco Bay, notably in the very attractive town of **South Freeport,** which like the rural, coastal side of Freeport attracted many affluent retirees and commuters in the 1980s. There are several spots where visitors can hike along the shore: at the **Audubon Society's Mast Landing Wildlife Preserve,** for example, and the larger **Wolf Neck Woods State Park.** The University of Southern Maine's **Wolf Neck Farm** is a favorite spot to take children to see the prize herd of Angus cattle.

■ FREEPORT TO BRUNSWICK

A few years ago, in response to complaints about traffic jams on coastal U.S. 1, the state put up a sign on the northbound side of I-95 suggesting in effect that motorists might get to Acadia National Park a lot sooner if they skipped the coastal route and traveled overland, so to speak, from the Augusta exit by way of Route 3 to Belfast. This is still good advice—rarely crowded Route 3 crosses some beautiful lake and farm country—but the howl from chambers of commerce and motel owners from Brunswick to Camden could probably be heard in farthest Madawaska. So the sign came down. The innocent still take the Brunswick exit onto fabled U. S. 1 and, if they are patient, can enjoy some of the most interesting towns in New England. The town of Brunswick is about half an hour northeast of Portland—or 15 minutes northeast of Freeport—on I-95, and makes a wonderful jumping-off point for this corner of the state.

■ BOWDOIN COLLEGE

Brunswick likes to think of itself as a small college town, though in fact its U.S. Naval Air Station dominates the local economy. But it is Bowdoin College, founded in 1794, that has carried the town's name across the world. The college, on a slight hill beyond the wooden Gothic tower of First Parish Church at the end of the village green, is one of the cultural and intellectual centers of the state, with much to offer the visitor interested in books, paintings, nineteenth-century architecture, Arctic exploration, or hockey. Although in the last 25 years the college has grown increasingly national in its student body, Bowdoin's traditional role as late as the 1950s was to train the social and professional elite of the state. This is precisely what its founders, many of them large landowners in the district, had in mind two centuries ago, for they worried that Maine was an unruly place that would never prosper until it had stable institutions and an educated, civic-minded ruling class. Most of them also sought an educated—that is to say, Congregationalist—clergy: by the 1790s the backcountry of Maine was filled with itinerant Methodist, Baptists, and Universalist preachers, whose reputations as radicals and evangelicals made them seem threats to the established order. (Though never officially Congregational, the college considered itself as "belonging" to that denomination throughout the nineteenth century, an allegiance that cost Bowdoin dearly when the new state government in 1820 turned out to be full of Baptists.) The college was chartered by the Massachusetts General Court in 1794. James Bowdoin III, an absentee proprietor of vast tracts of Maine land, became the new college's leading patron; with the other founders, he named the school for his father, James Bowdoin II, a

(following pages) Cold winter fog rises along the shoreline near Martinsville.

merchant-prince and amateur scientist whose decisive action as governor in 1786 squelched Shays' Rebellion in western Massachusetts.

In its first century Bowdoin College rarely enrolled more than 200 students at any one time. Yet, it has produced more people of note than any other college of its size in the country. The list is remarkable: writer Nathaniel Hawthorne and poet Henry Wadsworth Longfellow (both of the class of 1825) stand out, but they are joined by U.S. President Franklin Pierce, Sen. William Pitt Fessenden (Lincoln's secretary of the treasury), Congressman Thomas Brackett Reed (the most powerful speaker in the history of the House), Civil War generals Joshua Chamberlain and Oliver Otis

Henry Wadsworth Longfellow, Bowdoin College class of 1825. (Library of Congress)

Howard, Civil War Massachusetts governor John A. Andrew (who raised the famous black regiments), Arctic explorers Robert Peary and Donald MacMillan, U.S. Supreme Court Chief Justice Melville Fuller, the black editor and colonizationist John Brown Russwurm, and dozens of other writers and politicians famous in their day. In this century, the list includes expert on gall wasps (and human sexuality) Alfred Kinsey, poet Robert Peter Tristram Coffin, civil rights advocate Hodding Carter Jr., Olympic marathoner Joan Benoit Samuelson (the college went coed in 1971), diplomat Thomas Pickering, and U. S. senators George Mitchell and William Cohen of Maine.

Although the school's strong programs in the sciences and environmentalism have attracted students from far and wide, the college itself remains the quintessential

Maine college, small (1,400 students) and traditional (fraternities continue to dominate undergraduate social life, though they now are required to be completely coed). The campus itself exemplifies that New England icon: the large, maple-shaded quadrangle surrounded by dignified, historic buildings of brick and granite. Perhaps at its most beautiful early on a summer evening or after a fresh snowfall, the Bowdoin Quad offers a lesson in several architectural revival styles. Richard Upjohn's Romanesque chapel of the 1840s (a landmark in the history of "medievalism" on American college campuses) looks across the green to Henry Vaughan's Oxbridge-style Hubbard Hall (1903) and McKim, Mead & White's Renaissance Revival Walker Art Building (1894), which is probably the finest public building in the state. The oldest building on campus is Federal-style Massachusetts Hall (1802), which housed the president, the chapel, the library, and all eight students when the college opened, and which later was home to the now-defunct Medical School of Maine (an affiliate of Bowdoin, 1820–1921). Two other structures, across Maine Street, are of considerable architectural interest: the "carpenter Gothic" Boody-Johnson House (Gervase Wheeler, 1849), whose design was published by A. J. Downing and widely copied across the country, and the Shingle-style Psi Upsilon House (John Calvin Stevens, 1900), an imaginative adaptation of a seaside cottage for a fraternity club house. The college has not been so successful with its later twentieth-century architecture, although Hugh Stubbins's 16-story

Arctic explorer Robert E. Peary in 1909.
(The Peary-MacMillan Arctic Museum, Bowdoin College)

Coles Tower (1964) was for a little while the tallest building north of Boston.

The college's museums and library are worth a visit. The **Walker Art Building** houses an excellent collection of Colonial and Federal portraits; also in the museum are the massive winged genii excavated by Sir Austen Henry Layard at Nineveh and sent by missionaries in Mesopotamia to various American colleges in the 1850s as proof of the historical accuracy of the Bible. The group of European paintings and Old Master drawings (some of which were copies, as was the style among collectors at the time) comprise what is probably the earliest public collection of European art in the country; the pieces were bequeathed in 1811 by James Bowdoin III, who believed strongly that the visual arts should be part of a liberal education.

Bowdoin's other tourist attraction, and a good one for kids, is the **Peary-Mac-Millan Arctic Museum** in Hubbard Hall, where you see the sled that took Peary and his colleague Matthew Henson to the North Pole in 1909. The navigational instruments with which Peary made his still-controversial calculations are also on display, along with stuffed polar bears, narwhal tusks, Inuit folk art, and other examples of material culture from the Far North.

*This painting by John G. Brown, ca. 1822, shows the Bowdoin campus in
the age when Hawthorne and Longfellow were students.
(Courtesy of Bowdoin College Museum of Art)*

■ OFF-CAMPUS BRUNSWICK

Brunswick has several other attractions. In the open field where Hawthorne and his classmates picked blueberries and shot pigeons now sprawls the **Naval Air Station,** responsible for anti-submarine patrols over much of the North Atlantic and occasionally open for air shows. At the opposite end of Maine Street from the college is the late nineteenth-century **Cabot Mill,** a Florentine fortress in red brick overlooking the Androscoggin (and now being rehabbed under the name Fort Andross, a reminder of an early eighteenth-century garrison on the site at the time of the Indian wars). The distinction between uphill and down was, until World War II, more than geographic. The mill area near the river was working class and Catholic—and largely French speaking as the result of the arrival of workers from rural Quebec starting in the 1860s—while the hill was "Anglo" and Protestant. Noisy brawls between Bowdoin students and boys from town ("Yaggers," in the local slang) were a regular feature of nineteenth-century Brunswick life. Up the hill, First Parish Church (1846) is one of three Medieval Revival ecclesiastical buildings designed by Upjohn (in addition to the college chapel there is St. Paul's Episcopal Church, on Pleasant Street); the First Parish interior offers an intricate complex of wooden arches, suggesting to some people the hull of a ship, and the pew in which Harriet Beecher Stowe had the "vision" of Uncle Tom's martyrdom that inspired part of her novel. The church was also the scene in 1875 of Longfellow's reading of his "Morituri Salutamus," written for his fiftieth Bowdoin reunion. Stowe's house, now a gift shop and inn, can be visited at 63 Federal Street; there in 1850–51, while her husband Calvin taught theology at Bowdoin, she wrote *Uncle Tom's Cabin,* completing parts of it in her husband's quiet study in Appleton Hall. Federal Street is lined with many attractive Federal and Greek Revival houses, several of them the work of the talented local housewright Samuel Melcher.

The Pejepscot Historical Society, overlooking the Mall (as the village green is called), runs not only the increasingly popular **Chamberlain House** (see essay, "Joshua Chamberlain"), but a lesser known yet quite fascinating property on Park Row, the **Whittier House.** Dr. Frank Whittier was a pioneer in forensic medicine in the state (his rather grisly tools are on exhibit), and his daughter Dr. Alice Whittier was the state's first female pediatrician. A few years ago she turned the huge house and its contents over to the society with instructions to change nothing, not even the unlit candles in the dining room chandelier (which were to be lighted, according to family tradition, when any of the three Whittier daughters married).

JOSHUA CHAMBERLAIN

Although never forgotten in Maine, where he was a college president and four-time governor, Joshua Lawrence Chamberlain did not in his own day enjoy the national acclaim given such other Civil War generals as Lee, Grant, Sherman, Jackson, Sheridan, and Howard. There is no statue of him on a battlefield, and little mention of his heroism or his skill as a field commander in most of the standard accounts of the war. When he was mentioned in such works, it was usually for his ceremonial role in receiving the Confederate surrender at Appomattox, and for his controversial gesture of saluting his defeated foe. Yet in recent years Chamberlain has emerged as

Joshua Chamberlain, Civil War hero of Gettysburg. (Library of Congress)

one of the most exemplary figures of the Civil War era. It is widely recognized now that his decisive action at Little Round Top on the second day of the battle of Gettysburg may have saved the North from defeat: about to run out of ammunition, he ordered his Maine riflemen to fix bayonets and charge the Alabama troops who were about to turn the Union's left flank. His quick thinking under fire and his ability to inspire troops earned him a place in the modern U. S. Army's leadership training manual.

After being graduated from Bowdoin in 1852, Chamberlain became a professor of rhetoric and modern languages, and his colleagues at Bowdoin were not happy when, in 1862, he decided to go off to fight. But Chamberlain insisted, and, after writing the state's war-time governor to ask if any posts were available, he was asked to serve as lieutenant-colonel of the 20th Maine Infantry Regiment. On the long boat ride to Virginia, he studied tactics. Despite his lack of training, Chamberlain had a dramatic career: 24 major battles and numerous skirmishes, six wounds (including, during the siege of Petersburg, a bullet wound through his groin—the complications of which eventually killed him in 1914), near-death at Gettysburg when a Confederate officer tried to shoot him at close range (only to have his pistol misfire), and several horses shot from under him. He was promoted to general on the field after Petersburg, and by 1865 was so admired by Grant that he was given the historic honor of receiving the surrender of the Army of Northern Virginia at Appomattox.

The place to which all Chamberlain admirers must make a pilgrimage is the **General Joshua L. Chamberlain House** at 226 Maine Street in Brunswick, which he occupied for much of his long life. Saved from being torn down for a fast-food franchise in 1980, the house has been partially restored after several decades of service as a slightly seedy off-campus rental for Bowdoin students. The house, whose upper floors are still rented as apartments, contains a good deal of Chamberlain memorabilia, including his wartime saddle and his boots.

Built at 4 Potter Street, half a block away from its current location, the house started as a typical mid-1820s Cape house; the young Henry Wadsworth Longfellow and his bride lived there in the 1830s. Chamberlain purchased the house just before the Civil War, and had it moved to its current location. (Given enough oxen and rollers, wood-frame houses were not difficult to lift off their foundations and move in nineteenth-century Maine.) When Chamberlain returned to Brunswick after the war, he made major changes to his house: in 1871, he had the Cape house jacked up and a new ground story built beneath it. The Greek Revival doorway that the Longfellows had entered became a decorative porch on the Chamberlain House's second-floor facade. He also added to the chimneys, which display the red Maltese cross ensignia of the 20th Maine, and had woodworkers ornament the house in a medley of Gothic and Italianate motifs.

Chamberlain's post-Civil War career, however, held its share of disappointments. Although well respected as a Republican governor, Chamberlain found that civilian life lacked the clear-cut nature of military duties. His marriage was troubled, his plans to modernize Bowdoin were thwarted by the traditionalists, and he did not seem to share the skill (or the lack of scruple) so many former Civil War generals had shown in making money. In 1914 he died in Portland, one of the last survivors of that dashing generation of young men who had gone off to command armies in the "War of the Rebellion," and was buried in Brunswick's Pine Grove Cemetery.

On the Bowdoin campus, Hubbard Hall includes Chamberlain's portrait in the presidential gallery, and Memorial Hall includes his name on the bronze tablets listing 228 alumni who fought for the Union. Note, too, the smaller plaque on the west stair landing commemorating the college's 18 Confederate alumni.

There are several historic inns in the area, the most luxurious being the **Captain Daniel Stone Inn,** at 10 Water Sreet. Two local gastronomic shrines are **Fat Boy's** (111 Bath Rd.), across from the Navy base, and **Tess's** (54 Pleasant St.), a neighborhood pizza shop whose amiable proprietor will also sell you vintage port, first-growth claret, or the latest bargain from Chile or Spain.

One underappreciated fact about Brunswick is that it probably has more books for sale per capita than any other Maine community; aside from the commercial and college bookstores, there is Gary Lawless's alternative **Gulf of Maine** (with a good Maine poetry selection) at 61 Maine, Clare Howell's inviting **Old Books** at 136 Maine, and the **Maine Writers & Publishers Alliance shop** just off Route 1 near Maine Street, a showcase for local authors.

■ TOPSHAM AND THE HARPSWELLS

The environs of Brunswick also have much to offer. Across the river is the smaller town of Topsham, with a historic district along Elm Street that retains much of its

Common murre decoys on Matinicus Rock offshore from Rockland. These decoys are used to attract murres to the island in hopes of restoring a nesting colony.

Environmentalist author Rachel Carson's cottage near Southport.

early nineteenth-century look (the town was once an important lumber and ship-building center) and a landmark, 1860-ish yellow-brick mill jutting into the river.

To the south of Brunswick are three long fingers of rocky coastline known collectively as the Harpswells. While in the Brunswick area, Harriet Beecher Stowe gathered material on her excursions in this neighborhood for *The Pearl of Orr's Island,* a sentimental novel of coastal Maine life that helped popularize the use of local dialect in American fiction. Today the Town of Harpswell, which includes the communities of Cundy's Harbor, Bailey Island, Orrs Island, North and South Harpswell, and some 45 small islands, remains largely rural in feeling, though affluent retirees are beginning to outnumber the fishermen. The "heart" of the area is Harpswell Center, where a handsome 1757 meetinghouse overlooks the cemetery, a general store, and the 1843 Elijah Kellogg Congregational Church, named for a nineteenth-century minister and writer. South of town are South Harpswell and Bailey Island, which offer several atmospheric places to eat lobster, including the seasonal **Rock Oven,** with its view of Ragged Island—summer residence of Edna St. Vincent Millay.

A 1915 photograph by Bertrand H. Wentworth captures a quintessential Maine coastal scene. (Library of Congress)

■ MALAGA ISLAND

One other landmark deserves mention, though few people ever visit there (it is privately owned and accessible only by boat), and many old-time Mainers would prefer never to hear it mentioned. Malaga Island is as much a part of Maine's maritime history, however, as Bath or Wiscasset. A half-mile-long island near the mouth of the New Meadows River, between Harpswell and Phippsburg, Malaga was settled about the time Bowdoin College began—by a black fisherman-farmer, Benjamin Darling. He was one of several hundred blacks, some of them sailors, some of them descendants of slaves brought to New England, who lived along the Maine coast in the decades following the Revolution. Darling's descendants intermarried with local white families and, like their neighbors, continued to eke out a meager existence through a combination of fishing, farming, and doing odd chores. The history of the island through the nineteenth century is obscure (residents of such remote places often escaped taxation, the draft, and the census). Other blacks may have joined the original settlers. According to local legend, sea captains from nearby Bath maintained mistresses and second families there, on an island where no one asked too many questions.

By the early twentieth century, however, places like Malaga were highly desirable coastal real estate, and the island's impoverished, racially mixed population began to draw comment. The rumor spread that the 50 or so islanders were "half-wits" and "degenerates." Local authorities began putting some of the islanders' children in state homes, and sentiment grew that this pocket of "shame" needed cleaning out. In 1912—in one of the most shameful incidents in Maine's modern history—the governor himself supervised the eviction of the remaining settlers' descendants (none of whom could prove title to any land on the island, though their families had lived there since before Maine was a state). Even Malaga's cemetery was dug up and its contents hastily reburied on the mainland, at an institution for the mentally "enfeebled." The "purification" was complete, and the island made safe for development.

■ LEWISTON AND AUBURN

The Androscoggin today is an underappreciated river, even though it's much cleaner and less smelly than it was a generation ago. Nevertheless, the flow of its waters shaped the growth of much of west-central Maine in the nineteenth century. Brunswick, Lisbon, Lewiston, Auburn—all were built at falls of the river to harness its power for their mills (first lumber, then textiles). Today, if you stand on the Longley Memorial Bridge between the twin cities of Lewiston and Auburn at the time of the annual spring freshet, you can still get some idea of the river's strength as its floodwaters, drained from melting snow on the White Mountains, crash and explode over the falls of the Androscoggin.

Lewiston is not a city that appears on many tourist itineraries, other than being part of the popular Bates-Bowdoin-Colby circuit each summer for parents and would-be students looking at Maine's best known colleges. But Lewiston, the state's second largest city and still an important manufacturing center, is as representative of one side of Maine's past as Wiscasset, say, is of another. If one is Yankee, maritime, colonial revivalized, the other is French-American, industrial, and densely settled in patterns of habitation—most typically, "three-decker" wooden houses—that no one to date has found picturesque but which shelter a closely bonded community. Settled in 1770, Lewiston has been a textile center since 1819. From the 1840s through the 1870s, its life was dominated by Boston-owned factories and mills, whose massive brick buildings still line the riverfront and its adjacent canal and whose need for cheap, docile labor encouraged the migration of young people from Quebec. Lewiston in fact rivals Lowell and Lawrence in Massachusetts as one of the great assemblages of mid-nineteenth-century industrial architecture, although the effect as you drive along the two miles of canals is less Victorian Italianate that it is de Chirico. The city is beginning to appreciate its remarkable stock of buildings; the Lewiston Mill System Project began in 1993 to survey the 654-acre mill and canal system (the earliest parts of which date from the 1850s) and make plans for adaptive re-use of its abandoned architectural marvels (it includes, for example 26 historic bridges). Lewiston also has one of the best twentieth-century buildings in Maine: the soaring, twin-towered Sts. Peter and Paul Church, built in 1936–38 of Maine granite in a modified French Gothic style and the second largest church in New England. Lewiston's *centre ville* has several other buildings of note; a drive on the downtown portion of Lisbon Street also offers a slice of sociology, with rough-looking "social clubs" at one end and professional offices at the other. Lisbon Street is also home of L.A. Arts, which brings world-class performers to what, in a brilliant if ambitious piece of marketing, is referred to now as the twin communities of "L.-A."

Interior of the State of Maine Building in Poland Spring, just west of the Lewiston-Auburn area.
(Brian Vanden Brink)

Bates College, one of the best small (1,500 students) liberal arts colleges in the country, was founded in 1855 by Maine's Free Will Baptists as the first co-educational college in the East. (It was later named for a local mill owner who liberally endowed it.) The pleasant leafy campus on the northern side of Lewiston blends into its residential neighborhood—many of the adjacent houses are now student residences or faculty offices—and includes nineteenth- and twentieth-century collegiate buildings in a variety of styles, perhaps the best of them being the new George and Helen Ladd Library. Another attraction is the Olin Arts Center, which houses a concert hall and small art museum whose collection includes works by Mary Cassatt, Walker Evans, and Lewiston native Marsden Hartley. Also open to the public is the Muskie Archives, the papers of Edmund S. Muskie (class of 1936), the former Maine governor, U.S. senator, and secretary of state. Each summer the college sponsors the well-regarded Bates Dance Festival as well as a Lakeside Concert Series. Two other features worth noting are Bates's strong tradition in intercollegiate debate and its connection with the sea, 40 miles away. The **Bates-Morse Mountain Conservation Area,** near the mouth of the Kennebec, is one of the few remaining undeveloped barrier beaches on the Atlantic coast. Although long non-denominational, Bates has preserved some of the earnestness and social commitment of its idealistic founders—Maine's antebellum Baptists overall were much more abolitionist, for example, than were Maine's well-established Congregationalists—while offering the curriculum of a progressive modern college. Moreover, unlike Colby and Bowdoin, it never welcomed undergraduate fraternities and thus avoided the problems they experienced in the 1980s in trying to figure out what to do with the "Greek" system.

Lewiston's early industrialists had high-minded ideals. In the 1840s they hoped to create a new Lowell on the banks of the Androscoggin, with Lowell's model factories, orderly tenements, and general air of paternalism. But by the time that Marsden Hartley was born (1877), conditions had reverted to the Dickensian norm. As Hartley's biographer Townsend Ludington has written, "Much of the utopian atmosphere—if ever there had been one—had disappeared amid the huge, red-brick mill buildings, the increasing grime of industry, and the system of class and caste that prevailed among the growing population." The Anglos lived on "English Hill" overlooking the river, the Irish in "Gaspatch," and the French in "Little Canada." A good deal of assimilation has taken place since then, although Lewiston—like Biddeford—still has a large bilingual Francophone community (as you drive into town from Lisbon, for example, it is interesting to watch the names on offices and shops change from Anglo to French.) It was the enfranchisement in the 1960s and '70s of this population of French Canadian and Irish Catholics that helped break the hold the Republican Party enjoyed in Maine since the Civil War, and Lewiston remains one of the two cities (Portland being the other) that any successful Democratic candidate for governor or senator needs to carry.

The smaller town of Auburn, the Androscoggin County seat, had its manufacturing side as well (shoes, mostly) but still conveys the impression that this was where the managers lived, while the workers settled in Lewiston. Built on hills between the river and two large lakes, Auburn has a somewhat roomier feel. Neither community has much to offer in the way of hotels and restaurants, although Lewiston's **Marois** (249 Lisbon)—a Greek-American landmark with a legendary pastry cart—and Auburn's **TJ's** (2 Great Falls Plaza) are agreeable spots to dine. Auburn's Main Street along the river has several blocks of handsomely restored Victorian office buildings.

For all its Early Industrial air, Lewiston is not far from the country—after all, *The Farmer's Almanac* is published there—and a short ride out of town to the northeast will take you, for example, to the small, lakeside town of **Monmouth**, whose ornate turn-of-the-century "opera house," Cumston Hall, is home each summer for the repertory company known as the **Theater at Monmouth.** The company stages well-regarded productions of the classics at modest prices. The nearby cemetery is a thought-provoking spot to picnic before performances.

KENNEBEC VALLEY
A N D M I D C O A S T

TO TODAY'S AMERICANS, the establishment of this country seems to have been so inevitable that we overlook how often the Europeans' first attempts at settlement ended in disaster or at least disappointment. In August of 1607, for example, just three months after a similar experiment had taken root at Jamestown in Virginia, some 100 Englishmen led by Sir George Popham landed at the mouth of the Kennebec River in present-day Phippsburg, an area that Norsemen and some adventurous Europeans may have already explored. The glory of a late Maine summer had, quite cruelly it would turn out, deceived them. The English held a service of Thanksgiving for having arrived safely and immediately set to work building a defensive palisade, which they named St. George, after their national patron.

Accustomed to the mild, damp winters of the British Isles, they were terrified when the harsh Maine winter arrived. Sir George himself did not live through it, and those who survived until spring were as disoriented as the shipwrecked sailors of *The Tempest*. But, unlike the tobacco farmers at Jamestown, they had managed to cut and

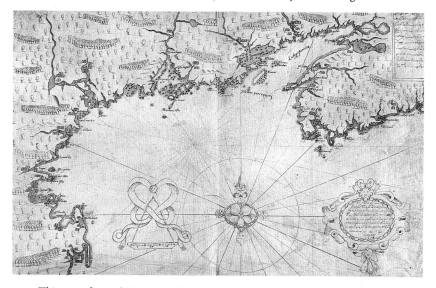

This map of coastal Maine was the result of two voyages that Samuel de Champlain made to America between 1603 and 1606. The Kennebec River and Valley can be seen in the upper left corner.

Carroll Thayer Berry's painting of the Bath Iron Works during World War II. (Farnsworth Art Museum, Rockland)

shape enough wood to build a sturdy little vessel, a pinnance they called the *Virginia,* which proved seaworthy enough to take them back to England. The Popham Colony was a disaster, but the *Virginia* made several more transatlantic trading voyages, the first in a long line of well-built ships to be launched on the banks of the Kennebec.

History books may claim that the Kennebec River is one of those places that never quite lived up to the promises people constructed for it. In the eighteenth century, for example, its absentee proprietors in London and Boston, basing their claims on nebulous royal grants and bargains struck with the Indians, saw the great river as another Hudson or Potomac, carrying settlers and merchants and soldiers far into the interior. Benedict Arnold saw the Kennebec as the back door to British Canada and military glory. William King, Maine's first governor and the Kennebec's richest merchant, ended his days in near poverty in the 1850s when his investments failed. Similarly, those sea captains and shipbuilders who could not make the transition after the Civil War from the age of sail to the age of steam were often to end their days sitting in some riverfront tavern. Even little Popham Beach, which tried in the 1890s to become another Bar Harbor, was doomed to relative obscurity.

Is it unkind to take some satisfaction in this long record of honorable failure? After all, it ultimately saved the beauty of the river. For much of the 150-mile passage of the Kennebec from its origin in Moosehead Lake until it flows into the sea at Phippsburg, the forests have reclaimed what used to be cultivated fields. How many other major rivers in the eastern United States can boast a landscape almost as pristine as the shore that greeted those ill-fated settlers in 1607?

The southern section of the river, navigable as far north as Augusta, was the site of considerable commerce during the nineteenth century. In fact, it's difficult to envision how much boat traffic there was on the Kennebec from Bath to the capital 150 years ago. The timber industry too contributed to river congestion in the nineteenth century: the stone pilings seen in several places in the river are not ruins of early bridges but supports to anchor the log booms, a sort of holding area for the timber merchants' spring log drives. Nor did winter's freeze end the river's usefulness: rather, it began the season of ice harvesting, a major business before refrigeration. The river's ice blocks were cut with large saws, stored in warehouses in sawdust, and then taken by boat when the river opened in the spring—occasionally as far away as India, but more commonly to East Coast ports. Our counterparts in the nineteenth century could enjoy views of all this river activity from trains between Bath and Waterville. Today's automobile traveler should stop in some of the towns along the way to get a flavor for the Kennebec Valley.

■ BATH, CITY OF SHIPS

There are many places around Bath to contemplate the river's history. For example, the nineteenth-century houses on Washington Street—unquestionably, still the handsomest residential street in the state—reflect the vast wealth that flowed through the city 150 years ago (and that reappeared at the height of the military build-up of the early 1980s). Ideas flowed here as well—for example, on nearby Middle Street, the columned Swedenborgian Church is one of the purest exercises in the Greek Revival style in the country, a classical temple re-invented in wood. You catch a glimpse of how present and past are linked as you watch the slow, stately pace of the giant crane at Bath Iron Works (BIW) assembling an Aegis destroyer, and as you observe the equally deliberate movements of an apprentice building a wooden boat at the historic Percy & Small shipyard.

■ MAINE MARITIME MUSEUM

The best place to pull all these thoughts together—and to reflect on how powerfully water has shaped human lives and human aspirations—is the new home, at the southern end of Bath's riverfront, of the Maine Maritime Museum, one of two such museums and research centers in the state (the other is the Penobscot Marine Museum in Searsport). The museum incorporates five buildings of the Percy & Small Shipyard, the site's original occupant, as well as Winton Scott's Maritime History Building (1988), widely regarded as the best example of postmodern architecture in the state. The stylized "Palladian" entry subtly echoes the neoclassical mansions erected by prosperous shipbuilders along the New England coast; behind that is the main hall, whose curved wooden ceiling suggests an inverted ship's hull.

Leading off from a series of small central galleries are larger rooms with exhibits telling the story of Bath's ships and sailors; the rooms' windows frame views of the swiftly moving Kennebec and the BIW yard about a mile away. The exhibits range from a nineteenth-century sailor's ditty bag to huge maritime paintings, and a glistening black model of J. P. Morgan's 344-foot *Corsair,* the largest power yacht ever made (built at BIW in 1929–30 for $1.5 million). Objects salvaged from wrecks include the main cabin door of the three-masted schooner *Joseph Luther,* which sank at sea, later drifting ashore at the mouth of the Kennebec in 1901. Several **Georgetown** houses were built from timbers salvaged from the wreck, while the cabin door served as the kitchen door of a modest dwelling for decades. If part of being a coastal Yankee was braving the dangers of life at sea, another part was being resourceful enough to know how to pick up the pieces—and use them.

Children will enjoy the exhibits on such trades as lobstering, as well as the variety of vintage craft that are moored on the river in the summer, just outside the museum. Some of the wooden boats you'll see there have been restored by participants in the museum's restoration apprenticeship program.

Among the more important exhibits in the museum are those that trace the history of **Bath Iron Works,** perhaps Maine's most famous company after L. L. Bean. Originally a foundry for marine hardware and deck machinery, the company later expanded to the manufacture of steam boilers, and eventually found itself building ships for the U.S. Navy during World War I. Unable to readjust to a civilian economy, BIW went bankrupt in the 1920s. Revived as yacht-builders in 1927, the company enjoyed perhaps its finest hours during World War II, when one out of

(following pages) The Warner *encounters rough seas as depicted in this recent acquisition by the Maine Maritime Museum in Bath. (Maine Maritime Museum, Bath)*

every four U.S. destroyers was "Bath-built" and when a large number of women entered the shipyard's workforce. At the height of the war effort, BIW launched a new destroyer every two to three weeks.

Today the state's largest employer, the company enjoyed boom times in the 1980s but now faces an expensive transition to the post-Cold War civilian economy. Closing or even significantly down-sizing BIW would be a severe economic blow to south-central Maine (as would be removal of the nearby Brunswick Naval Air Station, to a lesser degree). It is all a reminder that however much Maine's image is based on a rural and self-reliant past, this part of the state at least has come to rely heavily on a now-shrinking military-industrial economy.

If you find your energy shrinking after taking in so much maritime history, you might repair to one of Bath's better eateries. **Kristina's,** at 160 Centre, is especially renowned for its pastries, while the tiny cafe **Truffles,** at 21 Elm Street, fills up quickly for lunch and afternoon tea.

A number of excursions can be made easily from Bath. Just to the north of town, at the Chops, the Kennebec joins **Merrymeeting Bay,** a traditional hunting and fishing area whose wild-rice marshes are an important stopover for many migratory birds. Merrymeeting Bay is also fed by the Androscoggin, which was a stinking sewer within not too distant memory; though it's now a relatively healthy river, most Mainers refrain from eating its fish.

Directly south of town on Route 209 is an exceptionally beautiful drive by way of the historic village of **Phippsburg,** to **Popham Beach State Park,** which has some of the best sand dunes on Maine's midcoast. At the point where the river flows into the Atlantic, and within sight of the early lighthouse (1795) on Seguin Island, is the rather grim, Civil War-era fort that controlled the mouth of the Kennebec. On the opposite shore are Arrowsic and Georgetown islands as well as Robinhood Cove, a very scenic neck ending at **Reid State Park.** Overlooking the marina at remote Robinhood Cove is one of the area's better restaurants, the beautifully situated **Osprey.**

■ BOWDOINHAM AND VICINITY

From Bath, take U.S. 1 west to its junction with Route 24, then head north five miles to Bowdoinham. Situated on the marshy Cathance River, which also feeds into Merrymeeting Bay, Bowdoinham is a pleasant little town, known for its contra dances. **Richmond**, seven or so miles north on the Kennebec itself, offers some very beautiful old houses and a Russian Orthodox emigre community, described in the short stories of Willis Johnston. Swan Island is a slightly mysterious state park that discourages visitors in order to protect its wildlife. Across the river is historic **Dresden**, a hotbed of Loyalism on the eve of the Revolution, thanks in large part to its Anglican priest, the Rev. Jacob Bailey, whom the local patriots quickly expelled.

One of the great relics of eighteenth-century Maine is on the wooded bank of the river there: Gershom Flagg's very simple but somehow moving **Pownalborough Court House** (1761), where the young John Adams, among others, followed the judges on circuit in order to practice law. Lonelier looking today than it was when the river was a busy highway, the white-washed courthouse stands as an ambiguous symbol of life on the Maine frontier. On the one hand, it represented the rule of law, the hand first of British and then of Massachusetts civilization bringing order to the backcountry. On the other, it was a hated symbol of authority for the farmers who had settled along the Kennebec after the Revolution only to discover that some absentee landowner was trying to evict them for squatting on his land. Most of the land was owned by a group of holders and investors known as "Proprietors of the Kennebec Purchase" who had hoped to establish settlements in the valley. A sort of low-grade civil war simmered in the backcountry from the 1790s until statehood in 1820. Settlers dressed themselves as "wild Indians" and harassed surveyors, threatened land agents, and burned records, in order to protect the land they had settled on. The Pownalborough Court House is one of those undramatic, little publicized historic sites which suddenly prove very powerful when you encounter them. And there is a wonderful display upstairs on ice-harvesting on the Kennebec.

■ GARDINER

Not all the great proprietors were absentee. One Proprietor of the Kennebec Purchase, Dr. Sylvester Gardiner of Boston, settled with his family in the town that bears his name; his son Robert Hallowell Gardiner succeeded the scientist-physician-statesman Benjamin Vaughan as "first citizen" of the Kennebec Valley.

A landowner who for half a century encouraged the commercial development of the area, as well as a prominent Episcopalian, the younger Gardiner was a leading enthusiast of the new Gothic Revival style. Christ Church (1819), facing the town green in Gardiner, was one of the first churches in America to try to look medieval and English, an effect the architect Richard Upjohn achieved even more successfully at the Gardiners' 1835 house, "Oaklands." Glimpsed from the river road today, the crenellated, gray-granite manor house (private), with its sweeping lawn and its "hanger" of magnificent trees on a steep hillside, still looks more like a house in Northumberland, say, than in the middle of Maine.

The town of Gardiner was the childhood home of Edward Arlington Robinson, who seems to have hated it, although his family situation—including his mother's painful death and his father's failure in the lumber business—could not have made life there easy for him. The town in that post-Civil War period was sharply divided between poorly paid mill workers who lived near the river (an area now largely cleared) and proper folk "up the hill." Robinson transformed this Gardiner into his mythic Tilbury Town, a troubling place inhabited by the likes of Minniver Cheevy and Richard Cory. His house near the green is marked by a plaque.

Today, Gardiner is a bedroom community for Augusta. It is worth a stop not only for its nineteenth-century churches and houses but for an artifact of the early twentieth century, the **A1 Diner** downtown on Bridge Street. Its Depression-era interior is virtually untouched, but the food is eclectic, international, and cheap (most dinners are $6 or $7). "Latino-Moorish" might describe the cuisine, which includes Moroccan stew and Mexican chicken pie, alongside meatloaf and bread pudding.

■ HALLOWELL

Augusta and Hallowell were originally part of the same eighteenth-century settlement, the former being known then as "the Fort," the latter as "the Hook," short for Bombahook, a local stream. Today they still flow together, although you can tell when you cross the line: Hallowell, perhaps because of a stricter sign ordinance, just looks neater. For most of the nineteenth century, Hallowell remained the area's social and commercial center, thanks in part to the presence of the Vaughans, Hallowells, Pages, Hubbards, and other prosperous families in the area,

Benjamin Hallowell, scion of one of Maine's early influential families, as portrayed by artist John Singleton Copley. (Colby College Museum of Art, Waterville)

MARTHA BALLARD, HALLOWELL MIDWIFE

The "new" history has brought to vivid life a whole cast of Maine characters on the eighteenth- and early nineteenth-century frontier, people who did not have their portraits painted by Copley or Gilbert Stuart and who rarely left their names in the official local histories, but who shaped the future of the District of Maine. There is no better example of this than the story of the Hallowell midwife and healer, Martha Ballard, who between 1785 and 1812 attended 816 births and enjoyed a higher reputation for safe deliveries than the local, university-trained physicians. No one painted Ballard's portrait, but she sketched a self portrait of sorts in a diary she kept during those 27 years. In 1990, Laurel Thatcher Ulrich, a professor at the University of New Hampshire who specializes in women's history, found the diary, researched its historical context, and published it. Ulrich's richly annotated version won her a Pulitzer Prize, and guaranteed a virtually unknown woman in Hallowell an important role in our understanding of everyday life in the early Republic.

The diary entries are, at first glance, laconic and banal. They record visits with neighbors, births and deaths, weather, housework, the occasional odd event. A typical entry from 1788 reads:

> Clear. Mr Ballard gone to Mr James Pages on public business. Jonathan & Taylor went to see the execution of Oneal. I have been at home. The Girls washt. Gilbreath sleeps here. The wife of old Mr Springer Departed this Life this morn.

What Ulrich does with them, however, is near miraculous, one of the great technical and imaginative feats of recent American historiography. From these often cryptic diary entries, she brings back to life an entire community. Martha Ballard, it turns out, is not an obscure folk healer or a quaint village herbalist, but a strong-minded, independent woman at the center of a complex network of social, familial, and economic relationships. Neither from the top nor the bottom of local society, she and her husband (a surveyor for the Kennebec Proprietors) played a mediating role in the communal affairs of Hallowell's 100 or so families. She could not only see a neighbor through a difficult delivery, but perform in her own way a variety of healing tasks that in modern times would require the skills of a druggist, psychiatrist, and medical emergency technician. The local doctors respected her enough to seek her advice in difficult obstetrical cases and to invite her to attend autopsies and dissections, though both she and they knew that the age of the expert midwife was passing as the prestige of the trained medical profession grew. Both she and they probably knew, too, that a patient's chance of survival was sometimes greater given her gentle care and herbal remedies than it was from the so-called "heroic medicine"—which called for lots of purges and bleeding—of the medical school graduates.

Anyone traveling along the Kennebec near Hallowell today will see much of the same scenery that Martha Ballard knew intimately, though in her time there would have been less forest and more open farmland and much more traffic on the river. For eight months of the year, Hallowell was a seaport, connected to the Atlantic trade routes. The Kennebec froze with startling rapidity in early winter, however, and, as Ulrich points out, "Hallowell folks remembered openings and closings of the river the way people in other towns remembered earthquakes or drought." One year, the ice did not clear until May.

It was part of Martha Ballard's sense of vocation that she would take great risks to answer a call for help. As you speed in your car upriver from Gardiner toward Hallowell, imagine her walking across the ice on a winter morning, or in a canoe in April, a middle-aged woman breaking her way through the ice floes, then struggling to climb the steep and muddy bank to rush to someone's sickbed on the farther shore. Or imagine her tending her garden—the sound of the local sawmills in the distance—growing the food that sustained her family and collecting the herbs (camomile, catmint, lovage, pennyroyal, tansy, and two dozen others) that soothed the pain, killed the worms, cured the colic, and settled the bowels of her friends and neighbors. There is perhaps no other book since Thoreau's travel accounts which can so enrich a visit to the state. In short, *A Midwife's Tale: The Life of Martha Ballard, Based on Her Diary, 1785–1812* is the most important—and most readable —work on Maine history to appear in a generation.

who, with the Gardiners formed the well-educated, politically powerful gentry of the mid-Kennebec Valley. But what is now Augusta had a bridge over the river, and so it became the state capital in 1832, while the economy of the Kennebec began its slow post-Civil War decline. Today, reinvigorated Hallowell has the charm—and the good restaurants, bookstores, and antique shops—that Augusta in general lacks. Hallowell's attractive Water Street, whose red-brick shops seem to have one foot dangling in the river, includes **Slate's** at 167 Water Street, one of the most popular rendezvous for brunch in the area.

■ AUGUSTA

To the first-time visitor, Augusta may seem a nondescript city organized around two large traffic circles, one on either side of the river. Most of the state's bureaucrats are housed in buildings that do not look pompous or forbidding, just cheap, which is an approach to government Mainers have traditionally endorsed. Even the **State Capitol** (corner of State and Capitol) looks less imposing than many an American county courthouse. The old riverfront downtown has a depressed look, despite its postmodern office tower. (Maine cities and towns can be divided into two categories, those that have been able to keep such traditional shopping areas alive and those that have abandoned them for the malls.) There are a few notable buildings around—the "Romanesque-Renaissance" **Lithgow Library** (1898), for example, and the châteauesque downtown post office, which suggests what Portland's much-lamented Union Station (demolished 1961) might have been like. Yet Augusta is more than a traffic jam on the quick route to Bar Harbor. An easy day trip from many of the midcoast resorts, the capital has three major attractions for the historically minded visitor.

An early painting of the State Capitol in Augusta.
(Maine State Museum)

A collection of old pewter from a private collection in the Augusta area.
(Brian Vanden Brink)

On a bluff overlooking the river is the oldest of these, **Fort Western** (1754), the last of the original French and Indian War fortifications surviving in Maine. Its two (reconstructed) blockhouses are similar to those seen in the movie version of *Last of the Mohicans;* and the long eighteenth-century storehouse—divided into the comfortable dwelling of the Howard family at one end, and a re-creation of their store at the other—summarizes the history of the fort. Built by the Kennebec Proprietors as a supply station for British troops farther upriver, the fort eventually became the commercial center of the new community. When the town grew on the other side of the river, the buildings housed Irish immigrants brought in to work on the local mills and dams. The fort eventually declined into a tenement until bought by the Gannett family in 1922 and given to the city. Today, thanks to a combination of showmanship and scholarly and archeological accuracy, Fort Western is a major educational center for teaching people of all ages about life in

Maine on the eighteenth-century frontier. Staff members in period costume give regular demonstrations on such skills as weaving, sheep-shearing, dye-making, and open-hearth cooking, and visitors can peer through the pickets and try to imagine keeping watch for the French and their Indian allies.

Just south of the Capitol is one of Maine's hidden treasures, the **State Museum** in the State Capitol Complex. Sharing an almost unmarked building with the State Library, State Archives, and a remarkably silly foyer, the museum is one of the most imaginative and intelligently organized examples of its kind. Exhibits range from the feathery landscape murals of Rufus Porter—the last word in interior design in the 1820s—to "The Lion" (1846), a small steam-powered freight engine which carried lumber to the sawmills for 50 years. Here also is your chance to meet *Pertica quadrifaria,* the State Fossil, a plant that grew in the marshes of the Katahdin region 400 million years ago. The two major permanent exhibits focus on the caribou-hunting Paleo-Indians, and on the products and industries of nineteenth- and early twentieth-century Maine, complete with sound effects and period arti-facts. There's also an important early view of Augusta by the painter Charles Cod-man in 1836 showing Bulfinch's original Capitol (the columned facade was kept in later renovations). The almost brand-new neoclassical building arises from a romantic but thoroughly tamed wilderness—an image that reflected how Mainers thought about their state in its early years of independence.

The intimate, down-home quality of government in a small state is nicely cap-tured in another Capitol Hill landmark, the 1830-ish **Blaine House,** which since 1921 has been the official residence of Maine's governors, and whose reception

An iron rooster weathervane from the nineteenth century. (Colby College Museum of Art, Waterville)

rooms are open to the public. It bears the name of the state's most famous politician of the immediate post-Civil War period, James G. Blaine, a successful journalist, Congressman, and two-term U.S. Secretary of State who helped cement Maine's century of allegiance to the Republican Party. Despite his skills, Blaine ("the Plumed Knight") never got what he really wanted—to be President. In 1884 he lost decisively to Grover Cleveland, but he was always much honored in his home state, and his youngest daughter gave the house to the people of Maine. Its current look owes much to Colonial Revival remodeling by John Calvin Stevens, but Blaine's study retains its Victorian feeling.

There are other things to see in and around Augusta—the **State Arboretum,** the statue of Samantha Smith outside the State Library, and the view from across the river of the Capitol dome against the surrounding hills. But don't leave without tracking down one further delight. In a corridor of the Capitol, next to a yellowing display of shellacked salmon and the stuffed deer, moose, bear, and beaver that give the building a touch of the outdoors, there is a bronze plaque quoting a 1924 order "in Council":

> *O*rdered, that Governor Percival P. Baxter be authorized to erect at his own expense in the State Capitol a bronze memorial tablet to his devoted dog "Garry" (1914–1923) and that the State accept the same; the said tablet to serve as a constant reminder to the people of Maine of the faithful and unselfish services rendered them by their domestic animals and as an expression of the hope that the day will soon come in this state, when cruelty to, and neglect of animals will be no more, and when man will be kind and merciful to all of God's creatures however humble.

■ WATERVILLE AND ENVIRONS

Relatively few tourists follow the path of the Kennebec beyond Augusta, a historic route into the heart of the Great North Woods—and beyond. In September of 1775, Benedict Arnold (still at that time on the colonists' side) set out to persuade the French Canadians to join the rebellion. He brought 1,000 volunteers from the Continental Army besieging Boston, sailed up the Kennebec to Gardiner, where he transferred his men into 200 bateaux (large rowboats) ill designed for the rigors of the trip up river. As winter set in he crossed overland from the Kennebec to the

Chaudière, by which means he reached the St. Lawrence River. Some 650 men survived the trek and met up with their reinforcements as planned. On the night of December 30, they assaulted the fortifications of Quebec under cover of a blizzard. But they had been betrayed by a deserter. In the face of great losses, they fell back. The American expeditionary force was not finally expelled until spring, but Arnold's plan proved futile. The ill-fated and quickly forgotten campaign is remembered today chiefly in those towns in the Kennebec Valley in which Arnold and his men stopped on their way north. The original mid-eighteenth-century blockhouse at Winslow, **Fort Halifax,** washed away in a flood a few years ago, but some of the pieces were found at the mouth of the Kennebec, and the structure has been rebuilt.

On the west bank of the Kennebec River is Waterville, home of the Hathaway shirt (1847) and the Lombard Log Hauler, the forerunner of all caterpillar-treaded vehicles, including the tank. Today Waterville is no doubt best known as the home of **Colby College,** which was rebuilt in 1952 in neo-Georgian style on Mayflower Hill, at the edge of town. Founded in 1813 as the Maine Literary and Theological Institution, Colby was intended as a Baptist alternative to Congregationalist-

An early view of Colby College, at the time known as Waterville College, painted by Esteria Butler. (Colby College Museum of Art, Waterville)

From Seeing Cape Split *by John Marin is one of the many fine paintings in the collection of the Colby College Museum of Art in Waterville.*

dominated Bowdoin. The institution was chartered as Waterville College by a sympathetic legislature in 1820, but was renamed for a generous donor, Gardner Colby of Boston, in 1867. The original riverside campus was abandoned because the railroad tracks had made the area too noisy and dirty. Colby, a four-year liberal arts college of about 1,600 students, honors the martyred newspaper editor Elijah Lovejoy of the class of 1825 as its most famous alumnus. A courageous and outspoken abolitionist, he was shot dead in Alton, Illinois, in 1837 while trying to defend his printing press against a pro-slavery mob. The attractive campus is worth visiting, especially for its **Museum of Art,** one of the state's best small museums, particularly rich in twentieth-century American painting. Off campus, the local centers of civilization include the **Railroad Square Cinema** (near railroad tracks, call 872-5111), which shows foreign and high-quality American films and includes a cafe, and **Jorgensen's,** a wine, cheese, and coffee shop at 103 Main Street downtown.

Colby's strength in the arts owes much to its proximity to the **Skowhegan School of Painting and Sculpture,** a few minutes' drive upriver. Founded in 1946 on a poultry farm, the school conducts summer classes which have attracted some of the nation's leading artists, and which lend a temporary flavor of Manhattan to the surrounding farmland—locals don't usually wear so much black. The other famous landmark in Skowhegan is the **Margaret Chase Smith Library Center,** an extension of her home overlooking the river. It records some 40 years of public service, from her election in 1940 as a Republican Congresswoman (replacing her late husband in the seat) through her career in the 1950s and '60s as the first woman elected (a few had been appointed) to the U.S. Senate. Her finest moment came on the Senate floor in 1950 when she did what everyone else around her had been afraid to do—denounce Sen. Joseph McCarthy, in what came to be known as her "Declaration of Conscience" speech. A moderate conservative herself, Smith opened a door for women into the mostly male world of politics. Born in 1897, Smith, wearing her signature red rose, still greets visitors at her library.

Nearby **Norridgewock,** an attractive historic town at the point where the Indian trail linked the Kennebec and the Chaudière, is associated not only with Benedict Arnold but with the memory of Father Sebastian Rasles, the French Jesuit who composed a dictionary of the Abnaki language and whose dealings with Native Americans showed great sensitivity to their culture. Rasles's accomplishments in Maine are celebrated in William Carlos Williams's essay *In the American Grain.* After three decades of missionary activity in the upper Kennebec Valley (including training a choir of 40 young Norridgewock Indians to sing the Mass and learning how to make altar candles from bayberries), the scholarly Rasles was killed in 1724 by the British colonials, who pillaged and burned the Indians' village in what is now the pine grove at Old Point. Continuing upriver, you come to the town of **Bingham,** whose name commemorates the very rich Philadelphian, William Bingham, who in the 1780s owned some two million acres of Maine land. The Forks, a destination for many hunters and fishermen, is a tiny community at the confluence of the Kennebec and Dead rivers. The next settlement of any size (meaning perhaps 1,000 residents) is the North Woods town of **Jackman,** after which you will very soon find yourself crossing into the Province of Quebec.

■ EAST FROM BATH

If after a trip up the Kennebec Valley you yearn for Maine's rocky shoreline, a trip east from Bath along midcoastal Maine may be your best bet. While there are

PÈRE SEBASTIAN RASLES

[Rasles] tells of how [the Abnaki] laughed at his early attempts at the language. Failing to catch certain gutturals at first, he pronounced but half the words. He speaks of the comparative beauty of the Huron tongue.

In the spring the fish come up the river solidly packed, two feet deep—with flesh of the most delicious taste. They gather the fish, eat all they can and dry the rest—that serves them until the corn is ready to harvest. In the spring also, celebrating the Eucharist, Rasles saw the corn planted. In August this was ready to be plucked. When that was finished there must be other food.

For this it was the habit of the Indians to go to the seashore. It was always, says Rasles, the same formula. He knew what was about to happen. They would gather about their spiritual counselor and offer him a speech, saying that the corn was low, that the tribe must have food and that they begged him to come with them to the shore that they might not be deprived of his spiritual comfort while they were gone. Always he answered with the one word,—

Kekiberba (I am listening, my children).

When all cried together, *8ri8rie!* (We thank you). (Note, the figure 8 is used by Rasles in his alphabet of the Abnaki language to signify the unique guttural sound characteristic of the Indian dialects.) Then they would break camp.

—William Carlos Williams, "Père Sebastian Rasles," *In the American Grain,* 1925

many beautiful and interesting places to visit in coastal southern Maine, there is something tame, even suburban, about much of that part of the state now. But upon crossing Bath's Carlton Bridge over the Kennebec, you begin to feel that you have entered the ideal Maine of so many people's imagination. The experience is only intermittently satisfying. Indeed, the problem the unhurried traveler faces here is whether to be satisfied with rather commercial U.S. 1 and its succession of historic seaports, or to explore each neck of land along this much-fragmented coast. Not every fishing village or saltwater farm looks like the last one; the pleasure of wandering up and down the sea-pointed roads lies in finding the one that most meets your expectations. Travel is sometimes less about discovery than about confirmation.

Wiscasset has long billed itself as "Maine's prettiest village," a title that several towns might successfully dispute, and certainly one that depends on how you feel about the Maine Yankee Nuclear Power Plant looming on the other side of the harbor. (Most of the residents like it; its valuation is so high, it keeps property taxes among the lowest in the state, in what is a very well-heeled community.) The fact that U. S. 1 goes directly through the center of town is also a mixed blessing, depending on the time of year you travel there, but plans to build a new highway slightly inland have been fiercely opposed by residents concerned about the rural beauty of the backcountry. At any rate, Wiscasset is a very pleasant spot to get out of the car and explore its mostly nineteenth-century side streets.

Two architectural gems to visit are SPNEA's **Nickels-Sortwell House** (1807–12) at the corner of Federal and Main streets in the center of town—literally a textbook example of Adamesque Federal design (its entrance being copied from a design appearing in an 1806 architectural book)—and the suave **Castle Tucker** (1807–08), a Regency dandy facing off Maine Yankee across the cove. Nickels-Sortwell is a magnificent dwelling, though it conveys little of the personality of its builders (or its Colonial Revival rescuers); Castle Tucker, on the other hand, is still occupied by a descendant of the early owners and is full of the wonderful stuff—

The kitchen of Castle Tucker. (Brian Vanden Brink)

An interior view of the Nickels-Sortwell House in Wiscasset. (Brian Vanden Brink)

including an egg collection—that used to accumulate over the generations in an old seacoast house. For lunch or dinner, try **Le Garage** on Water Street, a converted 1920s-era garage. The restaurant's glassed-in porch offers a view of a maritime memento mori, the picturesquely rotting hulks of the *Luther Little* and the *Hesper,* two four-masted schooners half sunk in the mud of the pretty little Sheepscot River.

■ BOOTHBAY HARBOR

As you drive north, you'll have the chance to detour to several well-known locales. Just over the river at North Edgecomb the road beckons to Boothbay Harbor, a famous sailing town which in July and August seems on the verge of sinking beneath the weight of its tourists. The cafe-lined streets are especially densely packed during Windjammer Days, in late June or early July, when a dozen or so great sailing boats fill the harbor and the town celebrates three days of festivals. Thirty years ago, Boothbay Harbor must have seemed a charming fishing village (sixty years before that, it had been a bustling commercial and shipping center for the fishing and fertilizer trade). It remains a very popular destination for many tourists and recreational sailors, but, as Roger F. Duncan drily notes in his indispensable *Cruising Guide to the New England Coast,* "it is a port we are always glad to get into and delighted to leave." Apparently uncontrolled commercial and motel development along the narrow streets of the harborfront have given the town a circus atmosphere in high season. On the other hand, the view down the narrow harbor toward the sea is as beautiful as ever, the confusion of all those boats coming and going has its Raoul Dufy qualities, and you will not have trouble finding a place to eat or (if you book ahead) a nice Victorian house turned B&B in which to stay. Close to downtown is the **Spruce Point Inn,** a resort with pool, tennis courts, and cottages surrounding an old main building. The **Boothbay Railway Village,** one mile north of town on Route 27, is a delightful place, especially for children who have never ridden on a real live train.

For anyone whose idea of Maine involves fewer people, nearby **Southport Island**—just south of town on Route 27—is a welcome alternative to Boothbay Harbor. Indeed, with its cove-indented shore, its little white capes, and its stacks of lobster traps, it comes very close to being the *Down East* magazine version of Maine many people adore. For the moment, the mix of lobstermen and affluent retirees does seem to work—on Southport and in many similar Midcoast communities—although the inevitable increase in property values poses all sorts of long-range problems (perhaps at some point in the future the fishermen will be hired to mess about for a little atmosphere). The place to enjoy Southport is the **Newagen Inn,** a complex of buildings on the shore that conveys something of the timelessness of old-fashioned summers. Newagen can be enjoyed, more briefly, in the winter too: it is a superb place to watch the northern waters. The little tidal pool of a harbor is sheltered, almost toylike, but just beyond the barrier islands the Atlantic is churning, and when big waves hit the distant ledges, white water explodes like a geyser at sea.

Damariscotta, mercifully off the highway, is an unspoiled gem that manages to seem both a river and a seaport town. Nearby are the Damariscotta Shell Heaps, a shell midden left by Paleo-Indians 3,000 years ago (see essay, "Maine's Paleo-Indians"). Just across the river on the west side is **Newcastle,** and farther north lies **Damariscotta Mills.** Damariscotta Mills' Kavanaugh Mansion (private) inspired one of Robert Lowell's poems. A few miles farther inland are the villages of Alna and Head Tide. Alna is the site of the Old Alna Meetinghouse (1789) with its

"The Clamdiggers," photographed in 1895 by Emma D. Sewall illustrates an activity along coastal tidal flats still popular among Maine residents. (Courtesy of Abbie Sewall)

original ship-lapped clapboards, box pews, and raised hour-glass pulpit. Head Tide is the birthplace of the poet Edward Arlington Robinson. In a more thoughtful, less selfish society, those three villages, nearby Sheepscot, and the surrounding countryside would be as well protected from despoilation as any national park.

On the seaward side of Damariscotta, Route 130 leads south about 12 miles to the lighthouse at spectacular **Pemaquid Point,** whose thick strands of multi-colored volcanic rock seem in violent argument with the sea. Not far away on Route 130 are **Fort William Henry,** a replica of a 1689 structure built to fend off pirates and Frenchmen; the **Colonial Pemaquid Restoration,** an important archaeological site for understanding the area's seventeenth-century origins; and the **Harrington Meeting House** (1772), a museum of "Old Bristol." To continue east, take Route 32 north to its juncture with U.S. 1.

Back on U.S. 1, the next major historic town is **Waldoboro,** tucked into a fold at the head of the Medomak River's navigable waters. The town was settled in 1748 by Germans who had been lured across the Atlantic by the promise of prosperity, but were confronted, as a tombstone in the Old German Cemetery laments, with "nothing but wilderness." This is one of several New England towns that has "preserved" an old cattle pound, a slightly batty exercise in Colonial Revival nostalgia. Longings for a kinder, simpler, less diet-conscious America can also be fulfilled at Moody's Diner, a landmark known for huge helpings, a retro menu (which includes tripe), and creamy pies. Farther down east on Muscongus Bay is Friendship, famous for the sloops bearing its name. The whale's hump of **Monhegan Island** can be seen in the distance from Friendship's shore; ferries to the island, a popular summer residence and artists' colony, leave from Port Clyde.

Thomaston is next, offering along U.S. 1 two long rows of splendid Federal and Greek Revival houses and the less inviting domicile of the Maine State Prison, whose crafts shop is one of the state's most unexpected retail outlets (though it, too, attracts charter buses.) On a hilltop just beyond the town is "Montpelier," a replica of the mansion of the Revolutionary War hero and land speculator Maj. Gen. Henry Knox, whose unhappy business ventures in lumber, shipbuilding, lime-burning, and the like, combined with his personal extravagance, led to his ruin. His family's sudden decline and the legends that grew up about his heirs' land claims are believed to have inspired Hawthorne's account of the Pyncheon family "fortune" in *The House of the Seven Gables.* Side roads from Thomaston lead to Cushing and Andrew Wyeth country and, on the other side of the St.

St. Andrew's Episcopal Church in Newcastle. (Brian Vanden Brink)

George River, past Tenants Harbor to Martinsville and Port Clyde—the landscape which Sarah Orne Jewett described in *The Country of the Pointed Firs*. A little farther "down east" are Sprucehead, where the poet Wilbert Snow spent his youth on a farm (vividly and realistically portrayed in his 1968 memoir *Codline's Child*), and Owls Head, home of a transportation museum. As you leave the town of Thomaston, head toward the towns of Rockland and Camden on West Penobscot Bay; these shores mark the end of "Midcoast Maine,"—which began with one historic river, the Kennebec, and here meets another, the Penobscot.

Early views of Thomaston depict the village market (above) and town firehouse and brigade (right). (Thomaston Historical Society)

PENOBSCOT BAY
AND RIVER

NO ONE KNOWS HOW THE NAME ORIGINATED, but as early as 1548 a map of the "Tierra Nueva" published in Venice indicates a "Tierra de Nurumberg" on the northeastern coast of what is now the United States. The term—applied variously to a river, a city, and a region—may derive from the Algonquin word meaning "where the river is wide" as transcribed by Giovanni da Verrazzano, the Italian navigator who, in the service of the French, reached the Maine coast in 1524. By 1597, when Cornelius Wytfliet published a map of "Norumbega et Virginia" in a Flemish atlas, the idea was well established in the European imagination that somewhere on the North American shore was a river that offered a passage to the Indies as well as a fabled city at the head of that river rich with gold. The mapmakers may have heard that in 1525 a Portuguese captain employed by the Spanish had

A 1901 view of the Penobscot River Valley by Roy Homer.
(Farnsworth Art Museum, Rockland)

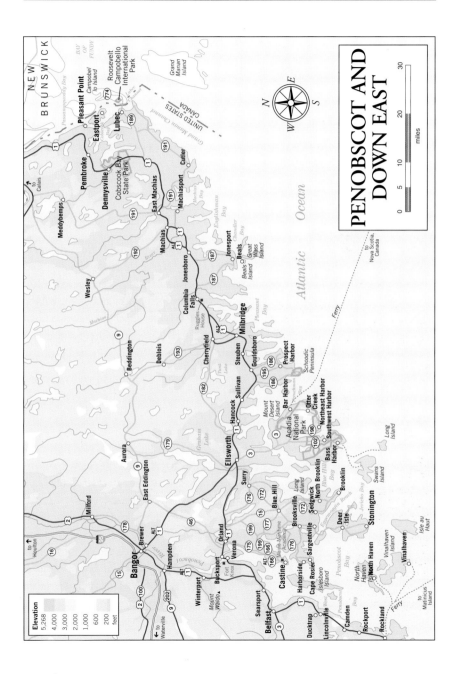

sailed up the Penobscot as far as modern Bangor in search of that Northwest Passage, and soon various European explorers, including Jean Allefonsce in 1527 and French geographer Thevet in 1556, had followed. Englishman David Ingram, who survived a 1568 shipwreck in the Gulf of Mexico, returned to England on a French vessel and wrote a colorful account of visiting the mythical city of Norumbega.

Although Wytfliet showed Norumbega extending as far south as the Chesapeake, the imaginary land was reduced on later maps to what is now New England and, at the time of Champlain's voyages in 1604 and 1605, was identified with the headwaters of the Penobscot in northern Maine. Although the territory along the Penobscot was to be fiercely disputed by the British and French and their respective Indian allies in the early eighteenth century, no one ever found gold there, much less a route to Asia.

From a vantage point in **Penobscot Bay,** or even glancing down from the roadside as U.S. 1 approaches the bridge at Verona, it is easy to understand how a river like the Penobscot could have caught the imagination of the first Europeans on the scene. More dramatic than the Kennebec, with steeper banks and fewer habitations in view, it cuts its way from the foothills of Mount Katahdin—with a western branch arising among the huge lakes of north-central Maine—and drains much of the eastern half of the state before flowing into the Atlantic at Penobscot Bay.

■ WEST PENOBSCOT BAY

Continuing on Route 1, you drive along the western side of Penobscot Bay, stopping by towns which serve as jumping-off points for some of the most beautiful islands on the New England coast. Between **Thomaston** and **Rockland,** the landscape abruptly changes; the Cianbro cement plant (now owned by the Passamaquoddy Indians) and the hillsides torn up to quarry limestone seem out of place in this otherwise pastoral part of the world. To be sure, Rockland is at first glance plainly utilitarian, best known to tourists and summer people for its ferry boats to North Haven, Vinalhaven, Islesboro, and Matinicus islands in Penobscot Bay. But the city, a busy fishing port, is much more agreeable now than it was in the last century, when its skies were darkened by the smoke of the lime pits and when travelers approaching from the sea at night compared its eerie glow to the gates of

Hell. It was the birthplace of the poet Edna St. Vincent Millay (200 Broadway) and the composer Walter Piston, as well as the childhood home of the Russian-born sculptor Louise Nevelson, whose constructions from wood scraps surely owed something to the jig-saw Victorian carpentry of her Maine youth.

Nevelson's work can be seen at the town's leading attraction, the **William A. Farnsworth Museum** at 21 Elm, where you'll also find pieces by three generations of Wyeths and by many other leading American artists who've painted in Maine. The Portland Museum of Art may one day outshine the rest of the state, but for the moment the Farnsworth shares with the Bowdoin College Museum of Art the distinction of being Maine's best art museum. Both museums offer high quality collections small enough to be absorbed in a single visit, yet interesting enough to make you want to return. If you want to see how Maine has looked to artists over the past 200 years, the Farnsworth is the place to begin. Attached to the museum is the **Farnsworth Homestead** (ca. 1840), preserved very much as it was in the long lifetime of Lucy Farnsworth. Having inherited a respectable fortune from her father, Farnsworth managed to increase it several times over through her shrewdness and frugality. In the dining room is the soup tureen in which her tenants are said to have placed their rent each month in summer—it sat in the window, they stood outside. When Miss Farnsworth died at age 96 in 1935, she astonished Rockland by leaving the city her $1.3 million estate to establish and endow an art museum and library and to maintain the family's homestead. Having spent a lifetime of monotonous stringency, one unrelieved (if the furnishings of her house are any indication) by literature or art, Lucy Farnsworth ended it with a magnificent act of largesse.

Continuing north, you pass the entrance to the waterfront Samoset Resort and, if you turn off into **Rockport** (of André the Seal fame), you re-enter the world of summer people. Nearby **Camden** is an attractive place long teetering on the verge of being ruined—so many boats, so many cars, so little space in summer—but never quite succumbing. For one thing, it has a year-round population of civic-minded retirees, many of them business executives and CIA veterans, whose political clout is best displayed in the impressive list of speakers they attract each winter to the Camden Conference, a series of seminars and lectures on foreign affairs, held in the town's old Opera House and nearby churches. Camden is packed with restaurants, most of them geared for undemanding tourists, and has possibly more bed-and-breakfasts and inns per block than any other Maine town south of Bar

Harbor. Among the former, **Chez Michel** in Lincolnville Beach is a welcome new-comer; among the latter, the castle-like **Norumbega** on 61 High Street is a pleasant change from the Martha Stewart look of most of its competition. Look also for the **Owl and Turtle Bookshop** on Bayview Street.

On the north side of town, U.S. 1 passes by some of the best Colonial Revival domestic architecture in the state, one of the finest examples being the historic **Whitehall Inn** (where Edna St. Vincent Millay was "discovered" in 1908). Famous for its harbor, Camden is also remembered for its circle of hills, a combination celebrated in Millay's poem "Renascence" ("All I could see from where I stood/Was three long mountains and a wood;/I turned and looked the other way,/And saw three islands in a bay . . .") Nearby **Lincolnville,** with ferry connections to Islesboro, is the retirement home of the great Brazilian soprano Bidu Sayao; the little town of **Ducktrap,** once a famous hunting and fishing spot, today gives its name to superb smoked fish and pâtés.

The tea room in the Farnsworth Homestead adjacent to the well-known museum bearing the same name. (Brian Vanden Brink)

(right) Marshall Point Lighthouse near Port Clyde, close to the entrance of Penobscot Bay.

■ BELFAST

Knox County, with its pockets of wealth in places like Camden and Rockport, gives way, as you drive north, to Waldo, one of the poorest counties in the state. A case in point is the town of Belfast, which still waits to recover from the collapse of the poultry business. Too far from Camden or Bar Harbor to share in their tourist loot, it sits on Belfast Bay waiting for the wave of prosperity that would put more life into its handsome Victorian downtown and its streets of superb Greek Revival sea-captains' houses. It is well worth a visit, if only to fantasize over the real estate ads, admire its **Opera House** (31 Main), support its growing arts community, or visit the **Fertile Mind Bookshop** (13 Main). You might even take the Belfast and Moosehead Lake Railroad excursion to the rural village of Brooks, along the—I am not making this up—Passagassawakeag River. Over the bridge, **Perry's Tropical Nut House** has been a landmark since the 1920s, a tourist trinket shop so filled with exotic tchotckes that it transcends the genre: during the 1920s, the Belfast man who owned it traveled throughout South America collecting rare nuts, as well as the stuffed tropical animals now on display.

■ SEARSPORT

Searsport is an under-appreciated town, and certainly a much quieter one than in the nineteenth century when its 17 shipyards launched some 200 vessels. The downtown is only two blocks long but charming nevertheless: the large old houses that aren't bed-and-breakfasts are antique shops. Nearby on Route 1 is a fine country restaurant, the **Nickerson Tavern,** where the imaginative menu attracts customers from Bangor and Camden. Above all, Searsport is known for its **Penobscot Marine Museum** on Church Street. Although the collection parallels that of the maritime museum in Bath, the exhibits are divided among half a dozen historic buildings, including three captains' houses, and they do an especially good job of explaining the history and ecology of Penobscot Bay. The museum has an important collection of marine paintings—including two rooms of Buttersworths, father and son—and what must be the country's largest display of pressed-glass butter dishes. Boats displayed include wonderful North Haven peapods, a Herreshoff sloop, even a smelt scow. Among the antique photos on view are scenes of domestic life at sea (including chickens roaming the deck), a reminder that many Maine captains took their families on their lengthy voyages.

Route 1 then offers you one of Maine's most spectacular highway views: the "gorge" where the Penobscot makes a near right angle below the battlements of Fort Knox (begun in 1844). Nestled on the opposite river bank, the small town of **Bucksport** would be the perfect locale for a David Lynch movie: it looks so innocent, with its beautiful nineteenth-century houses and churches, green hills, and majestically flowing river. Then you turn the corner and see the huge, steamy paper mill dominating the upper reaches of the riverbank. Closer examination of the town reveals the mysterious grave of Col. Jonathan Buck, the town's eighteenth-century patron. According to local legend, Buck presided over the condemnation of a local woman as a witch (this is quite a legend: no one was ever executed in Maine for witchcraft). On the scaffold she cursed him, and ever since his death the shape of a leg and foot appears on the side of his granite obelisk. After visiting this eerie site, you'd best repair to the historic **Jed Prouty Tavern** to rest.

The road to **Winterport** on the west side of the river crosses some beautiful grassy marshes, with Mount Waldo in the background. Winterport's 1831–32 **Union Meetinghouse** is a vigorous example of what Greek Revival church architecture could do on the right site. **Hampden,** birthplace of the reformer Dorothea Dix, is now a historic bedroom community for Bangor; **Brewer** on the river's right bank is the birthplace of Civil War hero Joshua Chamberlain.

■ BANGOR: QUEEN CITY

Not too many years ago, a German tourist whose English was at best shaky booked an air flight to San Francisco on a plane that made a refueling and customs stop at Bangor's modest but international airport. Suffering a little jet lag, the German visitor got off the plane and headed downtown. He found a place to stay and was able to point to things on the menu and for several days happily wandered through the city—under the impression that he was in San Francisco. Promoters of Bangor love to tell this story (which is true, by the way); when his mistake was revealed and widely publicized he was of course treated as a visiting dignitary. Not every visitor may be that immediately charmed, but Bangor is an important place historically— the self-styled "Queen City" of Maine's nineteenth-century lumber trade—and continues to enjoy its role as the metropolitan center of northern and eastern Maine, unwilling to defer to Portland in any regard.

Although perhaps best known today as the home of thriller author Stephen King—whose bat-winged fence and Victorian lumber baron's house on West Broadway have been frequently photographed—Bangor's real role is as the gateway to the Great North Woods. Much of its historic red-brick commercial district by the river was leveled by ill-considered "urban renewal" in the 1960s (about a decade before cities realized how such districts could be boutiqued and gentrified), though many splendid Victorian era residences remain up the hill. The best place, though, to see modern Bangor is amid the sprawling acres of new buildings—office parks, mini-malls, franchise restaurants—out by the gigantic Bangor Mall (which is a social as well as commercial mecca for much of northern Maine, by the way). If the summer retreats of Penobscot Bay are the version of an idealized Maine we are most accustomed to, here is the new Maine, and a harbinger of the future elsewhere in the state. It is all low, clean, orderly, spread out, relentlessly upbeat, and well heated indoors. And you'll drive, not walk, to get there.

Opening day for fishing Atlantic salmon at the Bangor Pool in Bangor.

(right) Bangor has benefited greatly over the years as the center of the lumber trade and gateway to the North Woods.

GROWING OLD ON EAST PENOBSCOT BAY

I have become a member of a very small communion of Episcopalians who meet for services in the American Legion Hall in Blue Hill. Most of them are sturdy, healthy retirees, professionals who have left cities all over the country and moved to this peninsula to live out their lives. There is not a black, Hispanic, or Oriental face among them. Throughout this homogeneous church, the thirty or so families have become friends as well as parishioners. After Sunday-morning Eucharistic service, they stay to have coffee and cakes and to talk about the 'outreach' programs many of them engage in. One works in an old people's home on Saturdays, another is active in a program to build houses for homeless families, one is concerned with helping Hancock's adult illiterates learn to read. On the whole, they are well-to-do and extremely active. I am of the belief that Maine residents live a long time because, unlike Florida retirees, they rarely sit down. They walk, sail, garden, shop, go to the library, the post office, the bookstore, visit and assist their friends, go to restaurants, movies, concerts, lectures, classes in crafts. Yesterday I heard a neighbor talking about a friend in Camden who had died, "prematurely," she said. Turned out the gentleman was eighty-one. Not to reach ninety up here is regarded as a disappointing act of carelessness or accident. The slogan here seems to be the old German saw *Rast ich, so rost ich.* When I rest, I rust.

—Doris Grumbach, *Coming into the End Zone,* 1991

■ EAST PENOBSCOT BAY

After touring perhaps as far north as the university town of **Orono**, you'll probably want to head south along the east side of the river. On the eastern side of Penobscot Bay lies a modern sort of Norumbega, a lovely collection of villages and fields as mythologized by nineteenth- and twentieth-century writers and artists as the fabled Tierra de Nurumberg was by sixteenth-century mapmakers and explorers. The picturesque peninsula and island which form the bay's eastern side have been celebrated by the enthralled novelists, poets, and essayists who've lived in towns like North Brooklin, Blue Hill, Castine, and Deer Isle.

■ NORTH BROOKLIN

In 1933, *New Yorker* writer E. B. White came to North Brooklin and bought a Federal-period house, complete with 40 acres of farmland and the barn which would eventually inspire *Charlotte's Web*. During the 1940s and '50s White created a vision of Maine as a more perfect place than the rest of the troubled United States—provincial, slow-moving, set in its ways, to be sure, but gentle, thoughtful, decent, and eminently admirable. As idealized as this image might seem, White, a thoroughly sophisticated and deeply urban man, wanted to believe it, as did thousands of people who read his inimitable prose and shared his bucolic longings. All over his part of the country live newcomers, many of them retired from noisier places, who may have chosen to end their days on the Maine coast because they once read sentences like this one: "And when . . . I dip down across the Narramissic and look back at the tiny town of Orland, the white spire of its church against the pale-red sky stirs me in a way that Chartres could never do." White lived there year-round 1938–43 then retired to the farm for good in 1957. The author once described to a friend the "certain bleak, hard-bitten character which the sea gives to the land":

This Maine farm calls to mind the setting for E. B. White's story, Charlotte's Web.

*O*ur woodlot is full of hemlock, spruce, birch, juniper, and all the aromatic sweetness of a Maine pasture; yet it dips right down to the tideflats, where gulls scream their heads off and hair-seals bark like old love-sick terriers. . . . Many days are startlingly clear and blue, many are thick a-fog. The fog shuts in fast, catching you short when you are sailing. It settles like a cloud down around the Hackmatack swamp and the frog pond, and makes the earth mysterious and enticing.

North Brooklin was also home to Katharine White, though it seems at times she missed New York and the literary world in ways that her husband did not. Best known to her contemporaries as fiction editor of *The New Yorker*, she surprised many of them in 1958 with a book review column under the subhead "Onward and Upward in the Garden"—a review of the spring's new garden catalogues and the first of 14 such columns she was to write over 12 years. In part to assuage her loneliness in Maine, she joined a long line of people who had struggled with the Maine climate, the salt spray, the slugs, the deer, and all the other hazards of the field to make their particular desert bloom. In illness and old age she did not stop. In his loving introduction to the 1979 compilation of her columns, *Onward and Upward in the Garden*, E. B. White recalled his late wife's persistence in planting spring bulbs:

*A*s the years went by and age overtook her, there was something comical yet touching in her bedraggled appearance on this awesome occasion—the small, hunched-over figure, her studied absorption in the implausible notion that there would be yet another spring, oblivious to the ending of her own days, which she knew perfectly well was near at hand, sitting there with her detailed chart under those dark skies in the dying October, calmly plotting the resurrection.

Those wishing to make a pilgrimage to the Whites' North Brooklin should note that while the original Norumbega was an imaginary city which appeared on many maps, North Brooklin is a real town which does not. The community can be found, however, northeast of Brooklin on Route 175. Successful explorers can stay at **The Lookout,** a classic summer hotel, whose situation on Flye Point allows visitors to feel the same relationship of sea and land that White so often described.

■ BLUE HILL

In nearby Blue Hill (further north a few miles on Route 175) there lived a man a century and a half earlier than Katherine White who would have applauded her efforts, although horticulture was only one of his many interests. The Reverend Jonathan Fisher, a country parson in that village from 1796 until his death in 1847, brought to this remote part of coastal Maine an essentially eighteenth-century conviction that a well-educated man (he was Harvard, class of 1792) could do just about anything he set his mind to. In 1814 he built largely with his own hands the house that stands today as the **Jonathan Fisher Memorial**, Route 15 in Blue Hill. At five each morning, Fisher sat in the room to the right of the entrance to read his Hebrew Bible before giving lessons in Latin and Greek to the young men who came to board with his family. In the 1840s the tutor founded the **Blue Hill Academy**, which still functions today and is one of Blue Hill's 75 buildings on the National Historic Register.

Fisher was also a poet, wood-engraver, amateur scientist, farmer, furniture maker, and artist; his paintings appear in the house and at the Farnsworth Museum in Rockland. Ill paid and, in his later years, unable to keep some members of his Congregationalist parish from straying into less respectable (yet more emotionally satisfying) denominations, he nonetheless proved that distance from great cities would not stifle an active and curious intelligence.

Fisher's parishioners hoped, of course, that Blue Hill and its harbor would become a thriving commercial center. Today, almost everyone is glad it didn't. The blueberry-covered hill which stands behind the village (and for which it was named) is still a relaxing place to stroll—a delicious experience come August. And the town may be best known for the craftsmanship of its potters, many of whom use unusual local glazes; look for their wares at **Rowantrees** on Union Street and **Rackcliffe Pottery** on Route 172.

The **Blue Hill Inn**, an old tavern on a quiet street near the academy close to the junction of Main and Route 177, offers 10 antique-filled guest rooms. An excellent dinner of grilled swordfish or Egyptian chicken curry can be found around the corner on Main Street at **Jonathan's**, whose eponymous chef is co-author of *Saltwater Seasonings,* the best contemporary Maine cookbook. For a rural experience, Blue Hill Farm on Route 15 offers six guest rooms on 48 acres; guests often

Her Room, *by Andrew Wyeth, shows the light-filled interior of the Wyeths' living room in* Cushing, Maine. *Through an open door and wavy-glass windows, the St. George River can be seen, lit by the diffuse, oblique rays from a solar eclipse. Nearby is the Olson House, made famous by Wyeth's* Christina's World, *and now owned by the Farnsworth Museum, which opens it to the public in summer.*

Born in 1917 and the son of noted illustrator N. C. Wyeth, Andrew Wyeth had his first one-man show in New York in 1937. He is best known for his use of watercolors and tempera in the muted harmonies of grays and soft browns. Used with an almost photographic naturalism, these colors convey perfectly his vision of the rural life about him. For the most part, Wyeth painted the houses, hills, fields, and people of his home in the Brandywine Valley of Pennsylvania and of his summer home in Cushing. (Farnsworth Art Museum, Rockland)

meet each other at the wood-burning stove in the big kitchen, or over a breakfast of home-made breads and fresh fruit.

■ CASTINE

About 12 miles west of Blue Hill is the town of Castine. It is interesting to debate which is the more perfect Maine village, Blue Hill or Castine. Both places have much to offer: white Federal houses, soaring church steeples overlooking green lawns and blue water, and storefronts that look like old *New Yorker* covers. It would be hard to find a more placid and restful spot than either one on the Maine coast—it helps that both towns are far off U.S. 1. Castine has by far the more colorful history. Battled over by the English, French, and Dutch in the seventeenth century, the town was named for the Baron de Saint Castine, the young Frenchman who, after marrying a Penobscot princess, became a sort of feudal lord/Indian chief over Maine's eastern coast. In the Revolution, the town was so Tory that it welcomed the redcoats—even the 1400 troops and marines sent by Massachusetts could not drive them out. The British returned during the War of 1812, occupying Castine's Fort George for eight months; today, panels on the fort's earthworks complex tell the story. Across the road, the Maine Maritime Academy stands on the site of the British barracks, and offers visitors the use of its gym and pool for a small fee (326-4311).

If Blue Hill has Parson Fisher's artistic legacy, then Castine wins the literary honors. Robert Lowell inherited his cousin Harriet Winslow's house on Green Street and summered there with his second wife, Elizabeth Hardwick, through the 1950s and 1960s; Mary McCarthy spent much of the last part of her life there; and the poet Philip Booth continues to be associated with the town. Several important Lowell poems including "Skunk Hour" and portions of *Near the Ocean* have Castine settings, as do Booth's "This Day After Yesterday" (an elegy on Lowell), "Thinking About Hannah Arendt," and "Mary's, After Dinner." While communing with writerly spirits past and present, visitors will find several pleasant places to sleep and dine in this historic town: on Main Street are the **Castine Inn**, a summer hotel with large airy rooms built in 1898, and the **Pentagoet Inn**, a turreted Victorian with cozy rooms; on Battle Avenue you'll find **The Manor**, a stately summer home set on five acres. All three serve breakfast, and are open to the public for excellent dinners.

■ DEER ISLE AND CAPE ROSIER

Between Castine and Brooklin is the winding road that will take you past the writer Doris Grumbach's Sargentville, across Eggemoggin Reach to Deer Isle, where the fishing town of Stonington faces the sea and where you can take a boat to Isle au Haut (pronounced "I'll a hoe"), much of which is part of Acadia National Park. Deer Isle's heavy losses of young men as the Civil War dragged on formed an especially poignant episode in the island's history.

If at North Brooksville you elect to take Route 176, you can visit Cape Rosier, where lived one formerly urban couple who managed to set up a truly alternative way of life. Helen Nearing and the late Scott Nearing turned their house "Harborside" on Cape Rosier into a center of the rural homesteading movement and a witness to what they called, in the title of their best known book, *Living the Good Life*. In his youth a controversial radical—he was fired as an economics professor by the University of Pennsylvania for having accused a rich trustee of exploiting child labor—Scott Nearing "dropped out" in the 1930s to try homesteading on a derelict Vermont farm. Their self-sufficiency, their reverence for music and art, and their Tolstoyan devotion to physical labor were greatly admired by the many people who came to pay the Nearings homage. Whatever their politics, they lived the lives of hardworking, old-fashioned Yankees, extremely rational and self-denying. Despite the success of the maple-sugaring business they ran on the Vermont farm, the Nearings were unable to fend off encroaching ski resorts and condo development. They sold out in the 1970s and came to Cape Rosier, where they turned to blueberries for their cash crop. Scott died at the age of 100, but Helen continues to live on Cape Rosier, for many of her admirers a beacon on Penobscot Bay.

For accommodations on Deer Isle, the elegantly furnished **Pilgrim's Inn,** built in 1793, is among the finest of Maine's country inns. In the simpler spirit of the Nearings, the **Hiram Blake Camp** on Cape Rosier offers a dozen cottages along the shoreline—each with kitchen, wood stove, and bath—where a family can spend a week or two. Still run by the descendants of Hiram Blake, who founded it in 1916, the camp also features rowboats, numerous hiking trails, and an extensive library.

MOUNT DESERT ISLAND

ONE FOURTH OF JULY A FEW YEARS AGO, I hiked with two friends up the southern face of Cadillac Mountain, the island's tallest mountain. Starting at the trail just beyond Otter Creek, near the Blackwoods Campground, we steadily made our way up the 1,530-foot lump of pinkish granite, pausing at those occasional spots where the trail leveled out for a few yards, allowing us to turn around and see where we had been. Mount Desert and Sutton Island glistened in the sunlight; The Eastern Way, the gray-green Cranberry Islands, the Baker Island lighthouse, and a broad expanse of Atlantic Ocean lay before us. Seabirds swooped below. The wake of tiny boats scratched the surface of the waters. As we climbed, the tree cover at Cadillac's base gave way to blueberry-scrub, which dwindled until the glacier-marked rocks were bare of all but their crinkled lichens. This was the balding peak that French explorer Samuel de Champlain had seen from his ship almost 400 years earlier. What an extraordinary place to observe the nation's birthday, to rediscover an entire world as fresh and unviolated as the continent the first Europeans found.

Otter Point in Acadia National Park on Mount Desert Island.

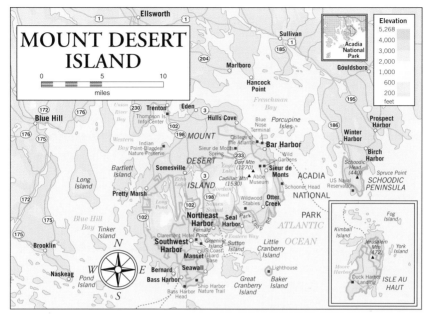

As we neared the summit of Cadillac—named for another French explorer—a metamorphosis took place, startling even for an island whose weather is notoriously changeable and whose landscape shifts from hour to hour with the sun and the wind and the fog. A phalanx of tour busses, hissing diesel, waited among many other vehicles at the top, spilling out humans who, after a quick look from the designated viewpoints, crowded into the gift shop before returning to Bar Harbor. We entered this cloud of people, paused again to admire the view, and descended into the deep ravine that separates Cadillac from Dorr Mountain. In a very few minutes, the people and their cars were out of sight; a couple of minutes more and they were out of hearing. On a steep, rocky face of granite we found a ledge, sunny but sheltered from the wind, where we unpacked our holiday lunch: sandwiches of local crabmeat, beer, and *tarte tatin* (an unwitting gesture of appreciation, I suppose, for the French role in securing our Independence). We were back in Eden.

That Fourth of July remains so strongly in my memory because it unexpectedly offered, within a few hours' walk, the essence of Mount Desert Island. It is a place that has been ill-used by some human beings, but cherished by others, including that second mountain's namesake, George Dorr, the conservationist who, early in this century, helped found Acadia National Park. Acadia is full of people, cars, and gift shops; it is also, despite its millions of visitors each summer, an island of secluded glens and little-walked trails, of real fishing villages and even a few surviving farms. People are everywhere, but you can escape them if you try. A century ago, the name of the island's leading town—Bar Harbor—was synonymous with ostentatious wealth and shameless snobbery. The island still attracts the rich, from the comfortably affluent to the downright famous, at least some of whom now stay year-round. It is also one of the East Coast's most popular family resorts, whether you drive over from Bangor for the day or come from New Jersey to camp out in the Winnebago for a week. Democracy arrived on Mount Desert, not as local legend would have it with the terrible fire of 1947, but with the ending of the gas crisis of the mid '70s when the nation took back to the highways in its campers and cars.

■ ISLAND HISTORY

In 1604, Samuel de Champlain discovered the island—or more accurately, ran aground on it. Champlain dubbed it the *Ile des Monts Deserts*—"the island of bare mountains"—none of them very tall even by Appalachian standards, yet *tout ensemble* a magnificent sight from the water. When the first French settlers arrived, they encountered and later traded with Abnaki Indians, who gathered shellfish on "Pemetic" (their term for the island) but lived on the mainland. French settlers traded with Indians on the island; in the eighteenth century, they used the island's harbors to hide their ships during the French and Indian War. After the British victory in Canada in 1760, English colonists were able to settle here.

By the mid-nineteenth century, the island had begun hosting summer residents; in 1858 the yachtsman-journalist Robert Carter commented on the growing number of "sea-side summer loungers" that M.D.I. was attracting. Over the next few decades, the island became the site of conflict over the degree to which nature should be tampered with. Carter himself believed the island needed the "hand of cultivated taste." Given the island's "mighty cliffs and sombre ravines and multitudinous ocean beaches," he noted, "it is impossible to conceive of any finer field for the exercise of the highest genius of the landscape gardener."

Carter had put his finger on a problem that was to animate luncheon conversation in summer cottages for the next generation: could—should—nature be improved? Did one approach the forest in a spirit of devotion, accepting as right whatever had naturally appeared there? Or did one treat nature with a gentle but firm hand, as if it were a willful child? When Percy Clark, for example, came to Northeast Harbor in search of a summer retreat in the early 1900s, he relished the wildness of the place and the physical challenges it offered the hiker and canoeist; the most that he and like-minded friends wished to interfere with the landscape was to lay out unobtrusive footpaths in the hills behind the village. Yet the very act of building rambling cottages along the shore had inevitably changed the balance of man and nature on Mount Desert Island.

■ NATIONAL PARK AND CARRIAGE ROADS

One person who realized this was oil heir John D. Rockefeller Jr., a summer resident of nearby Seal Harbor. Rockefeller helped George Dorr and Harvard University president Charles W. Eliot to assemble pieces of land in the area—all donated by private citizens—and handed them over to the federal government. In 1916, that land became Acadia National Park, the first national park east of the Mississippi. Meanwhile, between 1913 and 1940, Rockefeller designed and built 57 miles of carriage roads on Mount Desert Island, some of them on his own land, others on publicly owned property. (Not all of M.D.I. is national parkland.) Reserved then as now for hikers, equestrians, and horse-drawn carriages, they offered the best way, it seemed to him, to allow the public to discover and appreciate the beauty of some of the island's otherwise hidden places.

Percy Clark and others were deeply offended. They saw Rockefeller as a "spoiler of the wild," for the carriage roads had opened up parts of the island's interior that had previously been the domain of the solitary hiker. Clark agreed with naturalists like John Muir and John Burroughs that nature ought to be kept pristine. Rockefeller disagreed, preferring the view of Gifford Pinchot, the first director of the National Park Service, that people could be trusted to treat nature gently. Ann R. Roberts, the granddaughter of both Clark and Rockefeller, writes in her 1990 book on Acadia *(Mr. Rockefeller's Roads: The Untold Story of Acadia's Carriage Roads & Their Creator),* that the dispute "reflected a deep division in approach to conservation, one that persists to this day."

Ironically, the roads may have helped save the park's wild lands in several respects. For example, during the great fire of 1947 that burned some of the island's most beautiful scenery, the access the roads provided aided enormously in containing the fire. On a day-to-day basis, they probably curtail much potential damage to the environment by controlling and channeling the way humans penetrate the park's more remote sectors. More than 80 percent of the park's visitors today walk on Rockefeller's trails and carriage roads; others cycle, or ride horses or carriages on them (from the **Wildwood Stables** near Jordan Pond). In winter, they are popular routes for cross-country skiing and snowshoeing.

The network of carriage roads is distinctive in three ways. Although not always invisible on the landscape, the roads are carefully graded and their edges planted or terraced in ways that enable them to blend into the scenery. Rockefeller personally spent a great deal of time laying them out to open up vistas of the island's lakes and mountains that would otherwise be inaccessible to the casual visitor. And, while the design of the various bridges and edgings is subtly varied, they are built of local stone, often the distinctive, lichen-covered, pink Mount Desert granite, in a way that makes even the most elaborate of them seem always to have been there. As a design phenomenon, the complex system is unique to Acadia National Park and, though rarely studied, is surely one of the country's greatest achievements in this century in landscape architecture.

Unfortunately, the system is showing its age, and the hard-pressed National Park Service does not have the money to restore the shifting stonework or eroding surfaces. It is a tribute to the importance of the carriage roads to the Acadia experience, however, that private groups, like the Friends of Acadia and the Olmsted Alliance, are coming forth with the donations and the volunteer labor needed to make sure that this part of Rockefeller's legacy can be enjoyed by another generation.

■ GETTING TO MOUNT DESERT

There are several ways to approach the island. If you can manage it, come by boat. To see the Mount Desert range from a few miles out in the Atlantic is one of the great American experiences. It is like the first time you see a whale close at hand. There is something so improbable, yet absolutely right about it, that you can find yourself in tears at the sheer beauty of the sight. (Without your own boat, you can experience something of this effect by taking one of the nature cruises offered in

(right) A national park road snakes through fall foliage along Jordan Pond.

these waters, or perhaps the mail boat—a sort of *vaporetto*—that chugs from Northeast Harbor to the Cranberries.) In the days of Bar Harbor's social glory, the approach was from the other side of the island: the overnight express from Washington or New York delivered you and your servants early in the morning at **Hancock Point,** on the mainland, and a little steamer transported you across Frenchman Bay.

Most people today arrive by car over the bridge at **Trenton.** If you travel that way, the previous half hour can be a troubling one. The commercial sprawl on the Ellsworth "strip" is sometimes cited as a textbook case in how not to "grow" a city—although it's no worse than thousands of similar crowded stretches in other states, it seems more offensive in this part of coastal Maine. But the real assault to the senses is the 15 miles of Route 3 between Ellsworth and Trenton, through what used to be largely farmland and woods. This piece of the road has become one long, thin strip of neon-lighted entertainment park. In the distance the blue hills of Mount Desert watch, in silent reproach.

I used to have a cat who, after sleeping for hours in the back window of my car, would suddenly come to life again as soon as we crossed the bridge onto the island at Trenton. I would like to think it was his extraordinary powers of navigation, rivaling those of any migratory bird, but in truth it was simply low tide, and the distinctive smell of the great mud flat of Mount Desert Narrows—a major hazard for anyone trying to circumnavigate the island by boat. Percy the cat was a stray found in M.D.I.'s Southwest Harbor, and was probably the descendant of some feline who had jumped ship a century or two earlier: the memory of salt air was indelibly in his genes. Just past the **Thompson Island Information Center** (on a little piece, slightly detached, of the big island) the human at the wheel must make a decision: follow Route 3 into Bar Harbor, or continue on Route 102 toward the less busy part of M.D.I.

If you drive toward Bar Harbor from the Trenton bridge, you pass through **Hulls Cove,** whose cemetery holds the remains of the woman who once owned half the island. In 1688, Louis XIV granted all of M.D.I. to an officer named Antoine de la Mothe Cadillac. He never set foot on his island—he was busy settling Detroit—but his emigre granddaughter a century later pursued her claim and in 1786 persuaded the authorities in Boston to grant her the eastern half of Mount Desert (a letter from Lafayette is said to have helped). This Madame de Gregoire settled at Hulls Cove, where she died in straitened circumstances in 1811, a naturalized citizen who was also a final link in France's claim to this part of

North America. Also at Hulls Cove is Acadia National Park's visitor center and the beginning of the **Park Loop Road,** a 20-mile circuit of some of the island's most spectacular scenery. On the northern edge of town is the Blue Nose Ferry Terminal, with its frequent service to Nova Scotia, and the small, bayfront **College of the Atlantic,** a center for environmental studies, especially whale watching. (Biologists from the college lead whale watches from Seal Harbor, 276-5803). The fast-moving 1947 fire stopped at Eden Street (Route 3 at this point), and the college campus incorporates several former estates on the water that escaped the fate of their neighbors up the hill. The most imposing of these, a châteauesque pile known as **The Turrets,** welcomes visitors to the college's **Natural History Museum;** this is one place where you can experience, at least spatially, what the cottage era was like, and the terrace offers a splendid vista of Bar Island and the bay. Connoisseurs of local lore might also be interested to see the **Wonder View Motor Lodge,** on the site of mystery writer Mary Roberts Rinehart's summer home (the view of the bay is still a wonder), and the **Atlantic Oakes by-the-Sea Motel,** which incorporates what is left of the estate of Sir Harry Oakes, the gold-mining magnate whose sensational 1941 murder in Nassau has never been solved.

■ BAR HARBOR

Henry James, returning to the United States after many years in England, declared upon visiting Palm Beach that it was a "hotel civilization." Bar Harbor presents a motel civilization, an effect amplified by the way the hostelries hang from the hillsides as you enter town on the poignantly named Eden Street. For the first century of its existence, however, Bar Harbor literally was the Town of Eden, a small fishing and farming community, the only remnant of which is the town cemetery with its Civil War monument. The post-war years brought the appearance of the sprawling wooden hotels, which became so popular with fashionable rusticators that they grew and grew, one of them covering most of what is now the Village Green. (Another was built on top of nearby Cadillac Mountain, reached in those days by cog rail; both hotel and train disappeared when the summit became national park land.)

The era of the hotels (roughly, 1860 to 1885) was soon succeeded by that of the private "cottages," as beneficiaries of the country's great industrial fortunes arrived

The Breakwater in Bar Harbor is one of many formerly private homes that are now bed-and-breakfasts. (Brian Vanden Brink)

and began competing for status with their fellows. This was Bar Harbor's Golden Age, from the late 1880s to World War I, when J. P. Morgan's yacht *Corsair* was moored in the harbor, and the famous Mrs. Stotesbury of Philadelphia regularly entertained 40 at lunch in her palace by the sea. The less ostentatious of these cottages were constructed, sometimes quite fancifully, in the Shingle style, which is now recognized as one of America's most pleasing contributions to vernacular architecture. The most ponderous of them were melanges of every European style. Some summer residents tried to transform the landscape by sculpting Bar Harbor's hillsides into Italianate terraces and gardens. Today, on the overgrown sites of estates destroyed in the 1947 fire, you find traces of these elaborate schemes, in bits and pieces of wall and cyclopean blocks of dressed granite.

Remembering his childhood summers in Bar Harbor in the 1920s, the novelist Louis Auchincloss wrote of the "silly side" of fashionable life there and of his early realization that the summer colony's "big houses, their shining cars, and their glittering yachts were designed to impress just such onlookers as myself." As he recalled in *A Writer's Capital,* his Old New York parents were immune to this spectacle, even if their child was not: "Strong in their own innate decency, in their own high moral standards, they saw no reason why they could not live out a pastoral idyll in the very heart of Sodom or Gomorrah." Bar Harbor was still an idyllic place through the 1970s, despite the post-conflagration appearance of barracks-like motels and the slow erosion of the town's "social" cachet. It was not really until the '80s that everyone realized that the place had turned into Lobsterland USA. Some wailed and gnashed their teeth, others raked in the cash from the tourist herds.

Bar Harbor has received some bad press of late, "tacky" being one of the kinder adjectives used. Actually, the place is not that bad, especially outside the Fourth of July to Labor Day crush. The setting is still remarkable—the mussel-encrusted sandbar that allows you to walk at low tide across the inner harbor to Bar Island, the bristly-looking Porcupine Islands farther out in Frenchman Bay, the mountains standing like sentries along the southern flank of the town. And amid the modern clutter there are some charming survivors of an earlier day: **Butterfield's**

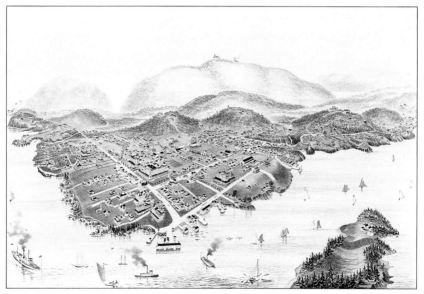

Bird's-eye view of Bar Harbor from an old lithograph. (Library of Congress)

Market, for example, with its air of the carriage trade era; the handsome **Jessup Memorial Library** (in the basement of which is the Bar Harbor Historical Society, filled with photos and other memorabilia of the town's Golden Age); and the **Reading Room** (now the dining room of the Bar Harbor Motor Lodge, and formerly the scene of much genteel tippling).

For first-time visitors to the island, Bar Harbor still offers the greatest range of places to sleep, eat, and shop while visiting Acadia National Park. It appears that almost every private house with more than two bedrooms has been converted into a bed-and-breakfast—if Laura Ashley had not existed, it would have been necessary here to invent her—but this at least assures some variety amid the more anonymous motels. (The hazard lurking in B&Bs is in having to talk to people at breakfast.) The town also has more to offer the out-of-season visitor than it used to, as cross-country skiing on the park's carriage trails grows in popularity and as more innkeepers discover that couples will pay to sip mulled cider in front of a log fire on romantic winter weekends. While there is no hotel of any real distinction, there is at least one very good restaurant, the **Porcupine Grill** on Cottage Street, whose slick, low-key decor includes photos of the Porcupine Islands just off Bar Harbor's coast. Otherwise, most of the restaurant menus seem to have been written by the same person (who also cooks all of the food), but there is something to be said for the blueberry pancakes at **Jordan's** and the restorative fish chowder at the no-frills **Acadia Restaurant.** The bookstore side of **Sherman's** is one of the island's cultural centers; the Art Deco **Criterion Theatre** is a good place to spend a rainy afternoon. Amid the tourist emporia on Main Street two stores stand out: the **Acadia Shop,** good for souvenirs and resortwear, and **Island Artisans,** a cooperative selling the work of local craftspeople in textiles, pottery, baskets, wood, metals, paper, and glass. The outskirts of Bar Harbor are still rural, thanks to the fact that the town is surrounded by national park land, though the amusement parks are beginning to encroach on Route 3.

Leaving Bar Harbor on Route 3 to the south, you pass the **Jackson Laboratory,** an internationally renowned center for genetic research. Soon you reach **Sieur de Monts Springs,** where the Bar Harbor Garden Club maintains its **Wild Gardens of Acadia,** a botanical collection demonstrating 12 habitats. Between the springs and the rather sinister-looking lake called the Tarn is one of the state's most interesting small museums, the **Abbe Museum,** devoted to Maine's Native American culture. Through changing exhibits, you can learn about pre-European life on the island (the museum has conducted archeological research since 1927), the Red

Paint People, the contact experience of natives and Europeans, and such traditional crafts as bark and quill basketry. Route 3 continues between the mountains to Otter Creek, whose cove was painted by Frederick Church in that first wave of rustication a century and a half ago. The village itself has a landlocked air, however; its vistas of mountains make you feel you've visited the American West, not Maine.

■ THE QUIET SIDE

It is a not very well kept secret that the nicest parts of Mount Desert Island today are on its "back" side, roughly the two-thirds of the island farthest from Bar Harbor and the Park Loop Drive. Visitors who complain that Bar Harbor doesn't look like the quaint Maine fishing village they'd expected should make the half-hour trip to Bass Harbor, say, or Bernard. These working communities, not quaint in the least, are only lightly touched by tourism. But as they snuggle around their shared harbor, they certainly live up to the image, romantic or not, of the self-contained coastal village. The relatively low-key nature of life on Mount Desert Island's "quiet side," with its mix of fishing and recreational sailing, of "real" Mainers and summer folk, does not quite disguise the fact that hidden down many of those piney drives are some of the richest people in America.

This is perhaps easier to comprehend when the shoreline is seen from a boat; the huge new houses, almost ancient Roman in their opulence, on the high granite cliffs near **Hunters Cove** are as much a monument to the Age of Reagan as their sprawling Shingle-style ancestors a century earlier were to the Age of Morgan, Gould, and Fiske. The same might be said of the new, quite controversial houses on Schooner Head, closer to Bar Harbor. But the authentic Mount Desert style is much more subdued, almost self-deprecating. Driving into Seal Harbor, for example—perhaps stopping at its small pocket beach, or hiking to Jordan Pond for tea—the visitor catches only glimpses of summer houses tucked into the woods. Long identified with the Rockefeller family, **Seal Harbor** may seem modest from the road, but its hillsides offer magnificent views over the Eastern Way past Sutton and the Cranberries and out to sea: the waters celebrated by Samuel Eliot Morison and so many other yachtsmen.

MAINE'S PALEO-INDIANS

As recently as 18,000 years ago, Maine was covered by a sheet of ice as thick as a mile in some places. This was the last gasp of the Wisconsin Ice Age, and it took 5,000 years for its glaciers to loosen their clutches on Maine. Then, before the land surface could spring back from the weight of so much ice, nearly half the state was inundated by the sea, leaving marine clay deposits north of Bangor.

The prehistory of Maine began another 2,000 years later—about 11,000 years ago—when land surfaces had rebounded from the weight of ice and the sea retreated, establishing a tundra similar to present-day interior Alaska. Then, wandering hunters now referred to as Paleo-Indians moved into the state, probably following big game such as caribou, and possibly mammoth, musk-ox, giant bison, and wild horses. They pitched camp on high, dry-soiled terraces that offered commanding views of the treeless landscape. These people, apparently well-adapted to the cold, traveled long distances to follow game herds and carried a kit of beautifully made stone tools. Among these tools was the fluted spearpoint, distinguished by the long channel flake removed from its center, which is the hallmark of Paleo-Indian technology. They often crafted their spearpoints out of chert, chipping this flint-like rock carefully to reveal its bands of color, usually shades of brown, blue, or red. The use of certain types of chert—types indigenous to New York, Pennsylvania, Vermont, and Massachusetts, but not to Maine—indicates the great distances traveled by the bands.

A forest environment more familiar to us was established about 9,000 years ago, when a change in climate ushered in the Archaic Period. At their sites along rivers, streams, and lakes, the Archaic People left stone tools including stone spearheads, net sinkers, and woodworking tools. Crafted from

Two slate spearpoints and an atlatl weight dating from about 3,800 to 5,000 years ago, during the Archaic Period. (Abbe Museum, Bar Harbor)

the local slate rather than chert, these artifacts indicate that these hunter-gatherers traveled far less than their forebearers. These peoples migrated more narrowly, adapting closely to the local climate and seasonal changes. Groups of hunter-gatherers moved up and down rivers, along the coast, and sometimes crossed water to offshore islands. They fished in the spring and fall, when the rivers were filled with migratory fish like salmon; hunted moose, caribou, and deer in the fall for their meat and skins; snared small fur-bearing animals; and probably collected a wide variety of seasonal plant foods and marine resources.

Porcupine quill over birchbark box.
(Abbe Museum, Bar Harbor)

One Archaic culture, popularly known as the "Red Paint People," entranced archaeologists during the early part of this century, when they discovered cemeteries of this group along the Penobscot, the Kennebec, and other major rivers. These archaeologists named the culture for the red iron pirite powder, or ochre, which covered the numerous stone tools—probably included as ceremonial offerings—among the gravesite remains. Because of the mysterious red powder and the lack of other data, these archaeologists and their contemporaries romanticized the "Red Paint People," describing them as a "vanished civilization" distinct from the Paleo-Indians before and after.

Modern research at living sites associated with the cemeteries reveals a more realistic picture of this culture of Archaic hunters and gatherers who lived from 3000 to 1800 B.C. We know that these people hunted and fished, and probably relied on other marine resources during some seasons. At coastal and island archaeological sites, abundant swordfish remains have been found—surprising, since today swordfish are infrequently found in the cold waters of the Gulf of Maine. But 5,000 years ago the climate had reached a post-glacial peak warming and the Gulf may have supported greater numbers. Archaic hunters probably traveled long distances from shore in large dugout boats to harpoon the fish—which can reach 15 feet and weigh nearly a ton—as they sunned themselves at the surface. The meat probably fed many people, and the bones and swords were used to make tools; swordfish bills were sometimes crafted into long daggers decorated with geometric designs.

The Archaic Period ended about 3,000 years ago, when the technology for making clay pots was adopted by Maine's native peoples. During the subsequent era, known as the Ceramic Period, people continued to hunt and gather the local flora and fauna—especially shellfish, as indicated by the many shell midden sites along the coast of Maine. The famous oyster heaps in Damariscotta, once mined for fertilizer but since preserved, are huge mounds measuring several hundred feet long and thirty feet thick. The piles of shells are conducive to the preservation of bone remains, providing us with detailed information about the variety of food resources during the Ceramic Period: in addition to shells of softshell clams, mussels, and sea urchins, the mounds are also composed of the bones of a variety of fish, birds, and mammals. Of interest to coastal connoisseurs today is the absence of lobster shells; there is little evidence that they were collected by prehistoric native Mainers.

The earliest contacts between native peoples and European explorers on the shores of Maine took place in 1604–1605, when Samuel de Champlain explored the coast and described the Abnaki (or Wabanaki, meaning "Downlanders" or "Easterners") in his journals. Beginning in the early seventeenth century, Indian tribes began losing their lands in a series of agreements which European explorers and settlers made and quickly broke. By the mid-eighteenth century, the Abnaki got caught in the middle of a conflict between European powers and found themselves designated allies of the French crown—and fair game for any British musket. Even after the European conflict ended, the Indians continued both to lose their land and to be wiped out from the diseases the Europeans brought with them. Meanwhile, heavy colonization destroyed much of the Natives' resource base. In the latter 1800s, an Abnaki confederacy was formed, but after years of political tribal conflict, the alliance dissolved by the end of the century. Today, descendants of the Abnaki still reside in Maine. The four federally recognized Indian tribes in Maine are the Penobscots, on Indian Island, Old Town; the Passamaquoddy tribe in Washington County; the Aroostook band of Micmacs in Aroostook County; and the Maliseet Tribe, also in Aroostook County.

—Rebecca Cole-Will, Curator of Archaeology, the Abbe Museum,
Acadia National Park, Mount Desert

■ NORTHEAST HARBOR

Route 3 leads on, suddenly offering a dramatic view of Northeast Harbor's narrow, boat-packed anchorage, where in high season the boats may range from the converted lobsterboat that is someone's summer toy to the late Malcolm Forbes's yacht *Highlander,* complete with its helicopter and brace of motorcycles on deck—the sort of vessel that seems to have sailed out of the pages of Petronius. The road turns sharply at the landmark **Asticou Hotel,** which commands the head of the harbor, and just past the serene Asticou Azalea Garden turns again into town.

For so famous a yachting center, the harborfront itself is rather bland, but a short walk uphill brings you to Northeast Harbor's **Main Street,** a very long block of modest yet festive shopfronts. The clapboards may look weathered, and no one really dresses up, but these little stores—the market, the fishmonger, the florist, the needlepointer, the paper store, the gift shop—despite their almost exaggerated plainness have in their own way as much cachet as anything on Worth Avenue or Rodeo Drive. It is not what they sell, it's who you see shopping there. Northeast Harbor is probably as fashionable an address in summer as any place you could find in North America. The town began as an obscure fishing village, was discovered in the 1870s and 1880s by college presidents and Episcopal bishops, and for much of the century was regarded as a sensible, if slightly dowdy, alternative to the more glamorous Bar Harbor. (The Asticou, a classic Maine hotel, seems to have preserved this quality, like a well-used country club.) After World War II, however, the focus of social life shifted. Today, the grandchildren and great-grandchildren of those early rusticators—many of them having had the good sense to marry into a major industrial fortune—now spend their summers *en toute simplicité* in a part of Maine they have tried (fairly successfully) to keep from ever changing, at least in terms of the way it looks.

In the early 1950s, the French writer Marguerite Yourcenar and her life-long friend Grace Frick bought a small farmhouse amid the summer cottages in Northeast Harbor and named it "Petite Plaisance." For years, few people on the island realized that Yourcenar was one of the greatest French prose stylists of the century —until she made headlines in 1981 as the first woman to be elected to the French Academy. This house is open July through August; call 276-3940.

■ SOMES SOUND

Northeast Harbor needs to be seen from a boat, but the corniche of Sargent Drive just to the north offers remarkable views of one of Mount Desert's most interesting bodies of water, **Somes Sound.** Said to be the only fjord in the lower 48 (a claim disputed by admirers of the Hudson River), Somes Sound cuts almost all the way through the island. On the opposite shore you can see, at the foot of Acadia Mountain, a stream of water dribbling down the granite—**Man o' War Brook**—where in Revolutionary times naval vessels took advantage of the deep water of the Sound to funnel fresh water aboard by means of sail cloth. Farther south is **Fernald Point,** today a handsome meadow, and in 1613 the site of St. Sauveur, the first Jesuit settlement in New England. It was quickly destroyed by the English, who buried one of the French priests they killed somewhere on the point. In the words of Francis Parkman—himself an early rusticator on the Sound—"In an obscure stroke of violence began the strife of France and England, Protestantism and Rome, which for a century and a half shook the struggling communities of North America, and closed at last in the memorable Triumph on the Plains of Abraham."

At the head of the Sound today is the remarkably peaceful-looking village of **Somesville,** so picture perfect that people get out of their cars in the middle of the road to photograph the little white footbridge next to the Higgins's general store. Somesville is a triumph of the Colonial Revival. For its first century and a half no doubt a scrappy outpost smelling of fish guts and drying cod, from the late nineteenth century on the village has been re-created and preserved as a reminder of how beautiful the country could have been, given a little thoughtful care. Admittedly, the location helps. One place to appreciate it is **Port in a Storm,** surely the most beautifully situated bookstore in America; one day, a few feet from its tiny waterfront parking lot, I saw a loon swimming.

■ SOUTHWEST HARBOR

Turning south on Route 102 the visitor passes hill-locked Echo Lake—a good, occasionally even warm, freshwater swimming spot—and soon reaches Southwest Harbor, the commercial center for the back side of the island. It is a town at the moment in perfect balance—working port, Coast Guard base, just enough tourists, a friendly Main Street, a world-famous assortment of boat builders—though out-of-scale condos already loom over part of the harbor. (If one notes that the huge nineteenth-century wooden hotels were just as obtrusive, the only reply is to ask if we've learned nothing since.) There are several places worth calling at. The **Wendall Gilley Museum**—devoted to a local plumber turned famous bird-carver—is a migratory stop for many birders, and of interest to anyone curious about modern techniques of making buildings energy efficient. In the center of town is **Sawyer's,** which from the street looks like a mom and pop grocery store but which on the inside proves a gastronomic landmark: the stock includes fresh goat cheeses from nearby Seal Cove, hand-picked vegetables from local farmers, farm-raised Atlantic salmon, the succulent local crab clawmeat, superb focaccia from the island's **Little Notch Bakery,** as well as the old-fashioned canned goods—aspic, hearts of palm, Indian pudding, and the like—that used to be found in every summer house pantry. Closer to the Coast Guard station is **Beal's,** where you can dine outdoors on the day's catch in an authentic dockside setting. Nearby in neighboring Manset is the **Hinckley Boatyard and Shop,** where visitors can see a video on how the dark, sleek yawls and sloops that fill the harbor are made.

The Claremont Hotel has long been one of Mount Desert Island's most evocative resorts. (Courtesy of The Claremont Hotel)

Southwest Harbor's most memorable landmark, however, is what I would argue is Maine's best hotel, the vintage **Claremont**, which has looked out over Somes Sound and Cadillac Mountain for more than a century. It is one of the few wooden hotels in Maine to have survived, and it won't be to everyone's taste: there are no telephones or TVs in the rooms, and you need a coat and tie for the dining room. But in terms of restful surroundings—the only public excitement comes from its famous croquet tournaments—superb views, good food, human scale, and a lightly worn sense of nostalgia, it cannot be equaled in the state. Actually a complex of old hotel and surrounding cottages, the hotel is usually booked well in advance for much of the summer. But you can always have a drink or lunch down at its boathouse and enjoy the scenery, directly across from Greening Island (private), the locale of May Sarton's novel *The Magnificent Spinster.*

Continuing on 102A from Manset, you drive around the southern tip of the island, passing the natural barrier at Seawall, where the Western Way enters the Great Harbor of Mount Desert, and the **Ship Harbor Nature Trail.** The latter offers a particularly good chance for a short hike through a coastal woodland, with views of the narrow inlet in which an eighteenth-century ship from Ireland is said to have been miraculously deposited by a life-threatening storm. Land ends at the **Bass Harbor Head Light,** after which you can drive up the quiet western side of the island, perhaps stopping at Pretty Marsh to hike in good seal-spotting territory.

Mount Desert can also be circumnavigated by boat, though getting through the tidal flats near the Trenton Bridge can be tricky even at high tide. For most visitors, a more practical excursion is to take one of the many whale-watching cruises offered from the island or to take the little mail boat which regularly plies the waters between Northeast Harbor's town dock and the islands known as Sutton, Great Cranberry, and Little Cranberry (where the fishing village of Islesford offers restaurants and a museum). For the more ambitious, a nature cruise to **Baker Island** and its lighthouse—or to the Audubon Society-owned **Duck Islands** about five miles out to sea—offers one of the greatest visual experiences on the North Atlantic coast. Don't look back until you are far offshore. Then turn around and look at Champlain's *Ile des Monts Deserts* rising from the sea, and imagine yourself a passenger on the Frenchman's boat—a man who, as F. Scott Fitzgerald wrote of another explorer, "must have held his breath in the presence of this continent . . . face to face for the last time in history with something commensurate to his capacity to wonder."

COCKTAILS ON THE POINT

*B*eing home down on The Point again after being away from Maine teaching in New York was strange. The place hadn't changed much, except for a few new houses here and there. How well I remembered most of the old places, since I had helped open them and close them all of my growing up summers. I had washed their windows, scrubbed their toilets, swept their floors, mowed their lawns, and delivered the milk from my grandfather's farm to their kitchens. My mother and most of my aunts cleaned the cottages and worked as cooks and did the laundries; and had done so all of their lives. My father and many of my uncles and other male relatives worked as caretakers and handymen servicing the summer places. Next to working at one of the town's two lobster pounds, or in the woods, or on the Maine Central Railroad, the summer colony was, for many of the town's families, something one could always count on at least for part-time work during the summer months, like worming or clamming.

I was really quite anxious to see everyone over drinks because this was the first party I had been invited to since my five-part radio series entitled "The Maine That's Missing," based on a previous article of mine in *Maine Life*, had been broadcast over the Maine Public Broadcasting System. I knew that some of the Point people had been tuned in and I was naturally anxious to learn of their reactions.

As I walked in the front door of the Clemson cottage, Marietta herself greeted me by saying, "I must take umbrage!"

"Must you, Marietta? Where shall we take it?"

"No further than this foyer. I just wanted to warn you that some people thought your radio series was very poorly edited and that the whole thing amounted to Andy Griffin's ego trip."

"Thanks, Marietta, That really makes me feel good."

—Sanford Phippen, *The Police Know Everything: Downeast Stories,* 1982

D O W N   E A S T

A FEW MILES EAST OF ELLSWORTH on U.S. 1, you realize that something remarkable has taken place. You have entered another time. While much is familiar, something is missing. The landscape is far from unspoiled, yet it seems to have a pristine quality that you don't associate with other coastal neighborhoods. It seems a place where people have begun to leave their mark—some of it raw and ugly, yet much of it slight and unobtrusive—only to have stopped. For older visitors, it seems like the Maine of the 1950s: a simpler, friendlier place, a world without fast food or shopping malls, traffic congestion or urban ills. Much of it is a very poor place—recalling the world of Carolyn Chute's novel *The Beans of Egypt, Maine*— a place that seems not only to have missed the prosperity of the 1980s, but to have never quite recovered from the Great Depression. Nonetheless, the stark beauty of its lakes and coastline and the almost toy-like quality of some of its towns (Steuben, say, with its postage-stamp of a post office and a few old houses and a church) give this easternmost corner of Maine a peculiar fascination. Fall is the best time to visit: the first touch of frost turns the blueberry fields all the shades of red of a Bokhara carpet.

Although all of the region might be seen on a daytrip from Bar Harbor, to appreciate eastern Hancock and Washington counties requires a few days' leisurely visit at the least. Starting at Hancock and Sullivan—with their stunning views across Frenchman Bay of Mount Desert—and continuing east (perhaps with a detour to see the Schoodic Peninsula, which is part of Acadia National Park), you will encounter the series of fishing villages and blueberry towns that represent what "Down East" means today.

■ HANCOCK TO COLUMBIA FALLS

A stop in the town of Hancock, nine miles east of Ellsworth, should be made around dinnertime: the understated **Le Domaine** restaurant offers a traditional French menu, including sweetbreads and coquilles St. Jacques. (Like many restaurants in the area it is open seasonally; call 422-3395.) About 12 miles farther down Route 1, the local fruit comes in an enticing form at the **Bartlett Maine Estate**

(right) The rugged shoreline of the "Bold Coast" near Cutler, far Down East.

Estate Winery in Gouldsboro: the dry Blueberry French Oak Reserve wine is highly recommended, and there is a tasting room open to the public. Close by on Route 1 is the tiny town of **Steuben,** just over the border into Maine's easternmost county, Washington—or more colloquially, "Sunrise"—County. The village is named for Baron Friedrich von Steuben, who served as inspector general of the Continental Army and was granted this land for his service in the American Revolution. (Today it is the home of food writer John Thorne.) Washington County's major industries are well represented in **Milbridge,** home both to one of the oldest wild blueberry processors and to one of the few remaining sardine canning factories; there's also a considerable Christmas wreath industry. Ten miles northeast is Columbia Falls, site of the **Ruggles House** on Main Street. Lumber dealer Thomas Ruggles built this Federal-style mansion, with its elegant flying staircase and palladian window in 1818, only to die soon afterward. The woodwork is so intricate that local legend tells of a woodcarver imprisoned there for three years with only a penknife to occupy his time.

■ JONESPORT AND BEALS

South of Columbia Falls on Route 187 are the towns of Jonesport and Beals, fishing villages which boast eastern Maine's largest lobstering fleet. The town of Beals comprises two islands joined by bridge: the more inland Beals Island, which is connected to Jonesport by bridge; and Great Wass Island, the site of **Great Wass Island Preserve,** a 1,540-acre tract maintained by the Nature Conservancy. With hopes of spotting eiders, scoters, razor bills, ospreys, and bald eagles, birders flock to the preserve's coastal peatlands. The island's jack-pine stands support several warbler and chickadee species, while its shores are visited by black-backed and ring-billed gulls, especially in August. The island is the largest of those within the Great Wass Archipelago, which the Nature Conservancy guidebook describes as being "in an unusual oceanic microclimate, where islands are colder and more moist than on the mainland, yet are buffered from the year-round temperature extremes of the interior." Because island weather is generally hard to predict, be prepared for various conditions.

■ MACHIAS

In 1763, settlers from Scarborough in southern Maine were exploring the coast in search of grazing land for their livestock when they discovered the site of present-day Machias and squatted there. It was not clear to them at first whether they were in Massachusetts or Nova Scotia—some indication of how vague a concept "Maine" was even on the eve of the Revolution. This group, like most groups of new settlers at the time, erected a sawmill; by 1774, there were 46 such mills between Cherryfield and Ellsworth alone. Within a year of its settlement, Machias had produced a million and a half board feet of lumber.

The last river drive in Machias took place in the 1960s, but the town remains prosperous-looking by Washington County standards—thanks in part to its wild blueberry industry—and it is in fact a very attractive community, with a branch of the University of Maine, a good bookstore, two good restaurants, a famous old academy (in East Machias), and a beautiful situation overlooking the Little Bad Falls of the Machias River. This is a good place to use as a base for exploring the easternmost piece of the United States.

The place to start there is the historic, gambrel-roofed **Burnham Tavern** on a slight bluff overlooking the river in the center of Machias. Thought to be the oldest building in the state east of the Penobscot and one of the most important sites in Maine to be associated with the War for American Independence, the tavern—today operated as a museum by the Daughters of the American Revolution—was in its first century not only a hostelry but an important meeting place in which much of the social and political life of the region was conducted. (The original sign over its door read: "Drink for the thirsty, food for the hungry, lodging for the weary, and good keeping for the horses.") It was in its public rooms that citizens gathered in 1775 to discuss the battles at Lexington and Concord and resolved to erect their own Liberty Pole in the village. More important, it was in the Burnham Tavern that the patriots of Machias planned the daring venture that turned into the first naval battle of the Revolution.

In the early summer of 1775, the situation in the Machias Bay region paralleled that in Casco Bay in one important respect: a local Tory sympathizer, Ichabod Jones, was supporting the British war effort by shipping desperately needed firewood and lumber to the royal troops occupying Boston. When the local Whigs threatened to destroy his vessels, the British naval commander in Boston sent an armed sloop, H.M.S. *Margaretta,* to protect Jones's business, just as the *Canceau* had been sent under Captain Mowatt to protect the Tory shipbuilder at Falmouth. The leading citizens of Machias proved more determined, however, than their Casco Bay counterparts. On the banks of a small stream later named "Foster's Rubicon," the local patriot Benjamin Foster, after a long debate over whether the town should furnish wood to the British in return for badly needed provisions, leaped across the stream, inviting those who agreed with him to follow him on his symbolic gesture. One after another, beginning with other fervent Whigs, followed by those who had wavered, and finally joined even by the would-be loyalists, the entire community crossed over.

The patriots first tried to capture the British commander and his local allies when they attended church, but they failed. The British quickly sought the protection of the sloop and its four guns. That night, Hannah and Rebecca Weston, two young women from nearby Jonesboro, became local heroines by carrying 50 pounds of gunpowder and lead through 16 miles of woods to aid the rebel cause. The next morning, 12 June 1775, some 40 men under the command of Jeremiah O'Brien sailed downriver in a sloop they had captured from Jones and were joined by Foster and about 20 more men in a small schooner. Poor sailing had delayed the *Margaretta* from reaching open sea; the Americans came alongside, attacked and boarded the British vessel, and mortally wounded the officer in command (he died later in the tavern). The crew quickly surrendered. Soon after, the rebels also surprised and captured the schooner *Diligent* and its tender and converted the three prize vessels into a small squadron to defend their river. It was on a mission to avenge this humiliation that Mowatt happened to burn Falmouth that autumn.

Punishment of the Machias rebels came in 1777, when Sir George Collier, with the *Ranger* and three other vessels, routed the local militia from their breastworks along the shore at Machiasport and burned several buildings. The British feared—correctly—that Machias itself was a staging point for a planned invasion of Nova Scotia and intended to destroy it, but for some reason withdrew when their goal seemed within their reach. One explanation is that the British commander, who had easily broken through a log boom placed to block the river and overcome the defenses of the port, thought his vessels were being lured into a trap upstream. Another factor was the presence of a large number of Penobscot, Passamaquoddy, and Maliseet Indians at Machias, some of whom helped fire on the British (overall, Indian support wavered between British and rebel forces during the Revolution in Maine, depending on local conditions and the Indians' sense of their self-interest.) History was repeated in 1814, when Fort Machias (now Fort O'Brien) at the mouth of the river was seized and its barracks burned by another British raiding party.

■ COBSCOOK BAY

East on U.S. 1 from East Machias is Cobscook Bay, and should you decide to remain on the same route, you'll arrive at **Cobscook State Park** on the bay's western shore. The park offers beautiful shoreside campsites, but there's always plenty of space available; few Maine visitors make it as far as Sunrise County, let alone its easternmost point. After continuing north on 1, head south on Route 190 at Perry. A few miles from Perry is Pleasant Point, homeland to the Passamaquoddies.

Buildings at Passamaquoddy *by Nellie Augusta Knopf.*
(Colby College Museum of Art, Waterville)

Formerly occupying the region around Passamaquoddy Bay and the St. Croix River, the Passamaquoddy by 1866 were restricted to the Perry area by the pressure of white settlement. The 100-acre reservation hosts a traditional Ceremonial Day, which features canoe races, traditional dances, and a pageant recounting Passamaquoddy history. The celebration is usually held on August 1; call the reservation office for information (853-2551).

MAINE'S AMERICAN INDIAN CRAFTS

The cultural distinctiveness of Maine's Abnaki—meaning "People of the Dawn," and including the Maliseet, Micmac, Passamaquoddy, and Penobscot tribes—is on the verge of disappearing. Although some of the tribal groups now enjoy a degree of prosperity (and public respect), thanks to settlement of their land claims with the federal government in the 1970s, their traditional culture seems increasingly fragile. Fewer people speak the tribal languages, and fewer young people in the tribal communities choose to resist the urge to join mainstream, non-Native America.

One aspect of Abnaki culture does show signs of survival, however: the traditional craft of basketmaking. While the number of people practicing this craft is small—probably only a few dozen skilled practitioners, scattered through northern and eastern Maine from Presque Isle to Eastport—public interest has revived. Even some non-Native craftspeople are learning the techniques and reproducing motifs the Abnaki developed over several centuries.

This trend actually marks a second "revival." About a century ago, the craft flourished when rusticators (city folks with Maine summer addresses) on the coast encouraged the efforts of the basketmakers. Each summer, members of the tribes would appear by canoe at shorefront cottages or at village fairs to sell that year's supply of baskets. To meet the domestic needs of their late Victorian customers, these Indians wove the baskets in special shapes and sizes, including thimbleholders, pillboxes, and picture frames. Examples surviving from that period can frequently be found in older summer cottages along the coast; the sweetgrass on the interior of the baskets often still emanates its distinctive smell.

Abnaki basketmaking and its related crafts require two things: a supply of ash, sweetgrass, and/or birchbark, and an unusual degree of patience and hard work. The brown or black ash tree *(Fraxinus nigra)* provides the splints, or thin strips of wood, used to make the larger, sturdier "rough" baskets—the all-purpose containers traditionally used in harvesting potatoes and hunting and fishing. The best trees for this grow in damp areas throughout northern Maine (although in modern times acid rain and clear cutting of forests has reduced the supply). A length of tree trunk is trimmed, peeled of its bark, and pounded with the blunt edge of an axe until the wood shatters into long, flexible strands that can be trimmed into strips for weaving.

Although today the distinction between male and female crafts is less rigid, customarily, "rough" baskets were the domain of men in the tribe. Meanwhile "fancy" baskets were women's work: centuries ago, Indian women collected sweetgrass—a tough, flexible, aromatic plant—on islands where their tribes stopped during the summer migration down river to the coast. Dried and twisted into strands, sweetgrass can be woven into intricate shapes and incorporated into "fancy" baskets for the tourist trade. Both ash and sweetgrass, which turn various shades of brown when aged, can be tinted with vegetable dyes for more complex work. While the antique boxes and baskets become dusty-looking and faded on the outside, they often retain their brilliant color on the inside if kept closed.

Birchbark, best known for its use in canoes, was also rapidly adapted by traditional craftspeople into merchandise for the rusticator market. Both the white outside bark and its reddish-brown inner layer were sculpted into popular items ranging from folding screens to children's toys. The craft survives today mostly in the form of wastebaskets, letter pouches (to hang on the wall), and other small receptacles.

Selling baskets and other household items to the tourists was a way of eking out a few dollars at times of the year when no work was available raking berries, trapping, or guiding hunters and fishermen "from away." Quite intricate work went for a pittance, and even today, when baskets sell for $25 to $125 or more, the earnings are modest given the amount of hours spent. (Non-Native basketweavers with access to urban markets command much higher prices.)

But basketmaking represents more than commerce. As Kathleen Mundell, an expert on the subject, writes, "Making baskets sustains and renews an individual's ties to family and tribe. Like the growth rings of the ash tree, the weaving tradition connects contemporary basketmakers to past and future weavers, joining them as a people and a community." Today, Abnaki baskets are sold through weavers' cooperatives in tribal communities and through a few high-quality craft shops around the state. Older examples can be found, in small numbers, in antique shops.

(following pages) West Quoddy Head Light near Lubec, is situated on the easternmost point in the United States.

You'll cross the causeway to historic **Eastport,** situated on Moose Island, a few miles beyond Pleasant Point. The city's proximity to the Canadian border allowed it during the Embargo Act (1807–09) to become a center for extensive smuggling between America and Canada. Meanwhile, the British insisted that all of Moose Island actually belonged to them, claiming it had been granted them by the Revolutionary War peace treaty in 1783. Consequently, the British army took Eastport during the War of 1812 and occupied the city for four years, a story you'll hear told at the **Barracks Museum** on Washington Street. In addition, in 1875, the town became the birthplace of the sardine industry when Julius Wolfe invented the canning process here. While today the island community hosts only one sardine cannery, at one time Eastport hosted 18 of them.

After years of decline and an almost eerie quiet, the old town of Eastport is showing some signs of revival. A major factor has been the success of aquaculture, particularly farm-raised Atlantic salmon. Smoked or poached, the fish is one of the most delicious products of Maine's coastal waters.

Eastport claims the country's highest tides, which, although generally ranging from 12 to 27 feet, have been measured at 40 feet. Between the city's shores and Dog Island, the St. Croix River and the extreme tides dispute passage, creating one of the world's largest whirlpools. Called "Old Sow," the whirlpool can sometimes be seen from the ferry that runs between Eastport and Deer Island, Canada.

■ CAMPOBELLO ISLAND

Circling back around Cobscook Bay, this time heading east on 189 at Whiting, you reach the town of **Lubec,** Eastport's sister city, and the easternmost town in the nation. In truth, the easternmost *point* is the piece of land on which **West Quoddy Head Light** stands. If you make it all the way to Lubec, you should continue across the bridge over the Lubec Channel to Campobello. This involves entering the Canadian province of New Brunswick, but border formalities are minimal, and U.S. citizens need only present some form of identification, such as a driver's license. Once you are on the Canadian side of the bridge, you are in the 2,800-acre **Roosevelt-Campobello International Park,** which occupies the southern fourth of the island. Established in 1964 under an agreement by President Lyndon Johnson

NEWS ITEM, JAN. 9, 1920—EASTPORT, MAINE

Maine Man a Hermit for 20 Years—Photo shows Al Parker, who has lived in a cave on Kendall's Head, Eastport, Maine, for 20 years. He sometimes sleeps in a dilapidated cabin just outside the cave entrance but he prefers the cave. Unlike most hermits he is cheerful and is most always whistling and has even been known to do odd jobs, more to help out someone who has been friendly to him than because he wants the money. He does not use tobacco or liquor and wrests his food from the sea and woods. He declares he prefers solitude to living among his fellow men because he likes to think undisturbed. He says there never has been a woman in his life. *(Underwood Photo Archives)*

and Prime Minister Lester B. Pearson, this unique international park commemorates the great World War II leader in a manner he would particularly have appreciated, for Franklin D. Roosevelt spent some of the happiest hours of his youth at the family's Campobello summer home, which was said to be second only to Hyde Park in his affections. The **Visitor Centre,** opened by Queen Elizabeth the Queen Mother in 1967, offers a brief introduction to FDR's life at Campobello and various exhibits related to the establishment of the park.

It is only a short walk from there to the **Roosevelt Cottage,** with its views of the islands and shores of Passamaquoddy and Cobscook Bays, and to the four other summer cottages (used now by the park commission for international conferences) formerly occupied by friends and neighbors of the Roosevelt family. The rest of the park is worth exploring, either by car (a round trip of about eight miles) or even better by foot, for it includes a remarkable variety of scenery, including several distinctive bog habitats. Visitors with more time may wish to explore the inhabited part of the island, including the village of **Welshpool;** despite its proximity to Maine, the island has a distinctly English feel, very different from nearby Lubec and Eastport. The old tales about why Campobello fell on the Canadian side of

The nest of a common grackle, set on a tree stump.

(right) Fog, lighthouses, and artists have all conspired to create an enduring popular image of coastal Maine.

the border—most of them involving Daniel Webster's being drunk during the treaty negotiations in the 1840s—are doubtless exaggerated. The actual reason has more to do with the fact that the Lubec Channel was the most important navigable waterway in the immediate area and as such had to be shared.

The broad outline of the role the island played in FDR's life will be familiar to anyone who saw the 1960 film *Sunrise at Campobello,* a dramatization of his struggle to overcome the crippling effects of the polio that struck him in the summer of 1921. James Roosevelt, the president's father, had joined a number of other New York and Boston families in purchasing land and building a summer house on the island in 1883 (in the days when the trains ran as far as Eastport, Campobello did not seem quite so far away). The house, which stood just north of the surviving Roosevelt Cottage, was home for the family each summer, and the athletic young FDR learned to sail in the tricky tidal waters of the bay. His mother, Sara Delano Roosevelt, purchased the cottage in 1910 and later gave it to Franklin and his bride.

The day that changed FDR's life, 10 August 1921, was a typically vigorous one for the future president and his five children. Roosevelt, having just campaigned unsuccessfully in 1920 as the Democratic vice presidential candidate, had settled in for a career as a New York banker—an occupation leisurely enough to allow a long summer vacation. In the morning the family went for a sail on the *Vireo,* and after lunch they helped put out a forest fire elsewhere on the island. Hot and exhausted upon his return, FDR ran with his children across the island to swim in Lake Glen Severn, followed by a quick dip in the chilly waters of the Bay of Fundy. "When I reached the house," he wrote later, "I sat reading for a while, too tired even to dress." He developed a chill, went to bed, and awoke with a fever. What seemed at first just a cold developed into a paralytic condition, which within two weeks was diagnosed as polio. In mid-September, local fishermen carried him by stretcher to a waiting boat, and 12 years passed before he saw Campobello again.

The cottage is filled with mementos of the president: the room used as his office during his 1933 visit, the large frame chair used to carry him after he was crippled, his fishing rod and canes, and a huge megaphone used to hail boats or call the family in to meals. The 34-room house, which faces Eastport, is also one of the few summer cottages of its era to have survived with its original furnishings intact and to be open to the public. Given the family's wealth and social and political prominence, it is striking how simple—and sensible—the furnishings are: wicker chairs and tables, plain brass beds, birch-bark Indian crafts. Nonetheless, a pervasive sense of luxury is created by the large, airy rooms and the sweeping view down the lawn and across the bay—and by the undeniable proof that this family must have enjoyed extensive leisure time.

For all the reminders of FDR here, one should remember that Eleanor Roosevelt lived here, too. While the summer house provided both recreation and escape for her husband, Campobello allowed Eleanor to form her own identity. As her recent biographer Blanche Wiesen Cook writes, Campobello was her first real home of her own (in New York City, the domineering Sara Roosevelt lived next door, in a connected townhouse). "Her romance with its rugged rocky shores, its intense mists and chill grey days, had much to do with the fact that on Campobello she and Franklin lived in a cottage that was well separated from Sara's by plantings and privets." Amid so much physical exertion, she welcomed the many foggy days when she could simply sit and read. Like many people who traveled "Down East" to spend their summers, she found the experience a healing one. To this day, opinions about Mrs. Roosevelt remain polarized—occasionally you'll overhear park visitors angrily disparage her advocacy of social programs and women's rights—but her reputation among admirers and historians seems to grow with each year. Although neither Roosevelt spent much time on the island during their busiest years, Campobello enabled them both to find a refuge from the cares of public life.

WESTERN LAKES

THE COASTAL-BORN POET Robert P. T. Coffin once wrote that there is a Maine that is "woods and mountains and sea" and another Maine that is "woods and lakes and mountains." The former, of course, has received the more glory; the artists and poets, the summer people and the vacationers flocked there, creating an image of Maine that has the distinct tang of salt water to it. But the other Maine—freshwater, inland, often less dramatic, certainly less celebrated—has much to offer as well. For one thing, it is rarely crowded, with the exception of a few aggressively promoted ski resorts on winter weekends. Although not exactly untouched by tourism—thanks to now defunct railroads, parts of it were once as popular as the coast—today the region as a whole is much less known than the state's coastal locales. Western Maine is full of inns and rustic hotels, the more southerly ones often being family-oriented and the more northerly catering to hunters and fishermen. And all of them seem to operate with a degree of friendliness not always in ample supply on the coast. The region is astonishingly beautiful in autumn, yet for some reason not as appreciated as comparable territory on the other side of the White Mountains. These western hills are an odd mixture of picture-book New England villages and rather grim papermill towns, of lush intervales and abandoned fields.

Much of this area is within a day's round trip from Portland (a rather long day, in the case of Rangeley). But to hurry through it—as many people do, on their way to the outlet shops in North Conway, New Hampshire—is to fail to savor the one part of Maine that has probably changed the least, visually, since the Civil War. There is no one highway that will give you a slice of it all the way U.S. 1 "delivers" the major coastal towns. There is no single compelling destination drawing tourists from afar, although places like the Shaker community at Sabbathday Lake and the Norlands "living history" complex at Livermore are like nothing else in the United States. But perhaps it's just as well: this is country for leisurely wandering and serendipitous delight.

Such a relaxing visit here might best be enjoyed by staying at one of the region's distinctive rustic resorts. These "camps" offer accommodation in guest cabins that often feature a wood-burning stove or screened porch, dining in a separate pine lodge and outdoor facilities ranging from hot tubs to rowboats.

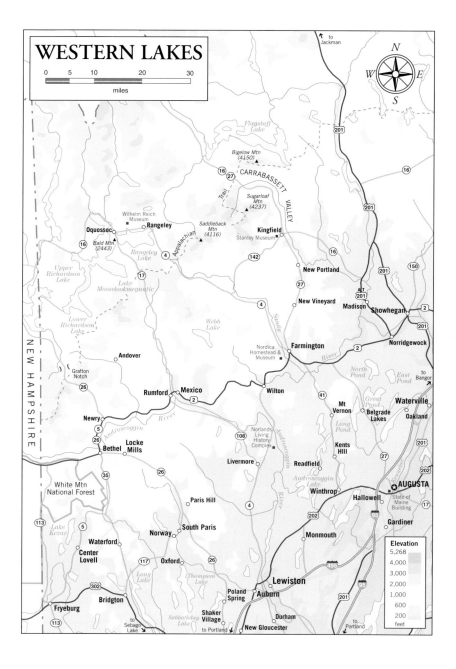

WESTERN LAKES

0   5   10   20   30
miles

to
Jackman

N
W E
S

201

Flagstaff Lake

16

Bigelow Mtn
(4150)

16   27   CARRABASSETT

Trail

Sugarloaf
Mtn
(4237)

VALLEY

201

Wilhelm Reich
Museum

Rangeley

Oquossoc

Saddleback
Mtn
(4116)

Kingfield
Stanley Museum

16   Bald Mtn
(2443)

Appalachian

Rangeley Lake

4

142

New Portland

16

201

150

*Upper
Richardson
Lake*

17

27

*Lake
Mooselookmeguntic*

New Vineyard

4

Madison

ALT
201

*Lower
Richardson
Lake*

*Webb
Lake*

Sandy

Showhegan

2

201

Nordica
Homestead &
Museum

Farmington

2

Norridgewock

Andover

River

*North
Pond*

*East
Pond*

to
Bangor

Grafton
Notch

26

Rumford   Mexico

2

Wilton

41

Mt
Vernon

Belgrade
Lakes

*Great
Pond*

Waterville

Oakland

NEW   HAMPSHIRE

Newry

5

Androscoggin

River

26

Bethel   Locke
Mills

Norlands
Living
History
Complex

108

*Long
Pond*

Kents
Hill

201

27

35

26

Livermore

Androscoggin

River

Readfield

202

White Mtn
National Forest

Paris Hill

4

*Androscoggin
Lake*

Winthrop

AUGUSTA
State of
Maine
Building

17

113   *Lake
Kezar*

5

Norway   South Paris

202

Hallowell

95

Gardiner

Waterford

Monmouth

Center
Lovell

117   Oxford

26

*Thompson
Lake*

*Long
Lake*

495

Elevation
5,268
4,000
3,000
2,000
1,000
600
200
feet

302

Bridgton

Poland
Spring   Auburn

Lewiston

201

95

to
Portland

Fryeburg

113

*Sabbatday
Lake*

Shaker
Village

Durham

to
Sebago
Lake

to Portland   New Gloucester

■ SOUTHWEST HILL COUNTRY

The hinterland of Oxford and western Androscoggin and Cumberland counties, a verdant region of forests and lakes, lies within an hour or two of Portland and Lewiston, making it the destination of choice for many Mainer day-trippers, as well as for the parents all over New England (and beyond) who send their children to the hundreds of summer camps there. Many of its nineteenth-century towns have some claim to fame, and merit a visit. While exploring the area, you might use one of Oxford County's pleasant old hotels as a jumping off point.

Your choice of "base camp" depends, of course, on personal tastes, and there is no lack of choices. The towns and villages are widely scattered, the roads meandering, and the recreational possibilities sufficiently mixed to render no single route or destination clearly better than another. Two choices on Kezar Lake near Central Lovell, for instance, are the rustic resorts **Farrington's,** where dinner is served in a pine-paneled dining room with white tablecloths, and **Quisisana,** where opera concerts are performed by the staff. Should you prefer staying in higher style, try the **Lake House** at Routes 35 and 37, a former stagecoach inn in Waterford.

A family cabin in the woods of Maine around the turn of the century is captured by the lens of photographer Emma D. Sewall. (Courtesy of Abbie Sewall)

THE SECRET OF SNOW

arm Diary: Yesterday in the cold and solitary winter twilight, I came upon a yoke of Holstein steers hauling an unloaded lumber sledge through the deep snow. Their driver, a middle-aged man, walked beside them in the dusk, all three pushing their way ahead along the unbroken road. / Every year the frost "heaves" the kitchen ell up about an inch and a half, the actual ell sliding up the fixed chimney like a ring on a finger. One latch no longer closes properly, and I shall have to readjust it. / From a sky full of sunshine but veiled to the west with a mere gauze of cloud descends the smallest snow I have ever seen, snow tiny as the dust of mica people buy to scatter on Christmas trees. It is falling with a brilliant and rather artificial twinkle through the sunlit air. /Elizabeth says that during the recent snowstorm, some half a dozen redpolls were perched on the tall weed stalks to the lee of the barn.

The secret of snow is the beauty of the curve. In no other manifestation of Nature is the curve revealed in an almost abstract purity as a part of the visible mystery and splendor of the world. What I think of, as I set down these lines, is the intense and almost glowing line which a great dune of snow lifts against the blue radiance of the morning after a storm, that high, clear, and incomparable crest which is mathematics and magic, snow and the wind. How many times have I paused to stare at such a summit when I have found it barring my way at a turn of the unploughed country road? It is when winds are strong, temperatures low, and the snow almost powder dry that you will see such monuments of winter at their best. Dunes of sand obey the same complex of laws, but the heavier sand does not have the aerial grace of bodiless and radiant crystal which builds the snow against the sky.

❖   ❖   ❖

What has today taken my interest are the colors in our winter world. There is color seen and unseen everywhere about: the universe is no duality of white and blue, and were I to stop and stare about awhile, I know that I should see more than I now see in a casual glimpse. In the landscape near at hand both grey trees and brown together with white birches rise above the snow; between me and the sun are faraway stone walls whose shadows are almost black; to the west, the pines stand dark, and withered and rusty autumn is still discoverable along the borders of the fields. At a turn of the farm road, moreover, I know there stands a copse of brush which during the deep of winter has turned itself into a thicket of red twigs whose color becomes a strange coral after a night of ice and freezing rain.

Henry Beston, *Northern Farm,* 1988

A spartan Shaker home interior at the Sabbathday Lake Shaker Community and Museum in New Gloucester. (Brian Vanden Brink)

Once comfortably settled, you can explore towns like **Paris Hill,** which has one of New England's most handsome assemblages of early nineteenth-century houses, including the home of Hannibal Hamlin, who was Lincoln's first vice president. Close to the New Hampshire border is **Fryeburg,** whose academy was once run by Daniel Webster and whose countryside was painted by Eastman Johnson; in the fall, when Fryeburg holds its famous country fair, the countryside is at its most spectacular. On the county's southern border is **Cornish,** with its splendid views across the Ossipee River towards the White Mountains.

Southwest of Oxford County's border is a chain of lakes, the largest of which is 46-square-mile Sebago Lake. **Sebago Lake State Park** is a popular day-trip destination for locals and out-of-staters alike. The lake is known to fishermen for its land-locked salmon. Coastal dwellers come for a swim in water that's cool enough to be refreshing, but not cold enough to turn their lips blue. Be forewarned that the park can become quite crowded in July and August. In fact, in recent years, environmentalists have grown concerned that Sebago and its neighboring lakes may be in danger of becoming polluted and their ecosystems harmed.

An alternative to the water might be a trip to one of the historic towns situated between the lakes. **Poland Spring,** near **Range Ponds State Park,** has gained international fame for its mineral water and its "State of Maine" Building, a relic of the 1893 Columbia Exposition in Chicago and once part of the sprawling Poland Spring Resort. About seven miles southwest is **New Gloucester,** itself a gem of a small town and the site of the **Sabbathday Lake Shaker Community and Museum.** The community was established in 1794, and today, with fewer than 10 "sisters" and "brothers," is the last remaining Shaker community in the country. Some of its 17 buildings are open to the public, and serve as illustrations of Shaker life and Shaker design. You can buy locally produced herbs, yarn, seed, and a Shaker cookbook, or even attend a Sunday service.

Bethel is the largest town in the northern part of Oxford County. The small city straddles the Androscoggin River not far from where the Appalachian Trail passes through scenic Grafton Notch on its long march towards Katahdin. Bethel is a center for hiking in the White Mountains, which spill over into Maine from New Hampshire, or for skiing at the **Sunday River** ski resort, about six miles north of town. When Bethel was founded in 1774, it was named Sudbury Canada for its original grantors—citizens of Sudbury, Massachusetts, who had fought to conquer Canada in one of the early Anglo-French skirmishes. In 1781 the town was the site

of the last foray into Maine by hostile Indians, who came down from Quebec, plundered the town, and carried off two residents for the duration of the Revolution. Near Bethel, you can relive history at the Newry and Andover covered bridges, as well as at Bethel's own **Moses Mason House,** a Federal-period dwelling noted for its Rufus Porter landscape murals in the front hall. While in town you might stay at the landmark **Bethel Inn,** which William Bingham II built in 1913 as a spa for wealthy patients. Known originally for its physical therapy program of strenuous exercise, the inn today offers golf, tennis, boating, swimming, and cross-country skiing.

Bethel is fast becoming a four-season resort town. Already busy on sunny winter days, the town has become more so with its new train connection to Portland. And it may get busier. Sunday River's developer, Les Otten, plans to extend the ski resort farther into the Mahoosuc Range with "environmentally friendly" year-round attractions and a sensitively redeveloped downtown Bethel. Meanwhile, the already intense competition between Sunday River and **Sugarloaf/USA** (about an hour northeast of Newry) is heating up even more, with the likely result being good bargains for skiers. Visitors from out of state in particular should not expect

Baldpate Mountain is in the Mahoosuc Range near Andover and, at 3,812 feet, ranks among the highest peaks in the state.

(left) The snow flies on the slopes and chairlifts at Sugarloaf.

too much off the slopes, though: the après-ski scene in Maine usually consists of hamburgers with the family. After a day of skiing, most people at Maine's ski resorts head back to the hotel or condo. In Bethel, there's something of a social "scene" at the Bethel Inn; slightly less family-oriented are the party atmospheres at the **Sudbury Inn** ("The Famous Suds Pub") and the **Sunday River Brewing Company.** But in general, skiing in Maine is family fun, and not a fashion show.

■ RANGELEY LAKES

The heavily wooded countryside around the seven lakes and innumerable ponds that make up the Rangeley Lakes region may seem familiar territory to anyone who has read Louise Dickinson Rich's very popular *We Took To the Woods* (1942), a sort of domesticated version of *Walden* written near Lower Richardson Lake. Doubtless greeted as a diversion among the strains of World War II, the book was more prophetic than its author may have anticipated; in the next generation, vanloads of people would be moving to the Maine woods to escape "civilization" and try to establish some sense of harmony with the natural rhythms of the world. Today, people in Rangeley like to point out that they are halfway between the equator and the North Pole, although to a new arrival the scenery seems so remote and coniferous that the Pole will feel much the closer of the two.

■ WILHELM REICH MUSEUM

Between the towns of **Rangeley** and **Oquossoc,** overlooking Dodge Pond and with a distant view of Saddleback Mountain, is one of Maine's least known major house museums. Its distinction is both architectural and biographical. Designed by the New York architect James Bell in 1948, the angular structure employs stones found on the property, but with a Bauhaus modernist effect that is all the more striking in this region of rustic camps and Victorian farmhouses. Its original inhabitant, the controversial psychiatrist and writer Wilhelm Reich, seems an equally unlikely phenomenon in rural Maine. But after many years of exile and misunderstanding, he thought he had discovered a refuge in these hills—only to find that the U.S. government was to succeed where the Nazis had failed in silencing his eccentric views on the nature of sexual energy. It's easy to feel sympathy for a man so poorly treated, yet in visiting his house—or the "Orgone Energy

Observatory," as he preferred to call it—you can glimpse what an exasperating and enigmatic individual he must have seemed to his contemporaries.

Born in Austria in 1897, Reich was an early associate of Sigmund Freud and a well regarded figure in Viennese psychoanalytical circles. Soon he went far beyond Freud, however, in attempting to link neurosis with a failure to achieve sexual satisfaction. While orthodox Freudians spoke easily of "drives" and "impulses," Reich produced an even more literal theory of "biological energy." To this theory he added a decidedly non-Freudian attack on the patriarchal social order of his day, and in 1933, Reich had to flee from the Nazis. He settled first in Norway,

Psychoanalyst Wilhelm Reich.
(Courtesy of The Wilhelm Reich Museum)

then accepted an invitation in 1939 to teach at the New School for Social Research in New York. Thanks to a sympathetic American colleague who owned a summer house on Lake Mooselookmeguntic (on the other side of Bald Mountain from Rangeley Lake), the émigré doctor discovered the beauty—and solitude—of western Maine. In 1942 he purchased the farm where he built his house. As a result of his investigations in the 1930s into the psycho-biology of sexual stimulation, Reich claimed he had discovered a hitherto unknown type of natural energy which he called "orgone." His 200-acre Maine property, which he named Orgonon, was to become his laboratory for a decade of research on how this energy manifested itself, both in the human psyche—where, he argued, it was the key to mental health—and in the external world, where he believed that with special instruments, this energy could be concentrated for useful purposes, such as controlling rainfall, for example.

Whether Reich was a genius or a crackpot—or some combination of the two—is still debated, but he might very well have lived out his life peaceably in the Rangeley Lakes region had it not been for the zeal of the U.S. Food and Drug Administration. Determining that his "orgone energy accumulators" (the devices which were to convert sexual energy into a usable resource) were fraudulent, the agency launched a full-scale investigation, in the course of which the government sought to ban works Reich had written earlier in his career (on the grounds that they were "promotions" for his "product") and block interstate shipment of his apparatus. Reich, denying the government's authority to judge his scientific work, lost in court in 1954. He abandoned his research and went off to study desert weather formations in the Southwest. When one of his students, however, transported some energy accumulators from Maine to New York (evidently without Reich's consent), the doctor was charged with criminal contempt. He was eventually sentenced to two years in a federal penitentiary, and in 1957, he was found dead in his cell. In retrospect, it seems likely that government officials punished Reich for challenging the sexual orthodoxy of the Cold War era, rather than for being a supposed pseudo-medical "fraud." Perhaps his great tragedy was not his ceaseless persecution but the fact that he did not survive into the 1960s, when he would been celebrated for the same views on sexual repression that in the 1950s brought him into such disrepute.

Before entering prison, Reich set up a trust which today owns and operates the **Wilhelm Reich Museum** and which is gradually publishing the doctor's writings. The museum was Reich's idea; he wanted to preserve for his students and future researchers his library, some 25 of his paintings, his unpublished findings, and his scientific instruments. The house, in other words, looks much as it did in Reich's lifetime; even the temporary wooden structure on the roof which he intended to replace some day with an observatory remains in place. The ground floor includes instruments used in his experiments and a model of one of his "cloudbusters," mechanisms which were supposed to use sexual energy to incite rainfall. The second floor includes his study, library, sunporch, and treatment room; on the top floor, his paints and easels are cluttered along with the scientific equipment. From this rural retreat, Reich held forth, part magus, part prophet of the sexual revolution. He is buried nearby, on a ledge with a panoramic view of the countryside, with a "cloudbuster" next to his tomb.

(right) A quiet dell along one of interior Maine's many rivers.

■ STANLEY MUSEUM

Between Rangeley and **Kingfield** rises Maine's second highest mountain, **Sugarloaf** (4,237 feet) and the site of its most fully developed ski resort area. A small museum in Kingfield commemorates the inventiveness and skill of the late nineteenth-century Stanley family, notably the twin brothers Francis Edgar and Freelan Oscar, who developed the Stanley Steamer, and their sister Chansonetta Stanley Emmons, who was a pioneer documentary photographer. The twins were enormously inventive from youth; before perfecting their jaunty little cars, they had already developed the dry photographic plate process (whose patent Kodak later bought) and invented the artists' airbrush. In 1896 they built the first Stanley Steamer, a vehicle whose lightness allowed it to achieve phenomenal speeds (unofficially, as much as 190 mph). F. O. Stanley astonished the world in 1899 by driving one up the dirt trails to the 6,288-foot summit of Mount Washington in New Hampshire. By tragic irony, F. E. Stanley was killed in 1918 when he crashed into a pile of cordwood in order to avoid hitting two farm wagons traveling side by side down the road. It was perhaps also a tragedy for succeeding generations that, after the Stanley Motor Carriage Company closed in 1925, few other people showed any interest in perfecting a steam-powered automobile. On view at the Stanley Museum are three of the twins' horseless carriages (models from 1905, 1910, and 1916) and the principal collection in the country of Chansonetta Stanley's photographs and glass plate negatives.

Kingfield, which was named for its early proprietor and Maine's first governor, William King, is a good point from which to explore the ski-obsessed Carrabassett Valley to the north (between Sugarloaf and 4,150-foot Bigelow Mountain) or the beautiful rural towns of **New Portland** and **New Vineyard** to the south. Both towns were settled by farmers forced out of the Kennebec Valley in the early nineteenth century by absentee proprietors, who disputed their land titles. New Portland owes its name, incidentally, to the fact that the township was given to the citizens of "old" Portland by the Massachusetts General Court to indemnify them for their losses suffered when the British burned their town in 1775. Kingfield also has what is widely regarded as the best restaurant in western Maine, **One Stanley Avenue.**

Nathan Noble of Norway, Maine, was a snowshoe "manufacturer" who hand-crafted over 4,000 pairs in the course of his lifetime. His father-in-law, Mellie Dunham, was the state fiddling champion at the time this photograph was taken in 1926. (Underwood Photo Archives)

■ CENTRAL HILLS

The lake-splattered hills north of Lewiston offer many hours of pleasant drives—say, from Monmouth (home of ornate Cumston Hall, a turn-of-the-century "opera house" now occupied by a much-praised theater company), north to such inviting country towns as Winthrop (center of the state's apple industry), Kents Hill (site of a well-known academy), and Mount Vernon (remembered as home of Elizabeth Arden's "Maine Chance" beauty spa). Beyond the Belgrade Lakes and to the northwest is Farmington, an important agricultural and educational center for much of the state's history. Today it is home to a branch campus of the University of Maine that has particularly good teacher education programs. Farmington was the home of Supply Belcher, who wrote *The Harmony of Maine,* a tune book published in 1794 that stands at the beginning of the state's musical tradition. It was also the birthplace of perhaps the most famous singer the state has yet produced, the "Yankee Diva," the toast of two continents in the 1890s, the "Lily of the North," "the great American songbird," the soprano Lillian Nordica.

Overlooking the Sandy River Valley is the **Nordica Homestead and Museum,** the 1849 farmhouse in which Lilly Norton was born in 1857. (An older sister, also named Lillian, had died at age two, so her parents gave their sixth daughter her

The lakes of central and northern Maine offer prime recreational opportunities year-round, but especially during the short but sweet summer months when fish bite—and mosquitoes swarm.

name, a New England practice called "repeating.") Like most Victorian families, the Nortons loved to sing and dance and play the piano. Edwin Norton proved a failure at farming, however, and the family moved to Boston when Lilly was six years old. She always liked to think of herself, however, as a child of the Maine countryside. In Boston, although the family was close to ruin, the fourth daughter Wilhelmina proved to be a singer of great promise—only to die suddenly of typhoid. Lilly also liked to sing, but no one paid much attention to her voice until she sang for a professor at the newly founded New England Conservatory of Music who agreed to take her as a pupil. She was trained as an oratorio singer, a more respectable pursuit than opera in the Boston of the 1870s, but one day she squeezed through a grating at the Boston Music Hall and heard her first opera, *Il Trovatore,* with Amalia Patti. She was afterwards able to sing much of it from memory. No one in the opera world took American voices seriously, and Norton might easily have been ignored, had not a famous bandmaster "discovered" her and taken her to Europe on tour. Norton began studying voice in Milan with Antonio Sangiovanni, who soon persuaded her to change her name—which Italians had trouble pronouncing—to Nordica. The Italian public adored her, and a brilliant European career ensued for "La Nordica." After three years abroad, she returned to what should have been a triumph in Boston. But the audience found her too "stiff," a stingy judgment of the artistic restraint that was to be one of her hallmarks as a singer.

In 1887 she established herself in London, where she sang the immolation scene from Wagner's *Götterdämmerung* with Hans Richter conducting. In 1893, Wagner's formidable widow Cosima (Franz Liszt's daughter) invited Nordica to sing the role of Elsa in *Lohengrin* at the Bayreuth Festival—an annual event begun by the composer himself, then continued as a tribute to Wagner after his death. It was the first time a non-German had been offered a major role at Bayreuth—and much of the intensely nationalistic Wagnerian public was furious at this apparent "desecration." Nonetheless, Nordica proved a radiant and flawless performer, and was applauded by no less a critic and Wagner fan than George Bernard Shaw. The decade that followed was marked by one triumph after another, especially when Nordica sang the roles of Isolde and Brünnhilde at New York's Metropolitan Opera. Her personal life was less happy: three disastrous marriages, to an Englishman (who disappeared over the Channel in a balloon accident), a Hungarian, and an American. This experience may have encouraged her to become active in the women's suffrage movement. Never forgetting her own penniless childhood in Boston, she also gave concerts at no charge for the poor. And on several occasions she revisited the family homestead in Farmington. She continued to tour into her 50s, and in 1914 died of a tropical fever while in Java.

The Nordica Homestead, which looks like any other nice, old Maine farmhouse, will win you over by its sheer unlikeliness: you step inside and suddenly confront Brünnhilde's feathered helmet and scarlet cloak. Scattered about the house are the trinkets of a major European operatic career, from an age when great sopranos had the celebrity of modern rock stars.

Madame Nordica in full dress.
(Courtesy of Nordica Museum, Farmington)

The elaborate costumes of a century ago may seem touching or tatty, depending on your feeling for the stage, but as John Dizikes writes in *Opera in America: A Cultural History,* Lillian Norton's Maine childhood stayed with her:

> She was much admired but never inspired audiences to erupt in paroxysms of adulation. She represented control, not abandon. By the early twentieth century, she had already come to represent a kind of "classic" singing which was rapidly disappearing, a spaciousness and nobility somewhat out of place in an operatic world dominated by realism. She was capable of fiery outbursts and conducted herself with a good deal of prima donna haughtiness, but Yankee down-to-earthness was always close to the surface.

■ NORLANDS LIVING HISTORY CENTER

"We don't get tourists here," says Billie Gammon, who slips in and out of the present century as easily as most people change their shoes. "We're so far off the beaten tourist path that you really have to want to find us." Each year, thousands of people show that determination, some of them on school tours that may last an hour or two, some of them to stay for three days and three nights as "live-in" participants in one of the most extraordinary museum experiences in the country. "Most museums tell you what to look at," explains Mrs. Gammon, who typically wears the clothing of a Maine farm woman of the 1870s. "Here we tell you to shovel the manure!"

In her twentieth-century incarnation, Mrs. Gammon is a scholarly former school teacher who some 20 years ago became enchanted by the Washburn family of nineteenth-century Livermore, Maine, a small community in the Androscoggin Valley about 20 miles south of Farmington, or 28 miles north of Lewiston. She is the founder of the Norlands Living History Center, a 445-acre site that includes a one-room school, a granite-walled library, a farmer's cottage, a church, a large barn, the Washburn family mansion, and an assortment of personable livestock that would have delighted E. B. White in his *Stuart Little* days. Each July and

Lunch at the Norlands Living History Museum (above) re-creates an atmosphere from the previous century, while a portrait of President Abraham Lincoln looms over a desk in the "men's study" in the mansion (right).

August, and on certain days the rest of the year, she and her staff greet visitors, some of them curious about Maine history or pre-industrial farm life, some of them simply eager to escape the stresses of modernity. In her nineteenth-century incarnation, Mrs. Gammon is quick to disabuse anyone of the notion that life in the past was a scene from Currier and Ives. She is Miz Lovejoy, the village pauper, widowed and heavily burdened. She tells you stories about her youth in Livermore, many of them about death and misfortune, yet the kindness shown her by the residents of Norlands is also a lesson of sorts, about how people survived in times past.

If you come there to stay a few days, you are greeted by name—not your name in the outside world, but the name of a villager of the 1870s, whose persona you are to occupy for the next 72 hours. You learn who your family was and what became of them by visiting the local graveyard, where you will discover how many years are left to you as well. Back in the house at nightfall, the lanterns are lit, you eat from blue willow-ware a huge meal of chicken and dumplings, with pitchers of milk and fresh butter from the farm, and you visit with the neighbors who come—in costume—to call. Over the next two days, you learn how to do farm chores—from ploughing to cutting ice, depending on the season—or to operate a nineteenth-century kitchen. There are other visitors like yourself there but you never learn their real names. You do learn a lot about how a family in rural Maine thought and behaved and interacted with each other more than a century ago. Nothing terribly dramatic happens. Some people are eager to leave at the end of three days. Others say that their lives—or at least their sense of time and of human companionship—have been changed.

The adult "live in" programs at Norlands are so popular that they're often booked a year or more in advance. But there are numerous other ways to experience the place. Some 20,000 school children each year come for day visits, sometimes just to see the kitchen and barn, sometimes to "role play" in the one-room school or on the farm. College students and school teachers can earn credits through research projects at Norlands, which operates as, among other things, an extension of the campus of the University of Maine at Farmington. The center takes its show on the road through outreach programs on such subjects as nineteenth-century childbirth, pre-modern medicine and health, funeral customs, and rural poverty. The emphasis is on increasing the public's understanding of rural life in nineteenth-century New England in ways which are, at the same time, dramatic and scholarly.

For many visitors, discovering the Washburn family itself is a revelation. On this remote farm grew up the seven sons of Israel and Patty Washburn. The eldest, also named Israel, became a U.S. congressman from Maine and then the state's governor during the Civil War. His brother Elihu served as a congressman from Illinois, Grant's secretary of state, and minister to France. William was a manufacturer, railroad builder, and congressman and senator from Minnesota. Samuel commanded a Union ship during the Civil War. Charles served as U.S. minister to Paraguay. Cadwallader was a banker, lumberman, flour manufacturer, Union general, and Wisconsin congressman and governor. Algernon was a well-known banker and merchant. The Norlands library has portraits and mementoes of the family, most of whose sons—like so many of their contemporaries—had to leave Maine in pursuit of a career. With them they took their New England ways and values into other parts of the United States.

Something of their ethos survives at Norlands, alongside the more practical lessons the staff have to teach about horse-shoeing, say, or quilting. The Washburn Humanities Center at Norlands holds scholarly seminars on New England history, but some of the wisest lessons are implicit in the very way the whole place operates. Everything is recycled, mended, reused. The frugality of old New England lives on, says Mrs. Gammon, in responsible stewardship: "Use it up, wear it out, make it do, or do without." Find a use for everything and create no waste seems a remarkably timely lesson from rural Maine.

A 100-year-old stained glass detail graces the door of the mansion at Norlands Living History Center.

FISHING IN MAINE

Maine offers something for fishermen of every skill level and preference. Fly-fishing purists can match the hatch on remote fly-in lakes where they can stalk the native squaretail trout in its only natural habitat. At a pond moments away, a boy and his dad equipped with nothing but cane poles, bobbers, and some hand-dug worms can relax and fish like characters in a Mark Twain story. You can get up before sunrise, fish some of the streams for trout, the rivers for salmon, hit the lakes for small and largemouth bass, then break for lunch and drive to the coast. There you might stand on a slab of pink granite, and cast into the ocean for flounder the size of doormats, or trophy bluefish and stripers strong enough to sap any arm strength you've got left. And if that's not an ideal fishing day, then I don't know what is.

Of course, there's more to a great fishing day than catching a net full of trout or snagging a massive salmon—achievements which you'll forget in a month or two. What you'll remember is the moment when, while casting into a quiet stream, you see a deer peeking through the brush. After pausing to make sure you mean no harm, it pushes aside some pine seedlings and lowers its head to take a drink. Or while sitting in a canoe on a calm pond, you spot a bald eagle cruising over the treetops, riding currents of air. Such captivating encounters make you forget what you originally came to do. And so much of Maine remains in its natural splendor, that getting to a beautiful lake or stream doesn't have to take long.

Once you've arrived at your fishing destination, take some time to roam or paddle around. Exploring these areas to find your ideal fishing spot can be both physically challenging and highly rewarding. For many of us the hours spent tramping about can amount to a fantastic vacation. If, however, time is at a premium and your sole objective is to catch your quarry, hiring a competent guide may be your best bet. These folks know the area and can tailor a trip to fit your own needs; some can give the beginning angler a lesson or two, insuring an enjoyable *and* productive trip. Many of these guides are listed in such publications as *Maine Sportsman,* as well as in magazines devoted to your favorite type of fishing. You can also inquire at local tackle shops. You'll end up with the equipment you need, and every now and then, the knowledgeable shopkeeper himself will take you to one of his secret spots, at no charge.

The true aficionado of angling may enjoy one of the many camps devoted exclusively to the sport. Some of the packages these fishing camps offer include meals, lodging, guides, boats, and even equipment. The people who run the camps are anxious to please even the most finicky sportsman, and will go to great lengths to ensure the success of your trip. Before booking a trip, make sure the camp provides exactly what you're looking for; for example, some camps lead only catch-and-release trips, while others conduct only fly fishing tours.

Grant's Kennebago Camps. Fly fishing only for brook trout, brown trout, and land-locked salmon up to six pounds. P.O. Box 786, Rangeley, 04970; 864-3608.

Libby Camps. Fish a different remote pond or wild river every day for trophy squaretails or land-locked salmon. P.O. Box V.R. Ashland, 04732; 435-8274/6233.

Penobscot Lake Lodge. Meals at your own convenience. Rare bluebacks and native brook trout. Eight full-facility log cabins. P.O. Box 155, Rockwood, 04478; 695-2821.

Weatherby's. Bait casting, spin casting, trolling. Guides; boat and motor rentals. Box FF93, Grand Lake Stream, 04637; 796-5558.

If you prefer fishing the wide open sea to catch your dinner, experienced crews man Coast Guard-inspected charter and head boats, which are equipped with communications and safety devices. "Charter" boats take up to six people on day for a fixed price per boat, per day. "Head" boats may take around 30, and may be chartered for private groups.

Anjin-San and **Devils Den** both operate half- and full-day fishing charter boats out of Portland Harbor. Anjin-San: 772-7168; Devils Den: 761-4466.

Bay Island Yacht Charters. Charters by day, week, and month. Box 639, Camden; 236-2776 or (800) 421-2492.

Cape Arundel Cruises. Full-day deep-sea fishing trips. Arundel Wharf, Route 9, Kennebunkport; 967-5595.

Cap'n Fish's Deep Sea Fishing. Half- and full-day trips, departing from Pier 1. Boothbay Harbor; 633-3244. Also in Boothbay Harbor, **Lucky Star Charters** operates half- and full-day charters for up to six people, departing from Pier 8; 633-4624.

For further information, contact the **Maine Publicity Bureau** in Hallowell; 582-9300 or (800) 533-9595.

—John Fuhrman

GREAT NORTH WOODS

FOR THE FIRST 300 YEARS or so that Europeans knew the land we now call Maine, it was in their eyes hardly more than a thin line of fishing settlements scattered along the Atlantic. The backcountry was a howling wilderness, inhabited by largely hostile tribes and the occasional French Jesuit or trapper. On the eve of the Revolution, English-speaking settlers began to travel up the major rivers, seeking good farmland in the rich intervales and slowly hacking away and burning the forest. But it was really not until the lumber boom of the 1830s that much of the interior was explored and surveyed. The woodsmen saw trees as a bounteous, ever-replenished commodity that, given enough manpower and waterways, could be converted into cash. They led the way into the Great North Woods. Thoreau was not an explorer of "virgin" lands, for everywhere he went in northern Maine he saw the evidence—the dams, the camps, the stumps—of a generation of logging. Yet for most people visiting the state, especially when seaside rustication became so fashionable after the Civil War, the upper half of Maine (an area larger than Vermont and New Hampshire combined) was as much terra incognita as it had been to the sixteenth-century mapmakers. It remains so for most visitors today, unless they have come to hunt or fish or hike the Appalachian Trail. U.S. 1 and I-95 channel tourists through southern Maine; from the viewpoint of Houlton, Bangor looks like a coastal town. This is unfortunate in the sense that Maine has become too identified with its towns "Down East." Try to build a McDonald's on Mount Desert Island and you will face an explosion of protest. Destroy an entire ecosystem north of Katahdin and only a handful of environmentalists will even notice.

It's true that most visitors do not have the time or curiosity to explore the north country, much of which, especially when seen from the highway, is a monotonous industrial forest. It smells good—year round, the lumber trucks perfume the air with their massive bundles of freshly cut hemlock and pine—but it fails to entrance the eye. There is little feeling of being in unspoiled nature, for only in some very inaccessible places has the mature forest been untouched by loggers. Nineteenth-century loggers went after the big trees, leaving the rest; modern ones go after the whole forest, the clear-cutting of acres and acres being considered more profitable (if only in the short run) than selective forest management. At the same time, there is even less a feeling in much of northern Maine of being on soil enriched by

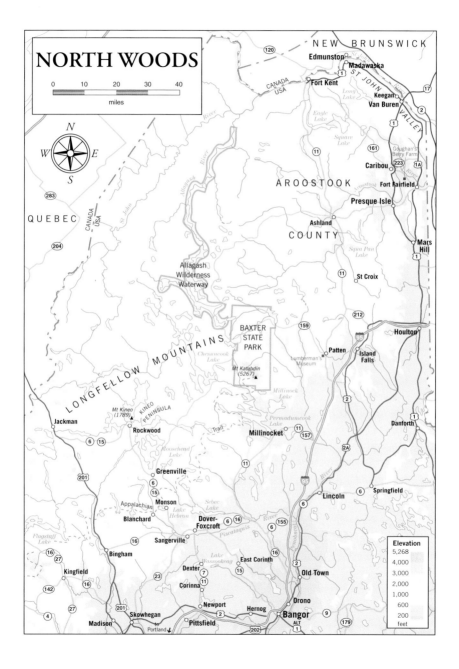

generation after generation of human experience. There is something provisional, frontier-like about many northern Maine towns, as if they might not be there the next time you drive through.

Why travel north of Bangor? Because the place is full of surprises. There are small Victorian towns that will delight you, and lakeside vistas that are among the most beautiful in New England. There is the biggest surprise of all at the very top of the state: the broad St. John Valley, whose rolling hills look more like the English Midlands than rocky Maine but where many of the people speak French. And there is Mount Katahdin itself, that giant granite paperweight holding the rest of the state on the map.

THE FAR NORTH COUNTRY

Speaking relatively, I live in the far north—in the top, left-hand corner of Maine, just below the Canadian border—and there seems to be something about that country that fascinates people, even people who have never been there and never intend to go. Perhaps it's an inheritance passed down through the centuries from the time when for those who ventured away from the known coasts, the familiar landmarks, there was only one fixed point to steer by, the Pole Star, only one sure thing to guide them, the trembling needle pointing North. Or perhaps the North represents an idea, a state of mind, cold, detached, lonely and austere, sanctuary from the heat and confusion and indulgence of the modern world. . . . So I try to tell [these people] what the North is like.

In the first place, it is very, very beautiful. It's a country of lakes and forested mountains and tumbling rivers. It's beautiful all the time. In the spring the new leaves of the birches and the blossoms of the maples look like wisps of green and red smoke blowing across the staid dark background of the fir and spruce, and the forest floor is carpeted with flowers—huge purple violets and tiny white ones, and the fragile wood sorrel, and the pink twin-sisters. The leafless rhodora blazes in the swamps. Then the thrushes sing high on the ridges in the arrowy light from the setting sun, and the red deer come down the slopes, stepping daintily, into the dusk of the valleys to drink.

—Louise Dickinson Rich, *My Neck of the Woods*, 1942

■ NORTH TO THE WOODS

For travelers who lack the time to explore this region at leisure, a very good glimpse of it can be had by driving about an hour north of I-95 at the Newport exit (which is roughly halfway between Waterville and Bangor). The first town you encounter, **Corinna,** was the birthplace of Gilbert Patten, who under the name of Bert L. Stadish wrote the Frank Merriwell series, an enormously popular group of some 1,000 adventure stories for boys. **Dexter,** on Lake Wassookeag, is a famous shoe-manufacturing town. **Dover-Foxcroft,** another manufacturing town, is typical of much of Maine in the way its two communities straddle a river (the Piscataquis) but unusual in that in 1922 they joined as one municipality.

Nearby **Sangerville** has the distinction of being the only New England town—probably the only American town—to produce two British knights, Sir Hiram Maxim and Sir Harry Oakes. Sir Hiram was knighted in 1901 by Queen Victoria for his inventions, among them the "Maxim gun," the first workable automatic machine gun. He had begun his career in a lathe shop in Dexter and had later become a British subject. Sir Harry Oakes, the swashbuckling mining tycoon, was knighted by George VI in 1939 for his charitable donations in England. His gold mines had made him the richest man in Canada. His brutal 1943 murder in Nassau—never solved—made for one of the more sensational stories of the war years. (The suspects ranged from the Mafia to the Nazis to members of his own family.) Sir Harry rests, with a suitable degree of pomp, in the Sangerville cemetery.

Maxim considered himself something of an art connoisseur, but the local resident with a much surer foothold in the twentieth-century art world lived until her recent death up the road at Monson (and earlier in the woods near Lake Hebron at nearby Blanchard). Berenice Abbott, who in the 1920s had photographed Joyce and Cocteau in Paris, and who in the 1930s shot some of the most famous images of New York City, chose in 1966 to live with her friend Margaret Bennett in this remote part of Maine. Her tribute to her adopted state was *A Portrait of Maine* (1968), a photo essay that—despite its many views of men working—captures the essential stillness of life here just on the verge of all the changes the 1970s would bring.

■ MOOSEHEAD LAKE

From Monson it is a fairly short drive to **Greenville**, at the southern tip of Moose-head Lake, the state's largest body of fresh water. An attractive town that manages to be both a corporate center for the lumber industry and the gateway to all sorts of outdoor adventures on the lake, Greenville is the logical point (and from a hotel-and-restaurant point of view, almost the only point) from which to explore the region. Wrapping itself around two coves, the town was a much livelier place a century ago, when the train brought fashionable vacationers, including the rich anglers who built many of the massive stone lodges or Adirondack-style "camps" around the lake. At the peak of the season, some 50 steamers crossed and recrossed its waters. One survivor of that era is the 1914 steamboat S/S *Katahdin*, re-launched in 1985 and maintained by the **Moosehead Marine Museum**, which offers 2 ½-hour cruises from late June through September. Since Moosehead and its ring of mountains can only really be appreciated from the water or the air, the boat ride is an important part of the local experience.

Wooden logs from the surrounding forest are employed in both the exterior and interior construction of this "Maine camp" in the North Woods. (Photo by Brian Vanden Brink)

The warm lights of an isolated home in northern Maine brighten a snowy winter evening. (Photo by Brian Vanden Brink)

Another major place to recapture the past is the **Greenville Inn,** a hotel with a well-regarded restaurant, built in a lumber baron's large house overlooking the lake. Like the town's other hostelries, the inn is open most of the year, since the Moosehead region now offers a range of winter sports. For those who prefer a different culinary experience, the much-publicized **Road Kill Cafe** at Greenville Junction gives new meaning to the notion of living off the land.

■ ROCKWOOD AND MOUNT KINEO

If you have traveled as far as Greenville, you ought to drive the extra quarter hour farther north to Rockwood, which is linked by road to Jackman and by the highway to Quebec. The drive will give you a sample of Moosehead's 350 miles of shoreline (though most vacation homes and camps are at the ends of long, wooded drives). Across the narrowest part of the lake from **Mount Kineo,** Rockwood offers dramatic views of the mountain's sheer, 760-foot cliff face, and has a public landing for launching canoes, which can be rented at many places along the shore. This part of Maine is renowned for its fishing; Moosehead is well supplied with landlocked salmon, brook trout, and lake trout (togue). In summer, the Kineo peninsula is accessible by ferry from Rockwood and—after being neglected for decades—once again offers lodging, dining, camping, and golf. Thoreau stopped to climb Mount Kineo on his trip across Moosehead Lake; there is a steep path which will enable you to do the same, for a spectacular view of the northern lakes and distant Katahdin.

■ THE COUNTY

Aroostook County—at 6,453 square miles, Maine's largest, and indeed the largest county east of the Mississippi—is not what in the tourist trade is known as a "point of destination." You go there to do business or to see someone you know; very few travelers visit "The County" for its own sake. To the dismay of its citizens, its major point of contact with at least a cross section of the rest of the American population is about to be shut down: Loring Air Force Base, near Limestone.

Yet northeastern Aroostook County, particularly the **St. John Valley,** is a unique piece of the American puzzle; it's worth visiting if you really want to know the

United States in all its variety. Unlike the wilderness areas in Aroostook's western interior, the valley is a series of softly folding hills, with the low, broad, often gray horizon of a Dutch landscape painting—an expanse of almost unbroken white after the first snowfall, and again in July when its famous potato fields are in bloom. The region shares its economy with the Canadians across the river, a border that has been peaceful since a brief flare-up in the 1830s. The people are a blend of Anglo-Saxon, Scandinavian, and Acadian French.

Wilderness areas make up 90 percent of "The County's" landmass. The more populated northeastern edge falls into three regions: southern Aroostook, with its center in the county seat of Houlton; central Aroostook, the center of the potato industry and the area most deserving of a claim to be "the garden of Maine"; and the St. John Valley itself, linked at its western end to the famed Allagash Wilderness Waterway.

■ HOULTON

At one end of the nineteenth-century military road that linked the border and Bangor, Houlton is a pleasant Victorian town which has long been the commercial

The scenery in Cossinghams, Snow Bound *by Paul Starrett Sample, resembles the landscape of St. John Valley. (Farnsworth Art Museum, Rockland)*

center of "The County." It enjoyed moments of considerable excitement in 1839–40 during the more or less bloodless "Aroostook War" between Maine and New Brunswick over their disputed boundary. Before the troubles were settled by the Webster-Ashburton Treaty in 1842, the young town was abuzz with militiamen. The arrival of the Bangor and Aroostook Railroad in the 1890s led to a short-lived business boom, but Houlton is a quieter place today.

One sign of spring in Houlton is the annual **Meduxnekeag River Race;** while watching the boats race down the river, you can imagine how important were those spring days in Maine's riverfront towns when the ice broke. Another is the appearance of **fiddleheads,** the delicious green cinnamon fern shoots that Mainers eat with fresh fish. Like most of "The County," this is a place untouched by tourism, but it offers a good jumping-off point for visiting Baxter State Park, or the extensive **Lumberman's Museum** at Patten. If there is a souvenir to be taken home from this part of Maine, perhaps it would be a traditional potato basket of woven splints of ash.

Rolling, fertile farmland produces the bulk of Maine's potato crop in the northeastern corner of the state.

(right) Wildlife rehabilitator Art Howell cares for a baby raccoon at his home in North Amity just south of Houlton.

THOREAU IN THE MAINE WOODS

"Two or three miles up the river, one beautiful country."
—An Indian, pointing to the Penobscot, speaking to
Thoreau on his first visit to Maine, 1838

That first trip of his was quick and business-like. Unhappy with his job as a public schoolmaster in Concord, Massachusetts, he looked into other teaching posts as far away as Kentucky. Having no luck, he decided in the spring of 1838 to continue the search in person in Maine. The trip began inauspiciously: he got seasick. Never comfortable on salt water—one of several ways he differed from many of his fellow New Englanders—Thoreau nonetheless knew that the overnight steamer from Boston to Portland was the most efficient way of reaching Maine. He made a quick tour through Brunswick, Bath, Gardiner, Hallowell, Augusta, China, Bangor, Old Town, Belfast, Castine, and Thomaston. It is interesting to consider what might have become of him had some district school teacher on that itinerary suddenly fallen ill or quit. But there were no jobs—it was a year of economic panic—and he returned, at age 21, to open a private academy of his own in Concord, a venture that attracted five students. He had caught a glimpse, however, of the wilderness that lay beyond Bangor, and it gave him some standard against which to judge Walden Pond.

Walden has become such a central text in the American perception of nature that it comes as a bit of a surprise that Thoreau did not think of the woods and pond he immortalized as being particularly wild. Symbolically, life at Walden Pond may have stood for everything that the materialistic "civilization" of Concord lacked. But in the back of his mind was what the Indian at Old Town had told him about the Penobscot.

In 1846, after a year at Walden and in the midst of his involvement in the anti-slavery movement, Thoreau left Concord to spend two weeks in the Maine Woods. He traveled by train to Portland, then took the overnight boat to Bangor. With his cousin George Thatcher and two other lumbermen, he traveled by stage to the end of the road at Mattawamkeag, where they continued in a batteau up the West Branch of the Penobscot to North Twin Lake, arriving by moonlight. Along Abol Stream they proceeded on foot to the south flank of Mount Katahdin. Thoreau twice climbed almost all of the way to the top. The second time he was so lost in the mist, he was no longer sure of his direction. "It was like sitting in a chimney and waiting for the smoke to blow away," he wrote of the ridge between Baxter and South peaks. "It was, in fact, a cloud-factory."

The ascent of the mountain proved to be one of the shaping events of his imaginative life. Accustomed to the tameness of Concord's woods, with their dappled sunlight and many traces of human habitation, he was suddenly confronted on Katahdin with an experience of nature as, in the words of his biographer Robert Richardson Jr., "vast, drear, and indifferent to humankind." Writing up his notes of the trip back home he reflected on this new perception of

Henry David Thoreau.
(Concord Free Public Library)

"nature primitive—powerful gigantic aweful and beautiful, untamed forever." The Romantic writers saw man as a heroic actor, able to subdue the natural world even while claiming to live in harmony with it. But in Maine Thoreau had witnessed a drama in which humans merely played bit parts. He felt exposed, at the mercy of the elements—but not fatalistic. That fall, he wrote not only the nature essay "Ktaadn" (this eccentric spelling alone suggesting the "primitive" quality of the mountain) but began work on one of his most radical political statements, "Resistance to Civil Government." It is as if the trip had cleared his mind and concentrated the power of his thought.

In 1853, he returned to Maine. Landing again at Bangor, he traveled by open wagon with his cousin and a Penobscot Indian guide, Joe Aitteon, to Greenville and Moosehead Lake; they then canoed to Chesuncook Lake, west of Katahdin, and back to Moosehead. This time it was the Indians who fascinated him. In camp at

continues

night, he would lie awake listening to them talk: "a purely wild and primitive American sound . . . I could not understand a syllable of it." In the essay "Chesuncook" based on this trip, Thoreau tried to balance in his own mind the conflict of the wild and the civilized (the killing and skinning of a moose played the role here that climbing the mountain had played in "Ktaadn"). As Richardson concludes, "Chesuncook" is "one of the founding statements of the conservation movement," a call for national wilderness preserves inspired not "by a distaste for human society or by a desire to escape it, but by a sense that true civilization will always require infusions of the spirit of wildness from time to time." In Thoreau's own words:

> Not only for strength, but for beauty, the poet must, from time to time, travel the logger's path and the Indian's trail, to drink at some new and more bracing fountain of the Muses, far in the recesses of the wilderness.

In 1857, he made his fourth and longest visit, which took him again to Chesuncook and then to the Allagash Lakes north of Katahdin, down the East Branch of the Penobscot, and back to Bangor. Traveling with a friend from Concord and a Penobscot Indian chief, Joe Polis, they covered 325 miles by canoe in just over ten days, in what was by far the most strenuous of his wilderness trips. (As the Thoreau scholar J. Parker Huber has written, "After repeating his Maine trips, I have a greater respect for his physical strength. This was no effete soul who in his thirties paddled the length of Moosehead Lake, carried a sixty-pound pack for five miles between Umbazooksus and Chamberlain lakes, and led the ascent of Katahdin through trailless woods by compass.") On this final trip it was Polis, age 48, who captured Thoreau's imagination: a Native American who, though a devout Christian and a representative in Washington for his people, never lost his ability to be at home in the woods.

The two essays, published ten years apart, were combined with an unpublished third essay, "The Allagash and East Branch," to form in 1864 the posthumous volume entitled *The Maine Woods*. Although Thoreau spent a total of only nine weeks in the state, the experience made an extraordinary impression on him (his last words were said to have been "moose" and "Indians.") In return, he left his distinctive mark on Maine: he constructed for his readers an image of Maine and the healing powers of its deep forests. Walden Pond may have been his true spiritual abode, but his words haunt Maine's northern lakes and woods.

■ CENTRAL AROOSTOOK

Say good-by to I-95 at Houlton—an old friend by this time—and rejoin U.S. 1 for its final stretch. About 40 miles north of Houlton, the triangle made by the towns of Presque Isle, Caribou, and Fort Fairfield defines potato-growing central Aroostook. Best known today for its branch of the University of Maine, **Presque Isle** is an important agricultural and industrial hub for the mid-county; the inland town got its name because Presque Isle Stream and the Aroostook River make it "almost an island."

Named for a variety of reindeer plentiful in Maine in pre-European times (and the subject in recent years of unsuccessful reintroduction attempts), **Caribou** is a major potato-shipping center notable also for its **Crown of Maine Balloon Festival** (second weekend in July) and its **Nylander Museum.** The latter is a collection formed earlier in this century by a Swedish-born geologist whose interests seem to have ranged over all of nature, including the cultures of Maine's pre-Columbian inhabitants, such as the Red Paint People. At Caribou you are only 20 miles from the Canadian border and closer to Quebec City (as the crow flies, 218 miles to the west) than you are to Portland (304 miles to the south).

On the way to **Fort Fairfield** is **Goughan's Berry Farm,** sort of a farm theme park that allows visitors to participate comfortably in local agriculture. You can pick your own strawberries, watch maple syrup or balsam wreaths being made, and show your kids the cows and pigs. A more austere site is Fort Fairfield itself, which includes a reconstructed blockhouse erected in 1840 to discourage an invasion by British troops from New Brunswick.

■ ST. JOHN VALLEY

Van Buren describes itself as "the gateway" to the St. John Valley. As you continue north and west, it is the first of a series of communities you'll encounter which were settled by French-speaking Acadians. Samuel de Champlain founded Acadia on an island in Passamaquoddy Bay in 1604, but the colony was relocated to Nova Scotia in 1605, becoming the center of the Acadian community. In 1713, the Treaty of Utrecht granted the island to Great Britain. In the early 1750s, realizing the imminence of war with France, the British demanded that the French farmers pledge allegiance to the Crown and the Church of England. The Catholic Acadians

(following pages) Mount Katahdin in Baxter State Park is Maine's highest peak at 5,267 feet.

refused, and most were expelled. The Acadians who moved to Louisiana and became "Cajuns" are far better known than those who sought refuge in what was then an ill-defined northern extremity of Massachusetts. But the St. John Valley families prospered, in a modest way, on this rich soil. They managed to preserve much of their culture, centered on the Catholic Church; its steeples continue to dominate the local landscape. Acadian French is a different dialect from the varieties of Quebecois French spoken in southern Maine. Similarly, the Acadians remained a predominantly agricultural people, while most of the state's other Franco-Americans arrived originally to work in textile mills.

The best place for the visitor to be introduced to the story of northern Maine's Francophones is the **Acadian Village,** a collection of typical early farmhouses, near Keegan, a few miles upriver from Van Buren, or at the **Acadian Festival,** held each year in late June in the papermill town of Madawaska, the northernmost town in the state. Nineteen miles farther upriver (but to the southeast) is another town preserving its Aroostook War blockhouse. Home to another branch campus of the University of Maine, **Fort Kent** welcomes visitors with a sign reminding them that "This Marks the Beginning of U.S. Rt. 1, Ending in Key West, Florida, 2209 mi. South."

Stretching from the town of Allagash in the north to Baxter State Park is the **Allagash Wilderness Waterway,** a 92-mile-long preserve comprising rivers, lakes, and streams. The waterway is a favorite destination for campers and canoeists alike.

■ BAXTER STATE PARK

This survey of Maine that began with one powerful symbol of the state—the placid Colonial Revival landscape of the lower Piscataqua Valley—now ends with another—the awesome bulk of **Mount Katahdin** in Baxter State Park. Between the two of them are many versions of Maine, some of them salt water, some fresh; some tradition-loving, some experimental. Some envision the state as a distillation of Old New England, a timeless refuge where work is hard and life is simple, untainted by the complications of modernity. Others see in Maine the essence of Nature, with unspoiled ocean, miles of rugged coastline, and acres of woods where lovers of the Great Outdoors can test their muscle and mettle. These two views are not mutually contradictory—many people are sympathetic to both—but they help explain why the state sometimes can't decide whether it's a museum or a wilderness preserve. (Many Mainers, of course, don't want it to be either, but that's another story.)

But back to the mountain. From miles around, its silhouette is unavoidable; on a clear day you can see it from much of north-central Maine. But it's not a place for the casual visitor. For one thing, you have to find a place to spend the night, probably in the mill town of **Millinocket** (more or less totally built by the Great Northern Paper Company to house its workers in 1901) or at a campsite in the park. And, unlike the mountains of Acadia National Park (none of which is too far from a paved road or too steep for a moderately active person to climb), the ascent and descent requires a day or more and perhaps a 16-mile hike, much of it in a semi-lunar landscape above the treeline. Like Thoreau, you may get swallowed up in the clouds. Unlike Thoreau, you may find—especially in July and August—that several hundred other climbers are sharing your epiphanies. (Remember that there are numerous other good climbs in Baxter State Park where you can be alone.) If you are serious about the climb, you need Stephen Clark's *Katahdin: A Guide to Baxter Park & Katahdin,* with its good maps and minutely detailed trail descriptions. And don't forget to check in with the park rangers.

Do climb Katahdin if you can. It's a rite of passage unlike any other physical challenge New England can offer. And when you reach the summit, think fondly for a moment of Gov. Percival C. Baxter. Between 1930 and 1967 he bought up the park's 314 square miles of forests, mountains, streams, and lakes and donated them to the people of Maine—to be kept "forever wild."

SIGHTING A MOOSE

If there is a rite of passage other than eating a freshly boiled lobster which introduces the newcomer to Maine, it is surely one's first sight of *Alces alces americana,* the North Woods' unmistakeable moose. While a lobster dinner can be planned in advance, a close encounter with a 900-pound cow moose—or an even heftier bull with his 60-pound rack of antlers—can only happen by chance. But the chances are getting better. Today an estimated 25,000 moose wander through the state, most of them in the heavily wooded northern half of Maine but with enough straying into more populated areas to justify those yellow MOOSE X-ING warnings which appear with increasing frequency on the state's highways. A collision at full speed

continues

with a deer is bad enough; with a creature the size of an adult moose, it can be fatal for you both. The only factor working against such accidents is that moose, unlike easily frightened deer, rarely leap out into the road.

The chances of seeing a moose on your own terms can be dramatically enhanced if you follow a few suggestions. First of all, choose one of their well-known habitats, many of which involve weedy freshwater and densely wooded shores. Bill Silliker, Jr.'s helpful paperback *Maine Moose Watcher's Guide* lists more than 30 such "haunts and hangouts," most of them accessible by road and most in the northerly counties. You can also ask locally. There is hardly a town north of Portland without its occasional visiting moose, and local residents can suggest some likely waterways. The best times to spot one are early morning, noon, and late afternoon (moose seem to like to eat three meals a day); the best season, late spring to summer near the water, and late summer in the woods. Be patient, spray yourself for black flies and other pests, and look for such signs of your prey as tracks, moose scat (which is larger than deer droppings), and places where seven-foot-high animals have browsed on leaves and twigs. Finally, enjoy the outing whether you spot a moose or not. Sooner or later, you will.

In general, moose are gentle, placid vegetarians with such poor eyesight that if you stand still they may not even see you against a wooded background (though if the wind is blowing toward them, they will quickly smell you.) There are two times, however, when you should make sure to keep your distance: during rutting season (mid-September to mid-October), when the bulls become very aggressive and unpredictable in behavior, and during nursing periods, when mother moose can become belligerent if they feel their calves are in danger. As awkward and lumbering as moose may seem, they can in fact run as fast as 35 miles per hour and can swim at about the rate most people can paddle a canoe.

Perhaps the human fascination with moose arises from the way they seem so oddly constructed—those immense bodies on such delicate legs—yet so obviously well adapted to their native woods and streams. They made Thoreau "think of great frightened rabbits, with their long ears and half-inquisitive, half-frightened looks." He understood why it was necessary for men to hunt moose, although the sight of a freshly killed cow being stripped of her hide ruined his day. He did try moose meat—"It tasted like tender beef, with perhaps more flavor,—sometimes like veal."

continues

(right) Moose are often observed in Maine's North Woods.

Plentiful in colonial times, moose had already begun to grow scarce in Maine by Thoreau's visit to the Chesuncook region in 1853; in 1830 the state legislature had already restricted the hunting season (though, as Thoreau noted, game wardens ignored the rules if the hunter gave them a shoulder of the meat). By the early twentieth century, a combination of over-hunting, disease, logging, and increased competition with white deer populations reduced the state's moose population to a few thousand animals. Beginning in 1935, hunting was prohibited outright. But increased herd sizes led in 1980 to introduction of a one-week moose season each October, with 1,000 permits being sold, many to out-of-staters. A referendum in the 1980s to ban moose hunting got much publicity but not enough votes, in a state where hunting is still regarded as less a sport than a way of life. Thoreau himself thought that shooting moose was "too much like going out by night to some wood-side pasture and shooting your neighbor's horses." He once noted that, if you encountered one face on, the moose would turn sideways as if to give you a better shot. "These are God's own horses, poor, timid creatures, that will run fast enough as soon as they smell you, though they *are* nine feet high."

Perhaps the best news for today's Maine moose is that they've become a tourist attraction, each one a symbol of pure and enticing wildness to visitors wielding cameras rather than shotguns. At Greenville, for example, biologists lead the curious to likely watering holes at dawn, and the local chamber of commerce has begun to market the town as a moose-watching center—including a month-long Moosemania festival in early summer.

Thoreau would have approved. Amid his detailed observations of Maine's flora and fauna, he allowed himself an occasional philosophical reflection. What did it mean to use nature for our own purposes, he asked—to cut down the pine tree as if its highest value was in providing us with lumber, or to think that discovering the value of whalebone and whale oil was "the true use of the whale"? He answered the question in these words: "These are petty and accidental uses; just as if a stronger race were to kill us in order to make buttons and flageolets of our bones; for everything may serve a lower as well as a higher use. Every creature is better alive than dead, men and moose and pine-trees, and he who understands it aright will rather preserve its life than destroy it."

PRACTICAL INFORMATION

NOTE: Compass American Guides makes every effort to ensure the accuracy of its information; however, as conditions and prices change frequently, we recommend that readers also contact the regional chambers of commerce for the most up-to-date information—see "Tourist Information."

■ AREA CODE

The area code for all of Maine is 207.

■ TRANSPORTATION

BY PLANE

Maine's major airports are **Portland International Jetport,** at 774-7301, and **Bangor International Airport,** at 947-0384; each has daily flights by major U.S. carriers.

Hancock County Airport, 667-7329, in Trenton, eight miles northwest of Bar Harbor, and **Knox County Regional Airport,** 594-4131, in Owls Head, three miles south of Rockland, are both served by Colgan Air.

Regional flying services, operating from regional and municipal airports, provide access to remote lakes and wilderness areas as well as the Penobscot Bay islands.

BY CAR

The **Maine Turnpike** and **Interstate 95** are the fastest routes to and through the state from coastal New Hampshire and points south. **U.S. 1** (also called **Route 1**), more leisurely and historic, is the principal coastal highway from New Hampshire to Canada.

In many areas a car is the only practical means of travel. The *Maine Map and Travel Guide* is useful for driving throughout the state; it has directories, mileage charts, and enlarged maps of city areas. It is available for a small fee from offices of the **Maine Publicity Bureau.** Call 582-9300 or (800) 533-9595.

BY TRAIN

Canada's **VIA Rail,** (800) 361-3677, provides northern Maine's only passenger rail service. The run between Montreal and Halifax crosses the center of the state three times a week, stopping at Jackman, Greenville, Brownville Junction, Mattawamkeag, Danforth, and Vanceboro.

Seaplanes on Moosehead Lake near Greenville gather for the International Seaplane Fly-In.

Fort Gorges and Portland Breakwater Light *by George M. Hathaway.*
(Farnsworth Art Museum, Rockland)

On weekends during the ski season, **Sunday River Ski Resort** operates the **Sunday River Silver Bullet Ski Express** through scenic terrain between Portland and Bethel. No reservations are necessary for the once-a-day run (lift tickets can be purchased aboard the train). For more information call 824-7245.

BY BUS

Vermont Transit, 772-6587, a subsidiary of Greyhound, connects towns in southwestern Maine with cities in New England and throughout the United States. **Concord Trailways,** (800) 639-3317, has daily service between Boston and Bangor (via Portland), with a coastal route connecting towns between Brunswick and Searsport.

BY FERRY

Marine Atlantic, 288-3395 or (800) 341-7981, operates a car-ferry service year-round between Yarmouth (Nova Scotia) and Bar Harbor; **Prince of Fundy Cruises,** (800) 341-7540 or (800) 482-0955, operates a car ferry between Yarmouth and Portland (May-Oct.).

Within Maine: **Casco Bay Lines,** 774-7871, provides ferry service from Portland to the islands of Casco Bay; **Maine State Ferry Service,** 596-2202 or (800) 491-4883, provides ferry service from Rockland, Camden (Lincolnville), and Bass Harbor to islands in Penobscot and Blue Hill bays.

From Acadia (Bass Harbor) to: Swans Island, 526-4273; Frenchboro, 244-3254. From Camden (Lincolnville) to Islesboro, 789-5611. From Rockland to: Vinalhaven, 863-4421; North Haven, 867-4441; Matinicus, 596-2203.

■ CLIMATE

Maine's weather is a topic of much discussion among its residents—"Nice day if it don't rain" being a not uncommon refrain. The widely held perception of Maine as a cold, snowy place with eternal winters is by and large correct. However, brief glorious springs, short but intense summers, and a month (usually October) of spectacular fall colors are the exceptions to "winter rules."

Cimate does vary within the state. In the far north, temperatures average 8 degrees F in January, while in Portland a balmy 22 degrees F is the average for the same month. During winters along the coast, northeasters frequently blow mild Atlantic air off the ocean and turn snowstorms into rain—a rare occurrence in the inland and northern regions. In summertime, onshore breezes bring fog and cool temperatures to the coast, while the inland areas warm up and frequently experience real summer heat. Precipitation is generally uniform across the state, ranging from 35 to 50 inches annually and spread more or less evenly over each month (but falling as snow from November to April). The following chart illustrates the climate for various regions of the state: Portland, Bar Harbor, and Eastport representing the coast; Caribou the far north; Bangor the "inland" region; and Millinocket the central part of the state.

CITY	FAHRENHEIT TEMPERATURE			ANNUAL PRECIPITATION	
	Jan. Avg. High/Low	July Avg. High/Low	Record High/Low	Average Rain	Average Snow
Portland	31 12	79 57	103 -39	42.05"	72"
Bar Harbor	32 15	76 56	98 -21	50.68"	58"
Eastport	30 14	68 52	93 -23	35.56"	66"
Caribou	20 1	76 54	96 -41	37.87"	112"
Bangor	30 10	82 60	104 -28	39.52"	103"
Millinocket	25 4	80 56	106 -41	41.60"	90"

■ ACCOMMODATIONS

Maine's tourism industry offers every type of accommodation, from inexpensive, old-fashioned roadside cabins for as little as $24 a night to luxurious seaside resorts where rooms cost ten times that amount and beyond. The listing below is merely a sample of what is available in the towns most visited by tourists. The number of bed-and-breakfasts seems to increase each year, offering a more personal (though rarely inexpensive) alternative to the standard motels. Another option, for anyone wishing to stay in one place for a week or longer, is to rent a house or cottage, which depending on size and location can range in high season (Fourth of July to Labor Day) from about $600 to $2,000 a week or more for luxury properties. Write to local chambers of commerce for rental listings or look at the back pages of *Down East* magazine. (A list of **"Classic Maine Inns"** appears on pages 248–249.)

Price codes are approximate for one room, one night, in summer, and are subject to change. Because of the vast number of competitively priced motels, any room for which you pay more than $100 a night can be considered "expensive" in Maine. Most year-round establishments offer considerably reduced off-season rates (if they don't, go elsewhere: innkeepers are desperate for winter and spring business). Breakfast is included in many rates, occasionally other meals. State taxes and service charges are not included.

Prices
B = Budget, up to $60. **M** = Moderate, $60 to $100.
E = Expensive, $100 and up.

AUGUSTA
Senator Motel. 284 Western Ave.; 622-5804. Power breakfasts and lobbyist lunches. **M**

BANGOR
The Lucerne Inn. RFD 2, Box 540, Lucerne-in-Maine 04429; 843-5123. Lakeside country inn and restaurant halfway between Bangor and Bar Harbor. **M to E**

The Quality Inn–Phenix Inn. 20 Broad St., Bangor 04401; 947-3850. Restored 1873 building on West Market Square. **M**

BAR HARBOR
Note: Although Bar Harbor has more than 3,000 tourist beds, the town is very crowded in July and August. Be sure to reserve a room in advance.

THE MAINE LOON

*W*e had hoped to see a moose even by now, but none has yet appeared in lake, stream, or river. Meanwhile, the loon will do. He is out there cruising still, in the spiralling morning mist, looking for fish, trolling. He trolls with his eyes. Water streams across his forehead as he moves along, and he holds his eyes just below the surface, watching the interior of the lake. He is gone. He saw something, and he is no doubt eating it now. When he dives, he just disappears. As a diver, there is nothing like him. Not even mergansers can dive like the loon. His wings close tight around his body, condensing everything—feathers, flesh—and he goes down like a powered stone, his big feet driving. He is known as the great northern diver. He can go two hundred feet down. He can swim faster than most fish. What he catches he eats without delay. His bill is always empty when he returns to the surface, and fifteen fish might be in his stomach. Because loons eat trout and young salmon, sportsmen (so-called) have been wont to shoot them—a mistaken act in any respect, because loons eat as well the natural enemies (suckers, for example) of salmon and trout.

—John McPhee, *The Survival of the Bark Canoe*, 1975

Common loons bask in the pink glow of evening light.

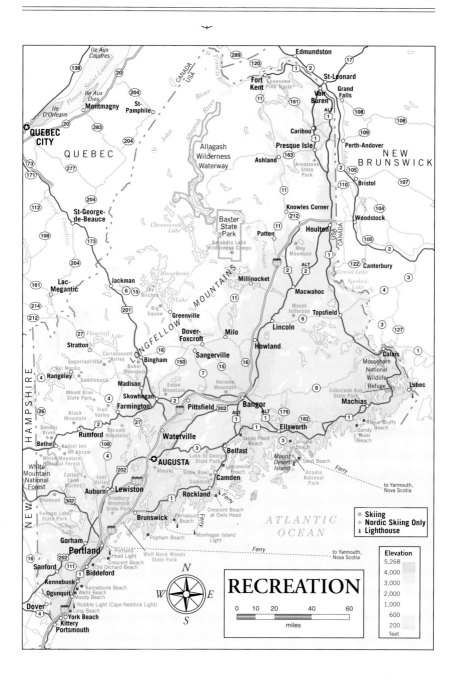

Balance Rock. 21 Albert Meadow, Bar Harbor 04609; 288-2610. Luxurious bayfront "cottage." **E**

Bar Harbor Inn. Newport Dr., Bar Harbor 04609; (800) 248-3351. Large bayfront motel in center of village incorporating part of 1880s men's club. **M to E**

Inn at Canoe Point. Box 216, Hulls Cove 04069; 288-9511. Near Acadia National Park entrance, good views in traditional setting. **E**

Ledgelawn. 66 Mount Desert St., Bar Harbor 04609; 288-4596. One of several in-town "cottages" along Mount Desert St. turned into comfortable inns. **M to E**

Nannau. Box 710, Lower Main St., Bar Harbor 04609; 288-5575. 1904 shingled "cottage" at Compass Harbor. **M to E**

The Tides. 119 West St., Bar Harbor 04609; 288-4968. 1880s Colonial Revival house near the "bar" connecting with Bar Island. **E**

BATH

Fairhaven Inn. North Bath Rd., Bath 04530; 443-4391. 1790s house on the Kennebec. **M**

The Grey Havens. See "Classic Maine Inns" page 249. **M to E**

The Inn at Bath. 969 Washington St., Bath 04530; 443-4294. Historic house on town's "best" street. **M**

Sebasco Lodge. Sebasco Estates 04565; 389-1161. Summer resort complex with golf course. **M**

BELFAST

Hiram Alden Inn. 19 Church St., Belfast 04915; 338-2151. 1840s house in historic downtown. **B**

BELGRADE LAKES

Bear Spring Camps. RFD 2, Box 1900, Oakland 04941; 397-2341. Family resort favorite (75% repeat business) with 32 cottages. Serious fishermen come here; tennis court and sailboat rentals. Rates include meals. **M**

Home-Nest Farm. Baldwin Hill Rd. Box 2350, Kents Hill 04349; 897-4125. Three historic homes (built in 1784, 1800, and 1830) available for rent as separate units. Breakfast included. **M**

BETHEL

Bethel Inn and Country Club. See "Classic Maine Inns" page 248. **M to E**

Sunday River Inn. RFD 2, Bethel 04217; 824-2410. Near Sunday River ski area, has its own cross-country trails. **B to M**

Sudbury Inn. Lower Main St., Bethel 04217; 824-2174. 1873 village inn with lively dining room and pub. **M**

Telemark Inn. RFD 2, Box 800, Bethel 04217; 836-2703. Country estate with herd of llamas (rides available). **M**

BLUE HILL

Blue Hill Inn. Near Main St. and Route 177, Blue Hill 04614; 374-2844. Attractive 1830s inn a few minutes' walk from Main St. **E**

BOOTHBAY HARBOR

Linekin Bay Resort. Boothbay Harbor 04538; 633-2494. Largest resort fleet of sailboats in New England, lessons offered. **M to E**

Newagen Seaside Inn. See "Classic Maine Inns" page 249. **M to E**

Spruce Point Inn and Lodges. Boothbay Harbor 04538; (800) 553-0289. Resort complex on 100-acre peninsula at eastern end of the harbor. **E**

BRUNSWICK

Captain Daniel Stone Inn. 10 Water St., Brunswick 04011; 725-9898. Hotel attached to Federal period house. **M**

Harpswell Inn. 141 Lookout Point Road, RR 1, Box 141, South Harpswell 04079; 833-5509. Attractive rural bayfront inn, popular with Bowdoin College visitors. **M**

Walker-Wilson House. 2 Melcher Place, Topsham 04086; 729-0715. B&B in handsome Federal house in Topsham historic district. **M**

BUCKSPORT

Jed Prouty Tavern. 52-54 Main St., Bucksport 04416; 469-1271. Maine's oldest continuously run hostelry (1798 building, renovated 1989). Also runs modern riverfront motel across the street. **M**

CAMDEN

Bed & Breakfast Society of Camden. P.O. Box 1103, Camden 04843. Provides detailed listings of local B&B's. **M**

Camden Harbour Inn. 83 Bayview St., Camden 04843; 236-4200. 1874 inn on hilltop overlooking harbor. **E**

Norumbega. See "Classic Maine Inns" page 249. **E**

Whitehall Inn. See "Classic Maine Inns" page 249. **E**

CAPE ELIZABETH/PROUTS NECK

Black Point Inn Resort. See "Classic Maine Inns"page 248. **E**

Inn by the Sea. Route 77, Cape Elizabeth 04107; 799-3134. New luxury resort at Crescent Beach. **E**

CASTINE

Castine Inn. See "Classic Maine Inns" page 248. **M**

The Manor. Box 276, Battle Ave., Castine 04421; 326-4861. 1895 summer "cottage" on five acres. **M to E**

Pentagoet Inn. See "Classic Maine Inns"page 249. **E**

DAMARISCOTTA AREA

Gosnold Arms. Route 32, New Harbor 04554; 677-3727. Rambling 1925 resort complex in picturesque village. **E**

The Hotel Pemaquid. See "Classic Maine Inns" page 249. **M**

The Newcastle Inn. River Rd., Newcastle 04553; (800) 832-8669. Popular inn overlooking Damariscotta River. **M to E**

FREEPORT

Freeport Area Bed & Breakfast Association. P.O. Box 267, Freeport 04032. Write for a description of more than a dozen local B&B's. **B to M**

Harraseeket Inn. 162 Main St., Freeport 04032; (800) 342-6423. Luxury hotel (54 rooms, 6 suites) in village, five minutes' walk from L. L. Bean. **E**

FRYEBURG AREA

The Cornish Inn. P.O. Box 266a, Route 25, Cornish 04020; 625-8501. Classic village inn, "Spirits Room" bar. **M**

Farrington's. Lake Kezar, Center Lovell 04016; 925-2500. Old summer resort with 16 guest rooms and 30 cottages; meals are served in the pine-paneled dining room. Water-skiing, movies, and tennis; rates include three meals. **E**

Oxford House Inn. Fryeburg 04037; 935-3442. 1913 house in village with views of Saco River and White Mountains. **M**

Quisisana. Lake Kezar, Center Lovell 04016; 925-3500. Lake resort of 16 guest rooms and 38 cottages; water-skiing and fishing guides available. The staff, recruited from top music schools, perform operas and concerts. Rates include meals. **E**

Westways. Lake Kezar, Center Lovell 04016; 928-2663. Lake Kezar resort complex with house and cottages, originally built by Diamond Match Company magnate. **E**

GRAND LAKE STREAM

Leen's Lodge. Grand Lake Stream 04637 (Oct. to May write Box 100, Brewer 04412); 795-5575. The most famous of the Grand Lake lodges; on a point that juts into West Grand Lake. Central lodge with library. 10 cottages equipped with fireplaces and fridges. **E**

Weatherby's. Box FF93, Grand Lake Stream 04637 (in winter write Box 256, Stratton 04982); 796-5558 (winter, 246-7391). Old rambling lodge on the stream with big sitting room. 15 cottages, most with a screened porch and woodstove or fireplace. **E**

GREENVILLE

Chesuncook Lake House. Box 655, Route 76, Greenville 04441; 745-5330. Rustic guestrooms and cabins at 1864 farmhouse. Price includes meals. **M**

Greenville Inn. See "Classic Maine Inns" page 249. **M**

Little Lyford Pond Camps. Box 1269, Greenville 04441; 695-2821 (radio phone). Ten shake-roofed log cabins without plumbing or electricity; main lodge serves three hearty meals. Sauna and paddle-tennis court; close to Appalachian Trail. Open year-round. **M**

Northern Pride Lodge. Box 588, HCR 76, Kokadjo 04441; 695-2890. Turn-of-the-century house with rooms and campsites. Price includes meals. **M**

HALLOWELL

Maple Hill Farm. Box 1145, RFD 1, Hallowell 04347; 622-2708. Rural setting only 4 miles from center of Augusta. **B**

KENNEBUNKPORT.

Captain Lord Mansion. See "Classic Maine Inns" page 248. **E**

The Colony. See "Classic Maine Inns" page 248. **E***

Kennebunkport Inn. Dock Square, Kennebunkport 04046; 967-2621. Pleasant, old-fashioned inn built around an 1890s mansion in center of town. **M to E**

The Shawmut Inn. P.O. Box 431, Kennebunkport 04046; (800) 876-3931. Large resort complex on 22 oceanfront acres. **M to E**

LUBEC

Home Port Inn. 45 Main St., Lubec 04652; 733-2077. Friendly B&B in 1880 house. **B**

Little River Lodge. Box 237, Cutler 04626; 259-4437. 1870s hotel with good dining room in fishing village. **B**

Peacock House. 27 Summer St., Lubec 04652; 733-2403. Another pleasant old Lubec house of the 1880s, convenient to Campobello. **B**

MACHIAS

Clark Perry House. 59 Court St., Machias 04654; 255-8458. Historic (1868) B&B. **B**

The Gutsy Gull. P.O. Box 313, Route 92, Machiasport 04655; 255-8633. 1850s house overlooking Machias River. **B**

MONHEGAN ISLAND

Island Inn. Monhegan Island 04852; 596-0371. Largest inn on famous island. **E**

The Trailing Yew. Monhegan Island 04852; 596-0440. Rustic, very basic, popular with artists. **B**

NORTH HAVEN

Pulpit Harbor Inn. North Haven Island 04853; 867-2219. Small country inn and restaurant. **M**

NORTHEAST HARBOR

Asticou Inn. See "Classic Maine Inns" see page 248. **E***

Kimball Terrace Inn. Northeast Harbor 04662; 276-3383. Large, modern motel-inn facing the harbor. **E**

OGUNQUIT

Aspinquid. Beach St., Box 2408, Ogunquit 03907; 646-7072. Condo-style complex just across bridge from beach. **E**

Cliff House. P.O. Box 2274, Ogunquit 03907; 361-1000. 162-room, 70-acre resort on Bald Head Cliff. **E**

Sparhawk, Shore Road. Box 936, Ogunquit 03907; 646-5562. Resort motor inn overlooking river and beach. **E**

Ye Old Perkins Place. Shore Rd., Box 324, Ogunquit 03907; 361-1119. 18th-century house with six B&B rooms, overlooking ocean. **B**

PORTLAND

Holiday Inn by the Bay. 88 Spring St., Portland 04101; (800) HOLIDAY. Convenient downtown location. 236 rooms. **M**

The Inn at Park Street. 135 Spring St., Portland 04101; 774-1059. 1835 townhouse on very attractive street. **M**

The Inn On Carleton Street Portland 04102; 775-1910. Western Prom area town-house. **B to M**

Pomegranate Inn. 49 Neal St., Portland 04102; (800) 356-0408. One of Maine's best B&B's, in the Western Prom neighborhood. **M to E**

Portland Regency. 20 Milk St., Portland 04101; (800) 727-3436. Restored red-brick armory (95 rooms) in great Old Port location. **M to E**

Sonesta Portland Hotel. 157 High St., Portland 04101; (800) 777-6246. Landmark in-town hotel (184 rooms) near museums. **M to E**

RANGELEY

Country Club Inn. P.O. Box 680, Rangeley 04970; 864-3831. Woodsy 1920s "cottage" with 18-hole golf course. M

Rangeley Inn and Motor Lodge. Rangeley 04970; 864-3341. Local landmark that is all to survive of a vanished grand hotel. M

ROCKLAND AREA

Craignair Inn. Clark Island, Spruce Head 04859; 594-7644. Originally built to house granite workers. Especially good hiking territory. **M**

East Wind Inn. See "Classic Maine Inns" page 249. **M**

Ocean House. P.O. Box 66, Port Clyde 04855; 372-6691. Good place to wait for the Monhegan ferry. **B**

ROCKPORT

Samoset Resort. At the Rockland Breakwater, off U.S. 1, Rockport 04856; (800) 341-1650. Very popular family-style resort in condo-like waterfront complex. Lots of sports activities, good restaurant. **E**

SEARSPORT

Captain Butman Homestead. Route 1, Searsport 04974; 548-2506. Inviting old houses with view of Penobscot Bay. **B**

Captain Green Pendleton Inn. Route 1, Searsport 04974; 548-6523. Vintage sea captain's house on 80 acres. **B to M**

Homeport Inn. Route 1, Searsport 04974; (800) 742-5814. 1861 sea captain's house overlooking bay. **B to M**

SOUTHWEST HARBOR

The Claremont. See "Classic Maine Inns" page 248. **E**

The Inn at Southwest. P.O. Box 593, Southwest Harbor 04679; 244-3835. Victorian "cottage" in village. **B to M**

Kingsleigh. 100 Main St., P.O. Box 1426, Southwest Harbor 04679; 244-5302. Colonial Revival house in village. **M**

The Moorings Inn. Route 102 A, Shore Rd., Southwest Harbor 04679; 244-5523. Waterfront restaurant and motel/cottage complex near Hinckley marina. **B to M**

Penury Hall. Box 68, Main St., Southwest Harbor 04679; 244-7102. Small village B&B with attractive garden. **B**

VINALHAVEN

Libby House. Water St., Vinalhaven 04853; 863-4696. 1869 house near Lane's Island Preserve. **M**

Tidewater Inn. Carver's Harbor, Vinalhaven 04863; 863-4618. Small waterfront motel near village center. **M**

WATERFORD

Kedarburn Inn. Route 35, Waterford 04088; 583-6182. 1850s house in attractive "preserved" village. **M**

Lake House. See "Classic Maine Inns" page 249. **M to E**

Moose Crossing Farm. RFD 1, Box 370, South Paris 04281; 743-7656. 18th-century farmhouse with flock of sheep, views of White Mountains. **M**

WELD

Kawanhee Inn. Weld 04285; 585-2243. Among the most beautiful Maine-style lodges, atop a slope overlooking Lake Webb. Open-beamed lobby with massive fireplace, pool table. 11 delightful cabins. **M**

WISCASSET

The Bailey Inn. Main St., Wiscasset; 882-4214. Newly renovated landmark building. **M**

Squire Tarbox Inn. RD 2, Box 620, Route 144, Westport 04578; 882-7693. Atmospheric 1763 farmhouse on Westport Island with good restaurant, serving the farm's own goat cheeses. **M to E**

YORK

The Anchorage Inn. Route 1A, Long Beach Ave., York Beach 03910; 363-5112. Large (178 rooms), overlooks beach, family friendly. **M to E**

Cape Neddick House. Box 70, U.S. 1, Cape Neddick 03902; 363-2500. Atmospheric 19th-century farmhouse despite Route 1 location. **M**

The Katahdin Inn. 11 Ocean Ave. Extension, York Beach 03910; 363-1824. 1890s guest house overlooking Short Sands Beach. **M**

Stage Neck Inn. York Harbor 03911; (800) 222-3238. Modern waterfront complex (58 rooms) on site of 19th-century Marshall House. **E**

York Harbor Inn. See "Classic Maine Inns" page 249. **M to E**

Fresh vegetables for sale at the Beveridge Farm in Camden.

CLASSIC MAINE INNS

If escapism is a large part of Maine's appeal, then why not stay in a place redolent of the past? The state has all sorts of historic hostelries, ranging from modest B&B's and out-of-the-way camps to sprawling seaside relics of the rusticator era. The list below includes many of the state's best known old-fashioned inns and hotels. Some of them are luxury resorts, some are just nice old wooden buildings. While they do not always offer every modern convenience, they have a patina that can't be faked. Those with a rather formal atmosphere in their public rooms—in other words, gentlemen will want to wear a coat and tie—are marked with an asterisk.

Asticou Inn. Route 3, Northeast Harbor 04662; 276-3344. The grande dame of Maine's hotels, with a commanding view of the harbor and a distinguished clientele. **E***

Bethel Inn and Country Club. Bethel 04217; (800) 654-0125. If the Asticou is a grande dame, this is her younger, much sportier sister, in western Maine's ski country. The yellow buildings are a particularly cheery sight in the snow. **M to E**

Black Point Inn. Prouts Neck 04074; 883-4126. As luxurious as a pre-war ocean liner, sailing in this case through Winslow Homer's seas. Guests have use of the Prouts Neck summer colony's yacht club and golf course. **E***

Captain Lord Mansion. P.O. Box 800, Kennebunkport 04046; 967-3141. If you can imagine a wing of Winterthur turned into a B&B, this is it, an antique-filled Federal house, complete with widow's walk. **E**

Castine Inn. P.O. Box 41, Main St., Castine 04421; 326-4365. A survivor from the 1890s, with harbor views and murals of one of Maine's most beautiful villages. **M**

The Claremont. Claremont Rd., Southwest Harbor 04679; 244-5036. Spectacular views, croquet on the lawn, an air of turn-of-the-century leisure. **E***

The Colony. Ocean Ave. and Kings Rd., Kennebunkport 04046; 967-3331. The sort of landmark hotel where guests ask for the same rooms their grandparents took each summer. **E***

Crocker House Country Inn. Hancock Point 04640; 422-6806. Views of Mount Desert across the bay, good food, a relaxed, unpretentious air, in a summer colony once famous for its college presidents and professors. **M**

The East Wind Inn. P.O. Box 149, Tenants Harbor 04860; 372-6366. Pleasant village inn in the country Sarah Orne Jewett made famous as "Dunnet's Landing." **M**

Greenville Inn. Box 1194, Norris St., Greenville 04441; 695-2206. Built as a lumber baron's luxurious house overlooking Moosehead Lake. Excellent dining room. **M**

The Grey Havens. Seguinland Rd., P.O. Box 308, Georgetown 04548; 371-2616. Attractive old hotel (built in 1901 by the Reid who donated Reid State Park) with panoramic ocean views. **M to E**

The Herbert. P.O. Box 67, Main St., Kingfield 04947; (800) THE HERB. Recently restored 1918 hotel in the Sugarloaf ski country. **M**

The Hotel Pemaquid. Pemaquid 04554; 677-2312. An 1889 farmhouse long ago converted into a country inn, not far from the Pemaquid Light. **M**

The Lake House. Routes 35 and 37, Waterford 04088; 583-4182. Former stagecoach inn in Currier & Ives-looking village, excellent wine list in small dining room. **M to E**

Newagen Seaside Inn. Box 86, Newagen 04552; 633-5242. Attractive, secluded complex of buildings on Southport Island, six miles from Boothbay Harbor. **M to E**

Pentagoet Inn. P.O. Box 4, Main St., Camden 04421; (800) 845-1701. Small Victorian summer hotel in village setting. **E**

Whitehall Inn. 52 High St., U.S. 1, Camden 04843; 236-3391. Handsome Colonial Revival inn associated with Edna St. Vincent Millay. **E***

York Harbor Inn. P.O. Box 573, York St., York Harbor 03911; (800) 343-3869. Colonial Revival ambience, overlooking famous harbor. **M to E***

(following pages) A sleeping harbor seal pup.

■ RESTAURANTS

Maine is not a place where most visitors expect to find exceptional cuisine. Many of its most popular restaurants are steakhouses that also happen to serve lobster. Listed here is a representative sampling of popular Maine eating spots. But there are a few restaurants that stand out—some for their use of local and seasonal ingredients, some for a willingness to experiment, some for the extraordinary care with which they treat their customers—and they have been listed separately as "**Maine's Dozen Best**" on pages 260–261. On pages 261–262 you'll find "**A Dozen Fun Places to Eat.**"

Price codes are approximate and subject to rapid change and are based on an average dinner, not including tax, tip, or drinks.

Prices
B = Budget, up to $10. **M** = Moderate, $10 to $25. **E** = More than $25.

AUBURN
TJ's. 2 Great Falls Plaza; 784-7217. Pasta, steaks, seafood; business lunches. **B to M.**

BANGOR
The Bagel Shop. 1 Main St.; 947-1654. Kosher bakery-deli-restaurant with best bagels in the state. **B**

The Pilot's Grill. 1528 Hammond St., Route 2; 942-6325. Traditional, very popular family restaurant near the airport. **M**

BAR HARBOR
Bubba's. 30 Cottage St.; 288-5871. Attractive pub serving light meals. **B**

George's Restaurant. 7 Stephen's Lane; 288-4505. Lively seasonal restaurant with a Greek flavor, just off Main Street. **M to E**

Jordan Pond House. Park Loop Rd., Seal Harbor; 276-3316. Very popular restaurant in Acadia National Park (book early). Large gift shop, attractive perennial garden, famous view of The Bubbles. **M to E**

The Porcupine Grill. See "Maine's Dozen Best Restaurants" page 261. **M to E.**

BATH
Kristina's. 160 Center St.; 442-8577. Locally famous for its baked goods, especially good for brunch. **M**

Truffles Cafe. 21 Elm St.; 442-8474. Tiny cafe serving very good lunches. **M**

BELFAST

Darby's Restaurant and Pub. 105 High St.; 338-2339. Storefront cafe with interesting menu. **B to M**

BETHEL

Michael's at L'Auberge. Mill Hill Rd.; 824-2774. Country inn, continental cuisine. **M to E**

Mother's. Main St.; 824-2589. Very popular restaurant-cafe in a Victorian house. **M**

BLUE HILL

Firepond. Main St.; 374-2135. Sophisticated village restaurant next to an old mill stream. **M to E**

Jonathan's. See "Maine's Dozen Best Restaurants" page 260. **M to E**

BOOTHBAY HARBOR

The Black Orchid. 633-6659. Classic Italian cuisine, less formal Bocce Club Cafe upstairs. **M to E**

Ebb Tide. Commercial St.; 633-5692. Old-fashioned fishing village cafe. **B**

BRUNSWICK

Dolphin Marina and Restaurant. South Harpswell; 833-6000. Excellent chowder, great fruit pies in attractive Casco Bay setting. **B**

Fat Boy's. See "A Dozen Fun Places to Eat" page 261. **B**

The Great Impasta. 42 Maine St.; 729-5858. Northern Italian cuisine. **M**

Richard's. 115 Maine St.; 729-9673. One of Maine's few German restaurants. Good beer list. **M**

The Stowe House. 63 Federal St.; 725-5543. Traditional restaurant in the house in which Harriet Beecher Stowe wrote *Uncle Tom's Cabin*. **M**

BUCKSPORT

MacLeods. Main St.; 469-3963. Dependable, unpretentious dining on the way to Mount Desert Island. **M**

Sail Inn. Route 1, Stockton Springs; 469-3850. Great little diner perched on the steep banks of the Kennebec, on the opposite side of the bridge from Bucksport-Verona. **B**

(following pages) A view of Camden Harbor by Alvan Fisher.
(Farnsworth Art Museum, Rockland)

CAMDEN

Cassoulet. 27 Elm St.; 236-6304. Small, storefront French restaurant, superb cooking. **M to E**

Chez Michel. Lincolnville Beach; 789-6500. A small bistro whose reputation for excellent French food is rapidly growing. **M**

Reunion Inn & Grill. See "Maine's Dozen Best Restaurants" page 261. **M**

The Waterfront. Bayview St.; 236-3747. Good value in photogenic dockside location. **B to M**

CAPE ELIZABETH

The Lobster Shack. Off Route 77 near Two Lights State Park; 799-1677. Seaside landmark since the 1920s. **B**

Dennett's Wharf. Sea St. near Town Dock; 326-9045. Seafood specialist. One of the few places in Maine you can try local sea urchin (almost all of it goes to Japan). **B to M**

CUNDY'S HARBOR

Holbrook's. See "A Dozen Fun Places to Eat" page 261. **B to M**

DAMARISCOTTA AREA

Coveside Inn Shore Restaurant and Dory Bar. Christmas Cove; 644-8540. Good coastal cooking, great harbor views, pleasant drive to get there. **M to E**

The Newcastle Inn. River Rd., Newcastle; 563-5685. Much-praised dining room with its own cookbook. **E**

FREEPORT

Crickets Restaurant. Lower Main St.; 865-4005. Popular family restaurant, good place to recover after shopping. **M**

Fiddlehead Farm and Country Cafe. Lower Main St.; 865-0466. Restored Greek Revival farmhouse not far from village center. **M to E**

Harraseeket Inn. See "Maine's Dozen Best Restaurants" page 260. **E**

McDonald's. 155 Main St.; 865-9566. Surely the only Greek Revival fast-food eatery in the world. **B**

GARDINER

A1 Diner. See "A Dozen Fun Places to Eat" page 261. **B**

GREENVILLE

The Road Kill Cafe. Route 15, Greenville Junction; 695-2230. Much-publicized roadside attraction with inventive menu descriptions. **B**

HALLOWELL

Bachelder's Tavern. Route 126 and Hallowell Rd., Litchfield; 268-4965. Sophisticated cuisine in old stagecoach inn in the center of a farming village. **M to E**

Slate's. 167 Water St.; 622-9575. Lively, popular cafe especially noted for its Sunday brunch. **B to M**

HANCOCK

Le Domaine. See "Maine's Dozen Best Restaurants" page 260. **E**

HERMON

Dysart's Truck Stop. See "A Dozen Fun Places to Eat" page 261. **B**

KENNEBUNKPORT

White Barn Inn. See "Maine's Dozen Best Restaurants" page 260. **M**

Cape Arundel Inn. Ocean Ave.; 967-2125. Continental cuisine emphasizing seafood. Especially good breakfasts. **M to E**

KINGFIELD

One Stanley Avenue. See "Maine's Dozen Best Restaurants" page 260. **M to E**

KITTERY

Cap'n Simeon's Galley. Route 103, Pepperrell Cove; 439-3655. Seafood restaurant with great views of Portsmouth harbor. **B to M**

LEWISTON

Marois. See "A Dozen Fun Places to Eat" page 262. **M**

LISBON FALLS

Graziano's. See "A Dozen Fun Places to Eat" page 261. **M**

MACHIAS

Helen's. See "A Dozen Fun Places to Eat" page 261. **B to M**

MACHIASPORT

Micmac Farm Restaurant. See "Maine's Dozen Best Restaurants" page 260. **M to E**

MILBRIDGE

The Red Barn. See "A Dozen Fun Places to Eat" page 262. **B to M**

OGUNQUIT

Arrows. See "Maine's Dozen Best Restaurants" page 260. **E**

Barnacle Billy's. Perkins Cove; 646-5575. Very popular informal waterfront eatery. **M**

Ogunquit Lobster Pound. Route 1, north of village; 646-2516. Classic "pick your own out of the tank" rustic lobster place. **M**

PORTLAND/SOUTH PORTLAND

Afghan. 629 Congress St.; 773-3431. **B**

Back Bay Grill. See "Maine's Dozen Best Restaurants" page 260. **E**

Cafe Always. 47 Middle St.; 774-9399. Small, imaginative restaurant just outside the Old Port. **M to E**

Cafe Brix. See "Maine's Dozen Best Restaurants" page 260. **M to E**

Hugo's Port Bistro. 88 Middle St.; 774-8538. **E**

Hu Shang. 29 Exchange; 774-0300. **B to M**

Katahdin. See "A Dozen Fun Places to Eat" page 262. **M**

Madd Apple. 23 Forrest Ave.; 774-9698. **M**

The Pepperclub. 78 Middle St.; 772-0531. Maine's best vegetarian menu (though not exclusively so). **B to M**

Raffles. 555 Congress St.; 761-3930. Attractive small bookstore serving light lunches. **B**

Ruby's Choice. Burgers plus. 116 Free St.; 773-9099. **B to M**

Silly's. 147 Cumberland; 772-0360. **B**

Street & Company. 33 Wharf St.; 775-0887. **B to M**

Uncle Billy's Southside & Bar-B-Que. 60 Ocean St., South Portland; 767-7119. A rarity: authentic barbecue in New England. **B**

Victory Deli. Monument Sq.; 772-7299. Popular bakery-cafe in center of business district. Second location near University of Southern Maine. **B**

Walter's Cafe. 15 Exchange St.; 871-9258. Trendy bistro in the heart of the Old Port. **M**

Westside. 58 Pine St.; 773-8223. Neighborhood bistro with inventive cuisine. **M**

ROCKLAND

Jessica's European Bistro. 2 South Main St.; 596-0770. Victorian house, continental cuisine. **M to E**

ROCKPORT

The Helm. Route 1, Rockport; 236-4337. French cooking plus Maine shore dinners, 1.5 miles south of Camden. Best take-out window in the state. **M**

The Sail Loft. Rockport; 236-2330. Popular traditional restaurant overlooking Andre the Seal waters. **M to E**

SEAL HARBOR

Jordan Pond House. See "A Dozen Fun Places to Eat" page 262. **B to M**

SEARSPORT

Nickerson Tavern. Route 1; 548-2220. Excellent cooking in attractive 1860s sea captain's house. **M to E**

SOUTHWEST HARBOR

Beal's Lobster Pier. Clark Point Rd.; 244-7178. Authentic dockside cafe. Also good place to get boiled and cracked lobster to go for a picnic. **B to M**

THOMASTON

Thomaston Cafe and Bakery. 88 Main St.; 354-8589. Good example of the friendly village cafe with tasty baked goods found in many Maine towns. **B**

WALDOBORO

Moody's Diner. See "A Dozen Fun Places to Eat" page 262. **B**

WISCASSET

Le Garage. Water St.; 882-5409. Pleasant, popular restaurant overlooking the wrecked schooners in the Sheepscot River. **M**

Montsweag Restaurant. Route 1, Woolwich, south of Wiscasset; 443-6563. A vanishing piece of Americana: the old-fashioned farm-turned-family restaurant. **B to M**

YARMOUTH

The Cannery Restaurant. Lower Falls Landing; 846-1226. Attractive modern seafood restaurant in a marina complex on the Royal River. **M**

YORK

Fazio's. 38 Woodbridge Rd., York Village; 363-7019. Traditional trattoria with fresh pasta and seafood. **M**

The Goldenrod. York Beach; 363-2621. Famous family restaurant since 1896. Saltwater taffy kisses made on the spot. **B**

MAINE'S DOZEN BEST RESTAURANTS

Arrows. Berwick Rd., Ogunquit; 646-7175. A 1765 farmhouse with kitchen gardens, inland from the popular beach resort. Maine seafood and other local products, imaginatively prepared with both classical and Oriental influences. Very expensive for Maine, but possibly the best restaurant in northern New England. Seasonal. **E**

Back Bay Grill. 65 Portland St., Portland; 772-8833. Restaurants come and go in Portland, but this one has consistently offered some of the best food in town, in a neighborhood better known for Bubba's Sulky Lounge. **E**

Cafe Brix. 343 Gorham Rd., South Portland; 773-2262. An improbable location (in a small shopping center across from Jordan Marsh at the Maine Mall), but serious cuisine in a surprisingly stylish interior. **M to E**

Harraseeket Inn. 162 Main St., Freeport; 865-9377. Under Sam Hayward's direction, Maine's pace-setting restaurant, especially in the rediscovery of traditional New England techniques and carefully chosen Maine ingredients. **E**

Jonathan's. Main St., Blue Hill; 374-5226. Chef-owner Jonathan Chase is co-author of the best book on the "new Maine cooking," *Saltwater Seasonings.* **M to E**

Le Domaine. Route 1, Hancock; 422-3395. Since the 1940s, a gastronomic landmark Down East. The emphasis continues to be on classic French country cooking. **E**

Micmac Farm Restaurant. Machiasport; 255-3008. The Platonic ideal of a Maine country inn: an 18th-century house in the woods, a warm fire, glistening antiques, amiable hosts, a short but perfect menu. The town is dry, so bring your own wine. **M to E**

One Stanley Avenue. Kingfield; 265-5541. Western Maine's best restaurant, in a big Victorian house near the Carrabassett Valley ski country. Imaginative use of Maine ingredients—fiddleheads, salmon, blueberries, even fir. **M to E**

The Osprey. Robinhood Marina, Robinhood; 371-2530. Perched over a small, secluded harbor near Reid State Park, in an osprey nesting area. The menu may be too ambitious for so small a place, but the standard is high. **E**

The Porcupine Grill. 123 Cottage St., Bar Harbor; 288-3884. Stylish, low-key decor and sophisticated home-cooking in a town better known for its lobster joints. **M to E**

Reunion Inn & Grill. 49 Mechanic St., Camden; 236-1090. The "new Maine cooking" at modest prices, in a relaxed setting, a block off Route 1 in downtown Camden. **M**

White Barn Inn. Kennebunk Beach, Kennebunkport; 967-2321. A renovated barn with a warm atmosphere. Specialties include unusual seafood interpretations and excellent desserts. **M**

A DOZEN FUN PLACES TO EAT

Well, you don't want to *dine* every day. Here's a list of places—some of them urbane, some of them very small-town—where the atmosphere is relaxed, the food is good and fairly cheap, and the locals may outnumber the visitors.

A1 Diner. 3 Bridge St., Gardiner; 582-4804. A classic steel diner that's gone to cooking school. Delicious, eclectic, cheap. **B**

Alberta's. 21 Pleasant St., Portland; 774-5408. Small, trendy, very popular bistro where Tex-Mex meets Maine coastal. **M**

Dysart's Truck Stop. Coldbrook Rd. (I-95, Exit 44), Hermon; 942-4878. A beacon in the darkness on I-95 just south of Bangor. Real food. **B**

Fat Boy's. Bath Rd., Brunswick; 729-9431. Munch on a Canadian BLT and watch the PC-Orions land and take off at Brunswick Naval Air Station. A classic 1950s drive-in. Seasonal. **B**

Graziano's. Route 196, Lisbon Falls; 353-4335. If you're running in a marathon on Saturday, this is the place to go to carbo-load on Friday night. Pre-trendy Italian dishes amid boxing memorabilia. **M**

Helen's. 32 Main St., Machias; 255-6506. A Washington County landmark famous for its high-rise pies. **B to M**

Holbrook's. Behind Holbrook's Store, Cundy's Harbor; 725-0708. Fried clams, lobster rolls, Indian pudding with ice cream at dockside in the Harpswells. Seasonal. **B to M**

continues

Jordan Pond House. Park Loop Rd., Seal Harbor; 276-3316. Not the restaurant (which is quite respectable), but the lawn, where amid the Acadia National Park scenery you can enjoy popovers and tea (although standards have fallen shamelessly since Grandmother's day: the staff no longer stands at parade rest or memorizes your order). **B to M**

Katahdin. 106 High St., Portland; 774-1740. Sophisticated home-cooking (a trend that ought to be encouraged) amid funky thrift-shop decor. Attracts Portland's upper Bohemia. **M**

Marois. 249 Lisbon St., Lewiston; 782-9055. Eccentric, eclectic, endearing downtown restaurant with Greek-American-United Nations cuisine and a killer dessert cart. **M**

Moody's Diner. Route 1, Waldoboro; 832-7468. Perhaps over-sentimentalized by its admirers, but a venerable U.S. 1 landmark that still packs them in. Even has its own cookbook on sale. **B**

The Red Barn. Main St. (junction of Routes 1 and 1A), Milbridge; 546-7721. The sort of solid, local, dependable restaurant—in this case, about halfway between Ellsworth and Machias—where the staff knows everyone's name and, on a Saturday night, you'll see half the town. **B to M**

■ FESTIVALS AND EVENTS

JANUARY

Greenville: Sled Dog Race. Sponsored by the Moosehead Riders Snowmobile Club at Moosehead Lake. 695-3901/2604.

Rangeley: Snowmobile Snodeo. Lakeside Park. Snowmobile displays, games, parade, and fireworks. 864-5364.

Sugarloaf USA/Carrabassett: Children's Festival Week. Fireworks, peanut carnivals, pool parties, torchlight parades. Special free skiing and lodging for kids 12 and under, some restrictions. 237-2000.

Sugarloaf USA/Carrabassett: White White World Week. Fireworks, torchlight parade, chili cook-off, broom ball, discount lift tickets. 237-2000.

Sunday River/Newry: Western Mountains Winter Wonderland Week. Skiing, fireworks, cuisine festival, hot air balloon lifts (weather permits). 824-3000 ext. 374.

FEBRUARY

Belfast: Winter Carnival. Bonfire, skating, cross-country skiing, snow sculpture, snow softball. 338-5900.

Bethel: Heritage Day-Dr. Moses Mason House. Winter festival, old-time crafts demonstration, historical videos, tours of the museum with hot Indian pudding from the hearth of the winter kitchen. 824-2908.

Bethel: Annual Wood Ski Day. Old-time wood ski parade. 824-3880.

Farmington: Winter Games. One week long of activities: skiing, ice skating, dog sled races, snow sculptures, snowmobiling, and races. 778-4215.

Orono: Annual Games Day. University of Maine Campus, Hudson Museum. 581-1901.

Oxford: Winter Carnival. 539-4848.

Shawnee Peak/Bridgton: Storybook Day. Skiing and games with costumed storybook characters. 647-8444.

Sugarloaf USA/Carrabassett: Children's Festival Week. Fireworks, peanut carnivals, pool parties, torchlight parades and more. Special free skiing and lodging for kids 12 and under, some restrictions. 237-2000.

Sunday River/Newry: Mardi Gras Festival. 824-3000 ext. 374.

MARCH

Island Falls: Log Drivers Bean Hole Bean Cookout. 463-2515.

Madawaska: Snowtime in the Valley. Winter Carnival activities.

Portland: Maine Boatbuilders Show. Portland Yacht Services, 58 Fore St.; 774-1007.

Rockwood: Ice Fishing Tournament. Moosehead Lake. 534-2261.

Shawnee Peak/Bridgton: Ski the Night for Sight. All proceeds benefit Maine Center for the Blind and Visually Impaired. Prizes, dinner. Non-competitive. Night skiing. 774-6273.

Shawnee Peak/Bridgton: Spring Fling. Slush cup, obstacle race, BBQ and music. 647-8444.

Sunday River/Newry: Eat the Heat Chili Cookoff & Firefighters Race. 824-3000 ext. 374.

Statewide: Maine Maple Sunday. Maple sugarhouses open to public. Contact Maine Dept. of Agriculture. 287-3491.

APRIL

Boothbay Harbor: Fisherman's Festival. City-wide. Miss Shrimp pageant, trap hauling, lobster boat races, fish fry, etc. 633-2353.

Houlton: Meduxnekeag River Race. 532-9541.

Newry: Pole, Paddle, and Paw Races. (skis, canoes, and snowshoes) Sunday River Cross Country Ski Ctr. 824-2410.

Ogunquit: Patriot's Day Weekend Celebration. Bazaar tents, tastings, and entertainment at the Beach. 646-2939.

Sugarloaf USA/Carrabassett: Country Music Festival Weekend and Reggae Skibash Weekend. 237-2000.

MAY

Augusta: Maine Mineral Symposium. Auction, displays, lectures, field trip to collecting site. Contact Robert Hinckley, Yarmouth Rd., Grey, 04039.

Lewiston/Auburn: Maine State Parade. 967-2800.

Old Orchard Beach: Apple Blossom Festival. Outdoor crafts, bake sale, and window box competition. 934-2500.

Sunday River/Newry: Ski Mania Day. Free skiing. 824-3000 ext. 374.

JUNE

Augusta and environs: Great Kennebec Whatever Week. Community celebration. 623-4559.

Bethel to Rockland: "Trek Across Maine," Sunday River to the Sea. Three-day, 180-mile bicycle ride. 622-6394.

Boothbay Harbor: Annual Windjammer Days. Parade, antique boat parade, concerts, exhibits. 633-2353.

East Millinocket: Annual Katahdin Family Bluegrass Music Festival. Scenic Sno Rovers Clubhouse along the River. Camping available. 746-5410.

Greenville: Moosemania. One month long of moose-related activities and events. 695-2702.

Kennebunkport: Taste of the Port. Charitable fund-raiser; area restaurants feature samples of their fares. River Green. 967-0857.

Madawaska: Acadian Festival. Celebrating the area's historic past. 728-7000.

Portland: Old Port Festival. Crafts and music; shops and restaurants display their wares. 772-6828.

Wiscasset: Annual Strawberry Festival and Auction. Hodge St., St. Phillip's Church. 882-7184.

J U L Y

Bar Harbor: Annual Summer Craftfest. Mount Desert High School. 794-3543.

Bath: Bath Heritage Days. Annual shipbuilders triathlon, carnival and museum. 443-9751.

Belfast: Maine Poets Festival. Institute for Advanced Thinking, 22 Salmond St., 04915.

Bethel: Mollyockett Day. Bethel Common. Frog jumping contest, lumberjack contest, parade, races, fiddler contest. 824-2282.

Caribou: Crown of Maine Hot Air Balloon Festival/Strawberry Festival/Arts and Crafts Festival. 2nd weekend in July. 498-6156.

Fort Fairfield: Maine Potato Blossom Festival. 472-3802.

Statewide: **Independence Day Celebrations.**

A U G U S T

Auburn/Lewiston: Annual Great Falls Balloon Festival. Hot air ballooning, balloon moon glows, carnival. 783-2249.

Brunswick: The Maine Festival. Thomas Point Beach. 772-9012.

Brunswick: Maine Highland Games. Bagpipe bands, dancing, arts & crafts, folk singers, fiddling, children's games, athletics. Thomas Point Beach. 549-7451.

Houlton: Houlton Potato Feast. 532-4216.

Machias: Blueberry Craftfest. 794-3543

Old Orchard Beach: Chowdafest. Memorial Park. 934-2500.

Old Orchard Beach: Festival of Lights and Illumination Night. Memorial Library Lawn. 934-2500.

Presque Isle: Northern Maine Fair. 764-1830.

Rockland: Annual Maine Lobster Festival. Exhibits, crafts, boat rides, children's activities. Harbor Park. 596-0376.

Skowhegan: Skowhegan Log Days. Week-long celebration with road race, canoe race, parade, professional logging events, beanhole dinner, fireworks. 474-3621.

Southwest Harbor: Celebration of Wooden Boat Magazine. Tours of boatyards, small boat gathering, cruise-in-company, parade of Classic Yachts along the Eggemoggin Reach. (800) 225-5205.

Wilton: Annual Blueberry Festival. Parade, crafts, lake tour, children's show. 645-3932.

SEPTEMBER

Augusta: Maine Made Crafts. Augusta Civic Ctr. 626-2405.

Brunswick: Annual Bluegrass Festival. Thomas Point Beach. 725-6009.

Kittery: Annual Kittery and Eliot Chowder Festival. Kittery Trading Post Co. 439-7545.

Old Orchard Beach: Tri-State Fishing Tournament. 934-2500.

Portland: Duke Ellington Festival. Portland Performing Arts Center. 761-0591.

OCTOBER

Boothbay: Annual Fall Foliage Festival. Craft fair, entertainment, photo show. Boothbay Railway Village. 633-4743.

Fryeburg: Fryeburg Fair. Largest agricultural fair in Maine. Harness racing; horse, ox, and tractor pulls; nightly country shows. 935-3268.

Livermore Falls: Apple-Pumpkin Festival. Livermore Falls Recreation Field. 897-6800.

Nobleboro: Applefest. The Oosoola Park Frog Jumping contest, chicken BBQ, booths, games and various contests for all ages.

Owls Head: The Great Fall Auction & Open House. 594-4418.

NOVEMBER

Portland: Victorian Holiday in Portland. Downtown, Congress St. and the Old Port. Costumed carolers, street musicians, horse drawn carriages, high teas, Victorian character actors, and Father Christmas. 772-6828.

Rangeley: Lighting of the Giving Tree. Lakeside Park. Entertainment, carols and reception at the Rangeley Inn. 864-5364.

Sugarloaf USA/Carrabassett: Thanksgiving Weekend concert. 237-2000.

DECEMBER

Eastport: Festival of Lights Christmas Celebration. 853-4644.

Kennebunk: Annual Walk through Bethlehem. 967-0857

Kennebunk/Kennebunkport: Annual Christmas Prelude. A weekend of Christmas activities: tree lighting, Christmas crafts, museum showcase, cocoa sale, book sale. 967-0857.

Ogunquit: Annual Christmas by the Sea. Tree lighting, caroling, chowderfest, ball, bonfire, Santa. 646-2939.

Rockport/Camden/Lincolnville: Annual Christmas by the Sea. Three days of events for all ages. 236-4404.

Sugarloaf USA/Carrabassett: New Year's Eve concert. 237-2000.

York: Festival of Lights and Parade. York Village. 363-4422.

■ MUSEUMS AND HISTORIC HOUSES

Maine is richly endowed with historic houses, museums, local historical societies, and other institutions devoted to the study and care of Maine's past. In addition to the selection listed below, remember that many public libraries also house a local historical society, with collections of old photographs, town archives, and genealogical records. Some of the institutions below are quite well known, with professional staffs and extensive outreach programs. Most of them, however, are small, low budgeted, and dependent on volunteers. Many are open only in summer; call ahead to verify days and times. Those described in more detail in the text are marked with an asterisk.

A C A D I A / F R E N C H M A N   B A Y

Bar Harbor: Bar Harbor Historical Society Museum. Jessup Memorial Library, 34 Mount Desert St.; 288-4245. Memorabilia of the town's Gilded Age in basement of attractive library.

Bar Harbor: The Natural Science Museum.* College of the Atlantic, Eden St.; 288-5015. Small science museum in large summer "cottage" with great views of Frenchman Bay.

Ellsworth: Colonel Black Mansion "Woodlawn"* (1827). West Main St., Route 172; 667-8671. Stately home, attractive grounds, beautiful mid-19th-century furnishings.

Ellsworth: Stanwood Homestead Museum (1850). Route 3. Memorial to pioneer ornithologist. Includes family furnishings and 100-acre woodland bird sanctuary.

Mount Desert: Robert Abbe Museum of Stone Age Antiquities.* Sieur de Monts Springs, Acadia National Park; 288-3519. Small but important collection on Maine's Native American history. Interesting gift shop.

Southwest Harbor: Wendall Gilley Museum of Bird Carving. Main St. and Herrick Rd.; 244-7555. More than 200 birds carved by local craftsman.

ALLAGASH / FORT KENT

Agatha: Ste. Agatha Historical Society (ca. 1850). Main St.-Route 162; 543-6364. Local and religious artifacts.

Allagash: Allagash Historical Society. Route 161; 398-3335. Log house with local artifacts.

Fort Kent: Fort Kent Blockhouse (1840). Block House St. off Route 1. Relic of "Aroostook War" with Canada.

AUGUSTA

Augusta: Blaine House* (1833). 192 State St. Originally, home of James G. Blaine. Since 1919, official residence of Maine's governors. Olmsted grounds being restored.

Augusta: Fort Western Museum.* City Center Plaza; 626-2385. Site of Pilgrims' 17th-century Cushnoc trading post. Reconstruction of blockhouses and palisade of 18th-century fort. Original barracks/store survives. Frequent demonstrations of colonial arts and crafts.

Augusta: Maine Military Historical Society Museum. Building 6, Camp Keyes, Upper Winthrop St.; 800-442-1157. Former stable now housing military memorabilia, 1763–1960s.

Augusta: Maine State Museum.* Capitol Complex, State St.; 287-2301. Encyclopedic collection of 12,000 years of Maine history.

Augusta: State Capitol Building (1829). State St.; 582-9500 Granite portico remains from original Bulfinch building. Civil War battle flags in rotunda.

Monmouth: Cumston Hall (1900). Main St. Ornate "opera house" with frescoed ceiling. Now summer repertory theater and town offices.

Pittston: Arnold Expedition Historical Society (1756). Off Route 27; 582-7080. Relics of Benedict Arnold's ill-fated march to Quebec.

BATH / BOOTHBAY / WISCASSET

Alna: Alna Center School (1795). Route 218; 586-5536. Second oldest one-room school surviving in Maine.

Alna: Old Alna Meetinghouse (1789). Route 218; 586-5643. Especially well preserved 18th-century building. Original box pews.

Bath: Maine Maritime Museum and Shipyard.* 243 Washington St.; 443-1316.
Complex of buildings on Kennebec illustrating how boats were built, used, and
salvaged, from colonial to modern times.

Boothbay Harbor: Boothbay Region Historical Society. 70 Oak St.; 633-3932.
Italianate house of 19th-century sea captain.

Boothbay: Boothbay Railway Village. Route 2. Complex of some two dozen
buildings. Rides offered on antique trains.

Newcastle: St. Patrick's Roman Catholic Church (1808). Academy Hill Rd.
Oldest surviving Catholic church in New England.

North Edgecomb: Fort Edgecomb (1808–09). Old Fort Road, Davis Island.
Sheepscot River blockhouse fort built to protect Wiscasset.

Wiscasset: Castle Tucker* (1807). Lee St. (at end of High St.). Regency-style
house virtually unchanged since late 19th century.

Wiscasset: Nickels-Sortwell House* (1807). U.S. 1. High-style Federal mansion
rescued in Colonial Revival period.

BANGOR

Bangor: Bangor Historical Society Museum* (1834). 159 Union St. High-style
Greek Revival house. Local history exhibits.

Bradley: Maine Forest and Logging Museum. Leonard's Mills in Penobscot
Experimental Forest, off Route 178. Reconstruction of 1790s logging community.

BERWICKS/KITTERY/YORK

Kittery: Kittery Historical and Naval Museum. Rogers Road, off U.S. 1; 439-1092.
Exhibits relating to local maritime history.

South Berwick: Counting House-Old Berwick Historical Society (ca. 1830).
Route 4; 384-8041. Greek Revival commercial building with collections on
local shipbuilding.

South Berwick: Hamilton House* (ca. 1785). Vaughan's Lane, off Route 236;
436-3205. Handsome 18th-century house overlooking Salmon Falls River,
with restored garden.

South Berwick: Sarah Orne Jewett House* (1774). 5 Portland St.; 436-3205.
Large in-town Georgian house with memorabilia of the famous writer.

York Harbor: Sayward-Wheeler House* (1718). 79 Barrell Lane Extension;
436-3205. Original furnishings of 18th-century merchant's family.

York: Old York Historical Society. 363-4974. Seven buildings are run by the Old York Historical Society in York, including **Elizabeth Perkins House** (ca. 1730) on South Side Road, a Colonial Revival restoration of an early house. On Lindsay Road are the **Emerson-Wilcox House** (1742) at York St. (Route 1A), a museum of local history and decorative arts; **Jefferds Tavern,** a mid-18th-century saltbox moved from Wells; **John Hancock Warehouse,** an 18th-century warehouse with exhibits on York River life; **Old Gaol Museum** (1719) at York St., one of oldest public buildings in North America; and the **Old Schoolhouse** (1745), a one-room schoolhouse.

BETHEL / WHITE MOUNTAINS

Bethel: Dr. Moses Mason House Museum* (1813). 15 Broad St.; 824-2908. Beautifully restored Federal house of U.S. congressman. Rufus Porter murals. Important research library for western Maine history and genealogy.

Bryant Pond: Woodstock Historical Society Museum (1873–74). Route 26; 665-2450. Barn converted into local history museum.

Fryeburg: Fryeburg Fair Farm Museum. Fryeburg Fair Grounds, Route 5. Demonstrations of early trades and crafts during Fryeburg Fair Week (autumn).

BELGRADE LAKES / FARMINGTON / WATERVILLE

Farmington: Nordica Homestead Museum* (ca. 1840). Holley Rd.; 778-2042. Birthplace of Lillian Norton, first American to sing at Bayreuth. Much opera memorabilia.

Livermore: Norlands Living History Center.* Norlands Rd.; 897-2236. "Live-in" 19th-century farm complex. Washburn family homestead and library.

Readfield: Union Meeting House (1827). Church St.; 685-3831. Extensive trompe l'oeil interior by Charles Schumacher.

Waterville: Waterville-Winslow Two Cent Bridge. Front St. Rare surviving toll footbridge over Kennebec.

BLUE HILL / CASTINE

Blue Hill: Jonathan Fisher Memorial* (1814). Main St. Built by polymath clergyman. Many of his paintings are on view.

Castine: Fort George (1779). Earthworks constructed by British to defend Penobscot Valley against colonials.

Castine: **John Perkins House** (1763–1783). Perkins St. (near Wilson Museum). Only surviving pre-Revolutionary house in town.

BRUNSWICK

Brunswick: **Bowdoin College Museum of Art, Walker Art Building*** (1894). Bowdoin College; 725-3275. McKim, Mead & White building. Especially strong in colonial and Federal portraits, Old Master drawings, antiquities.

Brunswick: **First Parish Church** (1846). United Church of Christ, Maine St.; 729-7331. Richard Upjohn's "Carpenter Gothic" church. Harriet Beecher Stowe had her "vision" of Uncle Tom's death here.

Brunswick: **Joshua L. Chamberlain Museum*** (1825). 226 Maine St.; 729-6606. Partially restored home of hero of Little Round Top at Gettysburg. Longfellow had lived in house earlier.

Brunswick: **Peary-MacMillan Museum.*** Hubbard Hall, Bowdoin College; 725-3416. Ethnographic exhibits on the Far North. Many relics of Admiral Peary's 1909 expedition.

Brunswick: **Skolfield-Whittier House Museum*** (1858). 161 Park Row. "Time capsule" house museum virtually unchanged since 1925.

Dresden: **Pownalborough Court House*** (1761). Route 128. Oldest court building in Maine. John Adams practiced law here on circuit. Good exhibit on Kennebec ice industry.

Harpswell: **Adm. Robert E. Peary Home.** Casco Bay, Eagle Island. Explorer's summer house, much as he left it.

CARIBOU/PRESQUE ISLE

Caribou: **Nylander Museum.** 393 Main St.; 493-4474. Extensive natural history collections.

Lille-sur-St. Jean: **Mont-Carmel.** U.S. 1; 895-3339. Restored Catholic church, now museum and Acadian cultural center.

Van Buren: **Acadian Village.** U.S. 1; 868-2691. Complex of 16 reconstructed or relocated buildings, 1785–1900s, illustrating Acadian culture in St. John River valley.

DOWN EAST

Columbia Falls: **Ruggles House*** (1818). One quarter mile off U.S. 1. Exceptional Federal house with intricate woodwork.

Lubec: **The Old Sardine Village Museum.** Route 189. History of local canning industry from 1830s through peak in 1930s.

Machias: **Burnham Tavern Museum*** (1770). Main and Free Sts., Route 192; 255-4432. Oldest surviving building in eastern Maine. Revolutionary War artifacts.

ISLAND FALLS/PATTEN

Patten: **Patten Lumberman's Museum.*** Route 159; 528-2650. Some 3,000 artifacts in 9 buildings.

KENNEBUNK/SACO

Kennebunk: **Taylor-Barry House** (1803). 24 Summer St.; 985-4802. Federal-style sea captain's house.

Kennebunk: **The Brick Store Museum*** (1825). 117 Main St.; 985-4802. Three adjoining 19th-century commercial buildings. Important collection of Federal decorative arts and Thomas Badger portraits.

Kennebunkport: **Seashore Trolley Museum.** Log Cabin Rd.; 339-4352. More than 200 electric trolleys and other vehicles.

Kennebunkport: **The Nott House ("White Columns").** Main St. Greek Revival house, Victorian furnishings.

Old Orchard Beach: **Old Orchard Beach Historical Society Museum.** Harmon Memorial, 4 Portland Ave.; 934-4484. Early resort history, including photos of transatlantic flights that landed on beach.

Saco: **York Institute Museum.** 371 Main St.; 283-3861. Important collections of 18th- and 19th-century decorative arts from northern York County. Frequent exhibits on local industries and architecture.

Wells: **Museum at Historic First Church.** Route 1; 646-4775. Local historical and genealogical collection.

Wells: **Wells Auto Museum.** Route 1. More than 80 cars.

MOOSEHEAD LAKE/BAXTER PARK

Brownville Junction: **Katahdin Iron Works*** (1843). From Route 11, 5 miles north of Brownville Junction, take gravel road (left) 6 miles to site. Partially restored 19th-century industrial site, near Baxter State Park.

Greenville: **S/S *Katahdin**** (1914). Moosehead Marine Museum, North Main St. Daily cruises on restored lake steamer.

ORONO/OLD TOWN

Old Town: **Penobscot Nation Museum.** Indian Island; 827-7776. Small collection of Penobscot artifacts and crafts.

Orono: The Hudson Museum*. Maine Center for the Arts, University of Maine. World-wide ethnographic collections, particularly strong in pre-Columbian art. Interesting gift shop.

Orono: University of Maine Museum of Art. 109 Carnegie Hall. Only publicly owned art museum in state.

PEMAQUID POINT

Pemaquid Point: The Fisherman's Museum. Terminus of Route 130; 677-2726. In former lighthouse keeper's house.

Pemaquid: Colonial Pemaquid (1600s). Off Route 130. Extensive archaeological dig, adjacent museum.

Pemaquid: Fort William Henry (1692). Off Route 130. Replica of second of three English forts built to discourage the French.

Pemaquid: Harrington Meeting House & Museum of Old Bristol (1772). Old Harrington Rd.; 677-2193. Restored 18th-century meeting house with local museum.

Phippsburg: Fort Popham (1861). Terminus of Route 209. Half-moon granite fort guarding mouth of Kennebec.

Prospect: Fort Knox (1844). Route 174; 469-7719. The "other" Fort Knox, looking over the Penobscot at Bucksport.

PORTLAND AND ENVIRONS

Portland: Children's Museum of Maine. 746 Stevens St.; 797-5483. "Hands on" exhibits of arts and sciences. Excellent gift shop.

Portland: Maine Historical Society.* 485 Congress St.; 774-1822. Founded 1822. Important collection relating to all aspects of Maine history. Popular genealogical research facility. In-town garden, exhibition space. Also operates adjacent **Wadsworth-Longfellow House*** (1785), the poet's boyhood home.

Portland: Neal Dow Museum* (1829). 714 Congress St.; 773-7773. Federal townhouse of famous prohibitionist and Civil War general.

Portland: Portland Fire Museum (1836). 157 Spring St. Early fire-fighting equipment.

Portland: Portland Museum of Art.* 7 Congress Square; 773-2787. New building (1983) links two earlier ones, including stately **McLellan-Sweat House** (1800). Major collection of American and European art. Notable State of Maine collection, including Winslow Homer.

Portland: Portland Observatory (1807). 138 Congress St.; 772-5547. Landmark watchtower on Munjoy Hill.

Portland: Tate House* (1755). 1270 Westbrook St.; 774-9781. Stroudwater house of colonial agent for mast trade.

Portland: U.S. Customhouse (1872). 312 Fore St.; 780-3328. Dignified French Renaissance Revival building.

Portland: Victoria Mansion/Morse-Libby House* (1858). 109 Danforth St.; 772-4841. Italianate summer house for Portland-New Orleans family. Lavish interiors, Herter furniture.

Scarborough: Hunnewell House (1684). Route 207, Black Point Rd.; 883-4301. Renovation of very early house.

Yarmouth: Old Ledge School (1738). West Main St.; 846-6259. One-room pre-Revolutionary school house with exhibits.

RANGELEY/SUGARLOAF

Kingfield: Stanley Museum.* School St.; 265-2729. Devoted to inventors of Stanley Steamer (and much else) and photographer Chansonetta Stanley Emmons.

Phillips: Sandy River & Rangeley Lakes Railroad. P.O. Box B; 353-8382. Restored narrow-gauge train offers one-mile rides.

Rangeley: Wilhelm Reich Museum.* Dodge Pond Rd.; 864-3443. Home, studio, and laboratory of controversial émigré psychiatrist.

Weld: Weld Historical Society. Weld Village; 585-2586. Complex of 19th-century buildings illustrating life in small mountain village.

ROCKLAND

Islesboro: Sailor's Memorial Museum and Lighthouse (1850). Grindle Point (ferry dock). Maritime relics.

Rockland: Shore Village Museum (Maine's Lighthouse Museum). 104 Limerock St.; 236-3206. Largest collection of lenses and other lighthouse artifacts in country.

Rockland: William A. Farnsworth Homestead* (1850s). 21 Elm St.; 596-6457. Well-preserved home typical of prosperous mid-Victorian coastal families.

Rockland: William A. Farnsworth Library and Art Museum.* 19 Elm St.; 596-6457. Major collection of paintings, especially strong in depictions of Maine. A must-visit for art-lovers who come to this part of the state.

Searsport: Penobscot Maritime Museum.* Church St.; 548-2529. Complex of historic buildings illustrating maritime history, especially in Penobscot region. Important collection of Buttersworth marine paintings, father and son.

Thomaston: **Montpelier*** (1793). High St. 20th-century replica of magnificent house that helped ruin Gen. Henry Knox.

S E B A G O   L A K E   R E G I O N
Bridgton: Bridgton Historical Society Museum.* Gibbs Ave.; 647-2873. Local history in 1902 fire station.
Casco: Friends Schoolhouse (1841). Raymond-Casco Historical Society; 655-4231. One-room school.
Naples: Naples Historical Society Museum. The Village Green, Route 302; 693-6528. Local history, including canal and Sebago Lake steamboat lore.
New Gloucester: The Shaker Museum. Route 26, Sabbathday Lake. Farming and religious buildings of Maine's only surviving Shaker community, including 1794 meeting house.
Newfield: Willowbrook at Newfield.* Main St. Restored 19th-century village of 37 buildings.
Paris Hill: Hamlin Memorial Hall (Old Stone Jail).* 787-2980. Mementos of Lincoln's first vice president. Famous view of White Mountains.
Poland Springs: Maine State Building* (1893). Route 26, located on the grounds of the former Poland Springs resort. Relic of Chicago 1893 Columbian Exposition.
Sebago: The Jones Museum of Glass and Ceramics. Douglas Mountain Rd.; 787-3370. Important collection of 2,000 years of glass and ceramics.
South Casco: Nathaniel Hawthorne's Boyhood Home* (1812). Hawthorne Rd. (off Route 302). Converted to community hall.
Standish: Daniel Marrett House* (1789). Route 25; 642-3032. Furnishings reveal family's history through two centuries. Attractive garden.

W A L D O
Liberty: Old Octagonal Post Office (1857). Main St.; 589-4393. Harness shop turned post office turned local museum.
Monhegan Island: The Monhegan Museum (1824). Lighthouse Hill; 594-5646. Housed in former lighthouse keeper's dwelling.
Unity: Maine Tribal Unity Museum Collection. Unity College; 948-3131. Native American crafts.

■ SANDY BEACHES

Despite its reputation for a rocky coastline, Maine has some spectacular sand beaches, most of them along the southern coastal plain. Just don't expect warm water. And don't be surprised if you have trouble in July and August finding a parking place. Although the beaches listed below are public, parking is often restricted to local residents with stickers. Call ahead to the town office to inquire to avoid disappointment and plan to arrive early. **Beaches are listed south to north.**

SOUTHERN COAST

Crescent Beach. Kittery. 625 yards long, on a narrow peninsula. On the other side of it is Seapoint Beach (550 yards).

Long Beach. York. Popular and often crowded crescent (2,180 yards). On the other, more protected side of Cape Neddick is Short Sands (410 yards).

Ogunquit Beach. Ogunquit. One of the two best barrier beaches in Maine (Popham being the other). Fine white sand (1,620 yards). Not crowded away from the motel end.

Moody Beach. Wells. Locus of a much-publicized lawsuit over public access below high tide mark in privately owned stretch (the public lost). Public part (2,750 yards) is accessible.

Wells Beach. Wells. Long (4,000 yards), very popular, good birdwatching along nearby salt marsh.

Drakes Island Beach. Wells. Dunes, nature area, swimming beach (940 yards). Connected to Laudholm Beach, near the nature preserve.

Crescent Surf Beach and Parsons Beach. Kennebunk. Fine white sand near salt marsh (totaling 1,700 yards).

Kennebunk Beach. Kennebunk. Popular surfing spot (820 yards). Nearby is Gooch's Beach (1,300 yards), with rocky point.

Goose Rocks Beach. Kennebunkport. Fourth longest stretch of sand in Maine (3,600 yards), just north of Cape Porpoise.

Fortunes Rocks Beach. Biddeford. Second longest (3,740 yards), just south of the Biddeford Pool summer colony. On the other side is Hills Beach (530 yards), a sand spit sheltering the Pool.

Ferry Beach. Saco. Longest of Maine's beaches (4,500 yards), just above the mouth of the Saco River. Part of Ferry Beach State Park. Ample parking (fee).

Old Orchard Beach. Old Orchard Beach. Very popular (3,320 yards, including adjacent Surfside). Fine white sand. Traditional "warm water port" for many visitors from Quebec.

PORTLAND AND ENVIRONS

Grand Beach, Pine Point Beach, Ferry Beach, and Western Beach. Scarborough. Group of beaches on both sides of the mouth of the Scarborough River, totaling 4,200 yards.

Scarborough Beach. Scarborough. Barrier beach (2,060 yards), freshwater marsh. Immediately north of Prout's Neck.

Higgins Beach. Scarborough. Mix of rocks and fine sand (910 yards) facing seaside summer colony.

Crescent Beach. Cape Elizabeth. Popular beach (1,560 yards) within a state park, about 15 minutes from downtown Portland.

Willard Beach. South Portland. Small, urban crescent beach near Spring Point.

MIDCOAST

Head Beach. Phippsburg. Crescent beach (360 yards) near the tip of the Phippsburg peninsula, about 15 minutes from Bath.

Popham Beach. Phippsburg. Maine's best, thanks to fine sand (3,640 yards), natural dunes, good swimming and fishing. Sufficiently remote (at the mouth of the Kennebec) never to feel crowded, but only a short trip from Bath and Brunswick. Ample parking (fee). Nearby is smaller Hunnewell Beach.

Half Mile Beach and Mile Beach. Georgetown. Part of Reid State Park. Half Mile Beach (650 yards) is a barrier spit protecting a salt marsh; Mile Beach (1,160 yards) includes rocky areas and dunes.

Pemaquid Beach. Bristol. Beautiful crescent beach (575 yards) on the Johns River, near Pemaquid Point.

Birch Point (Lucia) Beach. Rockland. Small pocket beach (220 yards), near South Thomaston.

Crescent Beach. Owls Head. Popular beach (1,100 yards) near summer colony.

Lincolnville (Ducktrap) Beach. Lincolnville. Popular beach (850 yards) near summer colony.

Sandy Point Beach. Stockton Springs. Beach (1,370 yards) and nature preserve on the Penobscot River, below Bucksport.

MOUNT DESERT AREA

Lamoine Beach. Lamoine. Popular state park beach (2,740 yards) with great views across Frenchman Bay to Mount Desert Island.

Sand Beach. Mount Desert. Pocket beach (290 yards) made of finely ground shell fragments in Acadia National Park.

DOWN EAST

Sandy River Beach. Jonesport. Sand and cobbles (500 yards), just north of Jonesport.

Roque Bluffs Beach. Roque Bluffs. Steep pocket (910 yards) in Roque Bluffs State Park, a few minutes from Machias.

■ HISTORIC LIGHTHOUSES

There are more than 60 lighthouses on the Maine coast, almost all of them today automated and "unmanned," to use the U.S. Coast Guard's phrase, or in a few instances recycled for civilian residential use. While some of the newer ones are purely utilitarian, the older ones are often of considerable beauty. Here is a listing of some particularly notable landmark lighthouses **listed southwest to northeast.**

SOUTHERN COAST AND PORTLAND

Cape Neddick Light. York. Built in 1879. Accessible by car. Much photographed, especially when lighted for the holidays.

Cape Elizabeth Light. Cape Elizabeth. Successor to the twin lighthouses ("Two Lights") erected in 1829 to mark the entrance to Casco Bay. Replaced in 1874, and since 1924 the only one to be operational. Accessible by car.

Portland Head Light. Cape Elizabeth. Maine's oldest (1791), commissioned by George Washington to guide vessels into Portland Harbor. Adjacent to Fort Williams, a few minutes from downtown Portland.

Spring Point Ledge Light. South Portland. Built in 1897, connected to mainland by breakwater in 1951.

MIDCOAST

Seguin Light. Off Georgetown. Built in 1795, rebuilt 1887. Guards the mouth of the Kennebec. Easily seen from Popham Beach.

Monhegan Island Light. Monhegan. Built in 1850. Much painted by 20th-century artists.

Pemaquid Point. Bristol. Built in 1827 at the entrance to Muscongus Bay. Stunning setting overlooking rocky Pemaquid Point, accessible by car.

Owls Head Light. Owls Head. Built of granite in 1826. Panoramic view of Rockland Harbor and the Camden Hills. Borders a state park.

Rockland Breakwater Light. Rockland. Built in 1888 on a granite pier, rebuilt in 1902. Accessible by foot via the long breakwater.

MOUNT DESERT ISLAND

Mount Desert Rock Light. 6 miles off Mount Desert Island. Most isolated lighthouse in New England. Formerly manned, now automated. A favorite subject for mid-19th-century painters.

Bass Harbor Head Light. Tremont. Built in 1858, at mouth of Blue Hill Bay. Accessible by car.

Bear Island Light. Cranberry Isles. Built in 1839, rebuilt in 1889, recently relighted. Familiar landmark at entrance to Northeast Harbor.

Baker Island Light. Cranberry Isles. Built in 1828, rebuilt in 1855, at entrance to Frenchman Bay. Exceptional views from tower.

DOWN EAST

West Quoddy Head Light. Lubec. Built in 1808, rebuilt in 1858, at the easternmost point of the U.S., now Quoddy Head State Park. Much-photographed candy-stripe tower. Accessible by car.

■ COVERED BRIDGES

Only nine covered bridges remain out of the 120 that once spanned Maine rivers; weather, fire, and neglect have taken their toll. Such bridges were originally roofed to preserve their floorboards from rain and snow and because cattle would cross more easily if they could not see the water rushing below. Today's survivors, a much loved symbol of old New England, are being kept in repair as historic sites.

Babb's Bridge. Gorham-Windham, Presumpscot River. Built in 1843, rebuilt 1976. Maine's oldest surviving covered bridge.

Bennett Bridge. Near Wilson Mills, Magalloway River. A newcomer, built in 1901.

Hemlock Bridge. Fryeburg, Saco River. Built in 1857.

Lovejoy Bridge. South Andover, Ellis River. Shortest in the state (70 feet). Built in 1868.

Low's Bridge. Sangerville, Piscataquis River. Rebuilt in 1990 after being swept away in the 1987 flood.

Porter Bridge. Porter-Parsonfield, Ossipee River. Built in 1876.

Robyville Bridge. Corinth, Kenduskeag River. State's only completely shingled bridge. Built in 1876.

Sunday River Bridge. Near North Bethel and Newry, Sunday River. Built in 1872. Most popular bridge in state for artists and photographers. Near a busy ski resort area.

Watson Settlement Bridge. Littleton, Meduxnekeag River. Built in 1911. Most northerly of the covered bridges.

■ STATE AND NATIONAL PARKS AND FORESTS

Maine's numerous state and national parks and forests offer myriad camping, hiking, climbing, fishing, and picnicking opportunities. The following sites are listed by region.

ANDROSCOGGIN

Bradbury Mountain State Park. Small camping area, playgrounds. On Route 9, 6 miles from Freeport exit of I-95; 688-4712.

Wolf Neck State Park. Shoreline hiking trails, salt marshes, bird sanctuary. Some nature trails can accommodate wheelchairs. Off U.S. 1 south of Freeport on Wolf Neck Rd.

DOWN EAST/MOUNT DESERT ISLAND

Acadia National Park. 44,000-acre preserve covering Schoodic Point, Isle au Haut, and about half of Mount Desert Island. Hiking, camping, swimming. Close to Bar Harbor. In Frenchman Bay; accessible by boat or drive Route 3 from Ellsworth; 288-3338.

Cobscook Bay State Park. Fishing, picknicking, hiking, camping. Close to Quoddy Head and Campobello International Park; 726-4771.

Lamoine State Park. Oceanside park with campsites and picnic areas and boat launching facilities on Frenchman's Bay. 8 miles southeast of Ellsworth on Route 184; 667-2778.

Quoddy Head State Park. Easternmost point of land in continental U.S. 400-acre oceanside park with rocky ledges along coast; Quoddy Head Light. 4 miles off Route 189 at Lubec.

Roque Bluffs State Park. 300-acre seaside park with hiking trails and swimming at both a freshwater pond and a saltwater beach. Off U.S. 1 south of Machias along an unnumbered road (Roque Bluffs is a relatively new park).

MIDCOAST/KENNEBEC

Damariscotta Lake State Park. Small lakeside park with sandy beach; picnic tables and grills. Route 32 in Jefferson.

Lake St. George State Park. Spring-fed lake provides excellent fishing for bass, salmon, perch, and brown trout. Bathing beach with bathhouse; overnight camping. On Route 3 in Liberty; 589-2131.

Peacock Beach State Park. Swimming at sandy beach; picnicking. Off U.S. 201 on Pleasant Pond in Richmond.

Reid State Park. Maine's largest oceanside park, with two long beaches. Surf casting for striped bass. 14 miles south of Woolwich on Route 127.

NORTH WOODS

Allagash Wilderness Waterway. 92-mile-long waterway between Baxter State Park's western edge and Twin Falls near the Canadian border. Write Maine Bureau of Parks and Recreation, State Office Building, Augusta 04330.

Aroostook State Park. Swimming, boating, nature trails, snowmobiling. Located on Echo Lake off U.S. 1, 1 mile south of Presque Isle; 769-8347.

Baxter State Park. 46 mountain peaks including Mt. Katahdin allow excellent mountain climbing. 130 miles of trails in a 200,000-acre preserve. Access to park at Greenville on the west, Millinocket on the south, and Patten on the east. Reservations must be paid in advance; 723-5201.

Lily Bay State Park. Excellent fishing for brook trout, togue, and salmon. On Moosehead Lake north of Greenville on Ripogenus Dam Rd.; 695-2700.

Peaks-Kenny State Park. Within a forested, hilly area along Sebec Lake; bathing beach in a quiet cove, nature trails. Fishing for small-mouth bass and land-locked salmon. North of Dover-Foxcroft on U.S. 153.

PENOBSCOT BAY AND RIVER

Holbrook Island Sanctuary. 1,600-acre preserve located off Routes 175 and 176 west of Brooksville on the Blue Hill peninsula.

Fort Point State Park. Small oceanside park on tip of a peninsula into Penobscot Bay. Off U.S. 1 in Stockton Springs.

Moose Point State Park. Seaside picnic area on Penobscot Bay. On U.S. 1 between Belfast and Searsport.

Camden Hills State Park. Beaches on salt or fresh water. Foot trail to summit of Mount Megunticook. 2 miles north of Camden on U.S. 1; 236-3109.

Warren Island State Park. The state's most secluded state park, reachable only by private boat. Campsites and hiking. Off mainland from Lincolnville, just south of Islesboro.

PORTLAND AND ENVIRONS

Crescent Beach State Park. Picnic tables, hiking, freshwater showers. 9 miles from Portland on Route 77 in Cape Elizabeth.

Two Lights State Park. Picnic areas overlooking rugged coastline. Hiking and surf fishing from rocks. Close to Crescent Beach. Off Route 77 in Cape Elizabeth.

WESTERN LAKES AND MOUNTAINS

Grafton Notch State Park. A series of natural attractions including Old Speck Mountain, Moose Cave, and Bear River. Appalachian Trail cuts through park. Along both sides of Route 26 between Upton and Newry.

Mount Blue State Park. Near Webb Beach; bathhouses with showers. Fishing for bass, perch, and pickerel. Hiking trails on Mount Blue and Tumbledown Mountain. Follow signs from Weld in Franklin County.

Rangeley Lake State Park. 700-acre park with camping and swimming facilities along the lake. Close to ski resorts and mountain climbing sites. Take Route 17 from Rumford, or Route 4 from Farmington; 864-3858.

Sebago Lake State Park. Really a combination day-use park with swimming and boating facilities, off U.S. 302 in Casco. Overnight camping is available (14-day limit) at the area off U.S. 302 in Naples; 693-2742.

White Mountain National Forest. 5 campgrounds within 42,000 acres. Hiking, climbing. Southwest of Bethel on U.S. 2 or Route 113; 824-3124.

■ NATURE CONSERVANCY PRESERVES

More than 100,000 acres of some of Maine's most scenic and most environmentally important land has been donated or purchased by The Nature Conservancy. Listed below are 41 sites that are open to the public in daylight hours or easily seen from roads or from the sea. Public use is limited to hiking, birdwatching, photography, and non-intrusive nature study. No fires, camping, pets, or collecting of specimens are allowed. Some islands with important bird colonies are off limits during nesting season (usually mid-April to mid-August); visitors should also avoid walking in fragile bog habitats, where it may take years for human footprints to disappear. Boaters visiting the Conservancy's islands should exercise caution because of strong currents and tricky tides.

Despite those restrictions, the Conservancy welcomes thoughtful visitors. A series of excursions to see most, or even all, of these sites would be an interesting way to organize a summer or fall in Maine. The listing below is by general region.

DOWN EAST

Flint and Shipstern Island Preserves. Harrington. A pair of rugged islands with nesting eagles in Pleasant Bay, near Milbridge. Best viewed from the water. Closed February 15 to August 15.

Great Wass Island Preserve. Beals. One of the Conservancy's most interesting preserves, extending into the Gulf of Maine from the Jonesport-Addison Peninsula. The windswept shorefront includes sub-arctic species, twisted jack pines, osprey, eagles, herons. There are two trails. Accessible by car from Jonesport.

Mistake Island Preserve. Jonesport. A treeless outpost at the entrance of Eastern Bay, with "coastal headland shrub" and "shrub-slope peatland" habitats found in the United States only in this part of Washington County. Lovely boardwalk across the heath; lighthouse at point. Accessible by boat.

Preble Island and Dram Island Preserves. Gouldsboro and Sorrento. Spruce-covered Preble is one of the four Porcupines off Bar Harbor. Preble Island protects Sorrento Harbor. Both can easily be seen from shore.

Turtle Island Preserve. Winter Harbor. 136 acres of a 150-year-old spruce-fir forest, with a blue heron colony, cobble beaches, and tidal pools. Reached by boat from Winter Harbor. Closed March 15 to August 15.

KENNEBEC

Indian and Fowl Meadow Islands Preserve. Embden. Two small typical flood-plain islands in the Kennebec north of Skowhegan. Accessible by canoe.

MIDCOAST

Bald Head Preserve. Arrowsic. An eagle nesting area between Phippsburg and Georgetown on the Kennebec, including 160-foot pine-covered cliffs above the Back River and tidal marshes. One of four major wintering areas for the bald eagle in Maine. Best observed from the river. Access to Bald Head is by river; be cautious of strong currents there.

The Brothers and Hay Ledge Preserve. St. George. A cluster of four small islands a mile off the Port Clyde Peninsula. Very important seabird nesting site, especially for laughing gulls, Arctic terns, and eiders. Closed March 15 to August 15.

Damariscove Island Preserve. Boothbay. A narrow, treeless island southeast of Boothbay Harbor inhabited since the early 1600s. An important nesting area for greater black-backed and herring gulls and the common eider. The Coast Guard station on the island is not part of the preserve. Accessible by private boat, but the northern part is closed during nesting season. (Northern portion closed March 15 to August 15.)

Musquash Pond Preserve. Jefferson. A variety of habitats touching three ponds near Alna and Coopers Mills, with extensive interpretive trails. Beaver dams.

Plummer Point Preserve. South Bristol. 71 acres on the Damariscotta River, including a mile of rugged, forested shore and evidence of 19th-century quarrying. Best reached by boat.

MOUNT DESERT ISLAND

Indian Point-Blagden Point Preserve. Pretty Marsh. A forested 110-acre preserve in a part of Mount Desert Island that escaped the 1947 fire. Some 1,000 feet of Western Bay frontage offers many good spots for watching harbor seals sun themselves on ledges. Good trails. Near Somesville on the "back" side of the island.

NORTH WOODS

The Hermitage Preserve. Northeast of Brownville Junction. 35-acre grove of
150-year-old white pines on a bluff overlooking the West Branch of the Pleasant
River, on the Appalachian Trail 81 miles south of Katahdin. Near Katahdin Iron
Works and Gulf Hagas Gorge. No camping. National Natural Landmark.

Seboeis River Gorge Preserve. Near Patten. Dramatic gorge on an 8-mile unspoiled
river corridor offering Class IV rapids canoeing, just east of Baxter State Park. No
good trails. Maine Forest Service Campground is 15 miles west of Patten.

PENOBSCOT BAY

Appleton Bog Preserve. Appleton. Part of a 680-acre bog containing one of the
northernmost stands of Atlantic white cedar in the country, 15 miles west of
Camden. No trails; a guide and a compass are needed. A National Natural
Landmark.

Big Garden and Big White Islands Preserve. Vinalhaven. Characteristic Penobscot Bay islands with granite shores, dark spruce and fir woods, nesting osprey.
Accessible by private boat or easily seen from the ferry. Big Garden Island was
donated in 1967 by Charles and Anne Morrow Lindbergh.

Crockett Cove Woods and Barred Island Preserves. Stonington and Deer Isle.
"Fog forest" habitats on the Deer Isle Peninsula. Crockett Cove can be reached
by car, Barred Island by boat.

Fernald's Neck Preserve. Camden. More than 1,800 feet of thickly forested shoreline on a large peninsula on Megunticook Lake. Especially impressive when
seen from a canoe. Good trails. Accessible by car from Route 52.

Lane's Island Preserve. Vinalhaven. 45 acres of windswept fields and rugged coast,
with spectacular surf on windy days, only a 10-minute walk across the Indian
Creek Causeway from Main St. in Vinalhaven. Ancient site of Susquehanna
and Red Paint People villages. No car is needed if you make a day-trip on the
state ferry from Rockland to Vinalhaven.

Smith Island and Sheep Island Preserves. Vinalhaven and North Haven. Two
small islands in East Penobscot Bay, the former moor-like (after years of sheep
grazing), the latter wooded. Accessible by private boat and easily seen from the
Vinalhaven and North Haven shore, respectively.

Wreck Island and Round Island Preserves. Stonington. Two islands just south of the Deer Isle Peninsula in the passage known as Merchant Row. Both were "cleared" by sheep grazing. Wreck Island was farmed from the 1700s until about 50 years ago. Accessible by boat from Stonington.

PORTLAND
Mill Creek Preserve. Falmouth. An important 20-acre saltwater marsh 5 miles northeast of Portland.

SOUTHERN COAST
Saco Heath Preserve. Saco. A parking lot on Route 112 is the starting point for a quarter-mile woods trail that leads to a half-mile boardwalk across this unusual heathland. It is the southernmost raised coalesced bog in North America, all the more remarkable for being in the heart of the state's most populous area.

The Waterboro Barrens. Waterboro. The best example known in the world of this rare pitch pine/scrub oak barrens. This natural community about 10 miles northwest of Saco thrives on an otherwise inhospitable base of 50 or so feet of glacial outwash (sand and gravel). Excellent for hiking and cross-country skiing.

WESTERN LAKES AND MOUNTAINS
Douglas Mountain Preserve. Sebago. Between Hiram and Sebago Lake. A 20-minute hike to the summit offers spectacular views of the White Mountains and the Atlantic (and on the clearest days, of the Green Mountains in Vermont). Good snowshoeing trails in winter.

Step Falls Preserve. Newry. A dramatic stretch of Wight Brook with cataracts and pools, near Grafton Notch State Park and the New Hampshire state line.

Sucker Brook Preserve. Lovell. Marshland near Kezar Lake, on the eastern edge of the foothills of the White Mountains.

■ GARDENS

Maine's climate severely tests even the hardiest gardener, but somehow the Canadians manage to do better under even worse conditions. Perhaps the reasons for the lack of a native horticultural tradition are cultural: in Maine, ambitious gardening is still identified with the rich summer people of an earlier time. Nonetheless, interest is growing as residents discover there is more to summer than a regimental array of marigolds. Meanwhile, here are a few public gardens that show what is possible.

CAMDEN

Merryspring. Conway Rd., off Route 1; 236-4885. A 66-acre garden and nature preserve on the Goose River, with frequent educational programs in summer.

FREEPORT

Tidebrook Conservation Trust. 38 Bartol Island Rd.; 865-3856. An idyllic 45-acre saltwater farm on the Harraseeket River with gardens and nature trails. Especially beautiful in late May when thousands of daffodils bloom in the orchard.

MOUNT DESERT ISLAND

Abby Aldrich Rockefeller Garden. Off Route 3, Seal Harbor. One of the greatest gardens in North America, though rarely open to the public now because of the sudden crush of visitors in the late 1980s (inquire locally for tours). Beatrix Farrand (who was Edith Wharton's neice) collaborated with Mrs. John D. Rockefeller Jr. in the 1920s to create a Jekyllesque garden about the size of a football field surrounded by a wall topped with glazed tiles from the Imperial Palace in Peking. It sits on a hilltop surrounded by scenic woods that manage to feel both Oriental and Maine-like at once. This orientalizing effect has had a major influence on late 20th-century Maine garden design.

Asticou Azalea Gardens. Route 3 near Route 198, Northeast Harbor. Charles Savage also designed this Japanese-influenced garden around a stream and pond. The azaleas (at their peak in late June) and rhododendron include rarities brought from Beatrix Farrand's famous Reef Point garden in Bar Harbor (which she had uprooted in a fury upon learning in 1955 that the town had declined her offer of the landmark as a horticultural center). Farrand gave her Reef Point library, which included English garden designer Gertrude Jekyll's papers, to the University of California, Berkeley.

Thuya Garden. Asticou Terrace, Northeast Harbor; 276-5130. Almost a century ago, rusticator Joseph Henry Curtis built a small house on the terraced side of Eliot Mountain; landscape architect Charles Savage later carved out Gertrude Jekyll-style perennial borders in back (recently restored by Patrick Chassé). The result is the most beautiful garden in Maine. With its botanical library, Oriental rugs, and cedar-log walls, Curtis's Thuya Lodge embodies the style (semi-rustic, semi-luxurious) in which the old summer colony lived. The garden and cottage can be reached by a narrow drive off route 3 or by a short hike up the hill from Asticou Landing.

The Wild Gardens of Acadia. Sieur de Monts Spring, Route 3 or Park Loop Rd., Bar Harbor. A small, well-labeled botanical collection near the Abbe Museum and the Tarn displaying more than 300 plants indigenous to Mount Desert Island.

PORTLAND

Deering Oaks. Forest Ave. A 51-acre city park designed by Frederick Law Olmsted to incorporate the famous grove celebrated in Longfellow's poem "My Lost Youth." Of special horticultural interest is the rose garden. The park is undergoing restoration to eliminate some of the auto traffic and to connect its green spaces with a city-wide system of trails and bike routes.

Several of Maine's historic houses have small gardens open to the public, notably the **Hamilton House** (South Berwick), the **Marret House** (Standish), the **Black Mansion** (Ellwsorth), and the **Longfellow House** (Portland). Gardeners whose interests are more culinary than horticultural may want to make the pilgrimage to **Johnny's Selected Seeds** in Albion (437-9294), a pioneer in the effort to preserve heirloom varieties of vegetables suitable for northern climates. For perennials on sale in a naturalized setting, the best display is at **Fieldstone Gardens** in Vassalboro (923-3836).

■ WHITEWATER RAFTING

Most outfitters operate from spring until fall.

BINGHAM

Maine Whitewater Inc. Trips to Kennebec, Penosbscot, and Dead rivers. Seasonal. Gadabout Gaddis Airport. 672-4814 or (800) 345-MAIN.

BRUNSWICK

Access to Adventure. Trips from one to six days on the Kennebec, Penobscot, Dead rivers. 725-2255 or (800) 864-2676.

C A M D E N

Viking River Expeditions. Personalized adventures on the Kennebec, Dead, and Penobscot Rivers. One-day and overnight trips. Instruction and sales. 236-8797 or (800) 244-8799.

C A R A T U N K

Action River Adventures. Trips to Kennebec, Penobscot, Dead. Accommodations available. Wyman Lake. 672-5506 or (800) 766-7238.

New England Whitewater Center. Kennebec, Penobscot, Dead. Accommodations available. 672-5506 or (800) 766-7238.

E A S T   V A S S A L B O R O

North County Rivers, Inc. Daily trips to Penobscot, Kennebec, and Dead rivers. No experience necessary. Accommodations available. 923-3492 or (800) 348-8871.

T H E   F O R K S / W E S T   F O R K S

AAA Whitewater Information. Trips run daily on Kennebec, Dead, Penobscot. Multiple day and overnight trips. 923-3492 or (800) 348-8871.

Adventure River Expeditions. Kennebec and Penobscot (daily), Dead (selected). Whitewater rafting, mountain biking, horseback riding, kayaking. Accommodations available. Route 201; 663-2249 or (800) 765-7238.

Crab Apple Whitewater Inc. Daily trips to Kennebec, Dead rivers. "Mild or wild" rafting. Accommodations available. Crab Apple Acres Inn, Route 201; 663-4491 or (800) 553-7238.

Downeast Whitewater Rafting, Inc. Kennebec (daily); Penobscot (daily); the Dead, Rapid, and Swift rivers (selected). Fishing, kayak and canoe trips and overnight trips. Accommodations available. Headquarters: Route 201, 2 miles south of The Forks. Office: Saco Bound/Downeast; (603) 447-3002 or (800) 677-RAFT.

Magic Falls Rafting Company. Small, personalized groups. 663-2220 or 873-0938.

Mountain Magic Company. One-day trips and packages to Kennebec and Dead. 663-2233 or (800) 464-2238.

North American Whitewater Expeditions. Kennebec, Penobscot, Dead. Daily and overnight trips. Guided mountain bike trips, canoe trips. Accommodations available. (800) 727-4379.

Northern Outdoors, Inc. Trips to Kennebec and Penobscot (daily) and Dead (selected). Professionally guided whitewater rafting, mountain biking, horseback riding, and adventure ropes course. Accommodations available. 663-4466 or (800) 765-RAFT.

Professional River Runners of Maine, Inc. Kennebec, Penobscot, Dead rivers. One to six-day canoe and/or raft trips. Professional guides. Smaller, more personalized trips. Overnight expeditions which combine canoeing and/or rafting with wilderness camping. Trips available for children, elderly, and physically challenged. Accommodations available. 663-2229.

Unicorn Rafting Expeditions. Trips from one to six days on the Kennebec, Penobscot, Dead and Moose Rivers. Guided hunting and fishing trips, mountain biking, horseback riding, and ropes course. Accommodations available. 725-2255 or (800) UNICORN.

Voyagers Whitewater. Small group trips, gourmet meals with trips on Kennebec, Dead, and Penobscot. Accommodations available. Route 201; 663-4423 or (800) 289-6307.

GREENVILLE

Eastern River Expeditions. Kennebec and Penobscot Rivers (daily). Highwater Dead trips (selected). Spring highwater trips: Moose River. Overnight rafting or "paddle your own craft" camping trips. Whitewater instruction for canoe and kayaking. Accommodations available. Moosehead Lake. (800) 634-7238.

ROCKWOOD

Wilderness Expeditions, Inc. Kennebec, Penobscot, Dead, Allagash, St. John. Accommodations available. 534-2242/7305 or (800) 825-WILD.

■ SEA KAYAKING AND OCEAN OUTINGS

Should you choose to see Maine from the Atlantic, several companies offer different types of ocean outings, including scenic cruises, whale and seal watches, lobster and deep-sea fishing excursions, and kayaking trips.

BAR HARBOR

Acadian. Daily 2-hour cruises in and around Acadia National Park. 2-hour Estate Cruise along Mount Desert Island. Sunset Nature Cruise around Frenchman

Bay. May 1 to Nov 1. Dpt: Frenchman Bay Co. 1 West St., Harbor Place;
288-3322.

Acadian Whale Watcher. Daily 4-hour cruises. Bay/Sunset Cruise leaves 2 hours
before sunset. Equipped for handicapped. Seasonal. Dpt: Golden Anchor Pier,
West St.; 288-9794.

Aunt Elsie. Seal watching, lobster-fishing trips. Seasonal. Dpt: Golden Anchor
Pier. 288-9505.

Coastal Kayaking. Kayaking trips. Wilderness expeditions. 48 Cottage St.;
288-9605.

Ebb Tide Sea Kayaking. Kayaking trips. 288-9624.

BATH

Hardy II. Historical river cruise. Daily, departing every hour. Dpt: Maine Maritime
Museum. 443-1316 or 882-7909.

BOOTHBAY HARBOR

Balmy Days II. All-day trips to Monhegan Island and 2-hour dinner cruises.
Seasonal. Dpt: Pier 8. 633-2284

Cap'n Fish's Cruises. Whale watching and deep-sea fishing trips daily.
Seasonal. Dpt: Pier 1. 633-3244.

Tidal Transit. Kayaking trips. 633-7140.

Whale Watcher. 4-hour cruises. 110-ft. vessel. Naturalist guide. Seasonal. Dpt:
Frenchman Bay Co., 1 West St., Harbor Place; 288-3322 or (800) 508-1499.

BOWDOINHAM

Dragonworks, Inc. Kayaking trips, instruction, and sales. RR 1, Box 1186,
Bowdoinham; 666-8481.

CAMDEN/ROCKLAND

Appledore II. Daily 2-hour cruises. Full moon 4-hour cruises. Seasonal. Dpt:
Camden Harbor. 236-8353.

Bay Island Yacht Charters. Deep-sea fishing. 236-2776 or (800) 421-2492.

Indian Island Kayak Co. Kayaking trips. 16 Mountain St., Camden; 236-4088.

Maine Sport Outfitters. Kayaking trips, instruction, sales and rentals. Off U.S. 1,
Rockport; 236-8797/7120 or (800) 722-0826/(800) 244-8799.

Outward Bound Hurricane. Kayaking instruction, courses. P.O. Box 429,
Rockland; 594-5548.

Sea Touring Kayak Center. Elm St., Camden; 236-9569.

EASTPORT

Anna. 3-hour cruises around Passamaquoddy and Cobscook bays. Seasonal. Dpt: Eastport Breakwater. West Pembroke Charter Co. 726-5151.

FREEPORT

L. L. Bean Outdoor Discovery Program. Kayaking instruction only. (800) 341-4341 ext. 7800.

KENNEBUNKPORT

Cape Arundel Cruises. Full-day trips. Deep-sea fishing. Dpt: Arundel Wharf, Route 9; 967-5595.

Elizabeth II, Nautilus. 5to 6-hour whale watching trips and 1 ½-hour scenic and deep-sea fishing cruises. Dpt: Arundel Shipyard, Route 9. Seasonal. 967-5595/0707.

Ugly Anne. Deep-sea fishing. Dpt: Perkins Cove. 646-7202.

Indian Whale Watch. Seasonal. Dpt: Arundel Wharf Restaurant, Ocean Ave.; 967-5912 or 985-5993.

NAPLES

U.S. Mailboat. 2-hour Long Lake mail delivery cruise. 3-hour Songo Locks to Sebago Lake cruise. Dpt: the causeway, Route 302; 693-6861.

NORTHEAST HARBOR

Isleford Ferry. Nature cruise. Baker Island cruise. Sunset cruise. Naturalist cruises to the Cranberry Islands. Seasonal. Dpt: Sea Street Pier. 276-3717 or 422-6815.

Seal. Northeast whale, puffins, seabird cruises. 38 max. Trips led by College of the Atlantic biologists. Dpt: Northeast Harbor Marina. Seasonal. 276-5803/3980.

ORRS ISLAND

H2 Outfitters. Kayaking trips and instruction. P.O. Box 72, Orrs Island; 833-5257 or 833-6606.

PORTLAND

Anjin-San. Deep-sea fishing. 772-2168.

Casco Bay Lines. Year-round service to Peaks, Chebeague, Long, Great and Little Diamond, and Cliff islands. Seasonal service to Bailey Island. Narrated cruises on Casco Bay. Dpt: Ferry Terminal, Commercial and Franklin Sts.; 774-7871.

Devils Den. Deep-sea fishing. Dpt: DeMillo's Marina; 761-4466.

Maine Island Kayak Co. Kayaking trips, workshops, and instruction. 70 Luther St., Peak's Island; 766-2373 or (800) 796-2373.

Norumbega Outfitters. Kayaking trips, tours, sales, rental, and repairs. 58 Fore St.; 773-0910.

Prince of Fundy Cruises, LTD. Nightly 11-hour trips to Yarmouth, Nova Scotia. Seasonal. Dpt: International Ferry Terminal, Commercial St.; 775-5616 or (800) 341-7450 (USA); (800) 482-0955 (ME).

Suellyn. Daily: 1 1/2-hour seal and island cruises. Dpt: Long Wharf, Commercial St. 1-hour harbor cruise. Dpt: Portland Head Light. (800) 437-3270.

R O C K L A N D

Bitter End. Lobster Dinner Cruise. Seasonal. Dpt: Middle Pier/Public Landing. 594-9040.

M/V Pauline. 3- and 6-day cruises with stops at fishing villages, islands, museums, and historic towns. Seasonal. Dpt: Windjammer Wharf; 236-3520.

W I S C A S S E T

Chewonki Foundation. Wilderness expeditions (ages 13-18). 882-7323.

■ MAINE'S MOST FAMOUS ISLANDS

Only less than one percent of Maine's population lives year-round on its coastal islands, but—thanks to several generations of artists, writers, and summer people—these once impoverished outposts today seem to represent "Maine" to much of the outside world. Perhaps because most of them are still hard to reach, they survive remarkably unchanged, at least visually (although many of them are having trouble maintaining economically viable year-round communities as fewer people want to stay). The islands are listed southwest to northeast.

The Isles of Shoals. Five of them are in Maine, four in New Hampshire. Several can be visited by boat from Portsmouth, NH; the largest, Celia Thaxter's Appledore and nearby Star, can be easily seen from Rye Beach, N.H. (look for the former's World War II submarine watch tower). See "SOUTHERN COAST AND YORK COUNTY."

Eagle Island. Several of the larger Casco Bay islands (Peaks, the Diamonds, Long, Great Chebeague, Cliff) can be visited on Casco Bay Lines' regular mailboats, but the most interesting of all—Eagle—requires joining a cruise out of Portland or renting a small boat in South Harpsell. The attraction is Adm. Robert E. Peary's 1904 summer home, where he planned several Arctic expeditions and which still looks as if he were about to return.

Monhegan Island. Probably the most famous Maine island in American art, thanks to Rockwell Kent, George Bellows, Jamie Wyeth, and others attracted by its dramatic cliffs. The year-round population of about 85 increases tenfold in summer, augmented by some 100 trippers daily in July and August. Reached by mailboat from Port Clyde, about an hour away, or by excursion boats out of Boothbay Harbor.

Matinicus Island. Most remote of the inhabited islands (23 miles from Rockland) and much less self-consciously "quaint" than Monhegan (no inns, yacht clubs, or restaurants). The year-round population of fishing families (about 45 people) is linked to the mainland by the Maine State Ferry Service (Rockland) one day a month or by private boat and plane charters.

Vinalhaven. Less artsy than Monhegan (although Robert Indiana is its most famous resident), this is perhaps the island that best conveys to the casual visitor the feeling of off-shore life. Its 1,200 people, many of them descendants of granite quarrymen of the 1880s, rely on fishing and tourism.

North Haven. Rather private island known for its Old Guard summer cottages "on the Thorofare" (the short cut if you're sailing to and from Penobscot Bay). There is a small knitwear business, using the local wool, and a few places for visitors to eat and sleep. About an hour by car ferry from Rockland.

Isle au Haut. One of the most beautiful, unspoiled, and little visited of the major islands, about half of it part of Acadia National Park. Reached by mailboat from Stonington.

Isleboro. One of the most accessible (20 minutes by ferry from Lincolnville Beach), though a place without a great deal to do (other than bicycling or picnicking) unless you know somebody there. Dark Harbor is another very private Old Guard summer colony. There are good views west to the Camden Hills and east to Cape Rosier and the smaller Penobscot Bay islands, including Great Spruce Head (private), made famous by the nature photography of Eliot Porter and the paintings of Fairfield Porter.

The Cranberries and Swan. See "MOUNT DESERT ISLAND."

Campobello. Well worth the drive all the way to Lubec and then across the bridge into New Brunswick, Canada. See "DOWN EAST" for details.

■ SKIING

A L P I N E

Baker Mountain Ski Area. Route 201, Moscow 04920; 672-5580.

Black Mountain of Maine. Glover Rd., Rumford 04276; 364-8977.

Camden Snowbowl. Box 1207, Hosmer Rd., Camden 04843; 236-3438.

Eaton Mountain. HCR 71, Box 128, Skowhegan 04976; 474-2666.

Hermon Mountain. Hermon Mountain, Newbury Rd., RFD 1, Box 1347, Searsport, 04974; 848-5192.

Hermon Mountain. RFD 1, Box 1347, Searsport 04974; 848-5192.

Lonesome Pine Trails. P.O. Box 372, Fort Kent 04743; 834-5202.

Lost Valley. Lost Valley Rd., P.O. Box 260, Auburn 04210; 784-1561.

May Mountain Ski Area. c/o Vacationland Estate Resort, P.O. Box 398, Island Falls 04747; 463-2002.

Mt. Abram Ski Slopes. RR 1, Box 1688, Howe Hill Rd., Locke Mills 04255; 875-5003.

Mt. Jefferson Ski Area. Route 6, Lee 04455; 738-2377.

Saddleback Ski and Summer Lake Resort. Box 490, Rangeley 04970; 864-5671 or (800) 685-2537.

Shawnee Peak at Pleasant Mountain. RR 1, Box 734, Bridgton 04009; 647-8444.

Ski Squaw. Route 15, P.O. Box D, Greenville 04441; 695-2272.

Sugarloaf USA/Carrabassett Valley 04947; 237-2000 or (800) THE LOAF.

Sunday River Ski Resort. Box 450, Bethel 04217; 824-2187 or (800) 543-2754 (reservations).

Titcomb Mountain. Farmington 04938; 778-9031.

THOMASTON POND

E very winter when I was growing up in Thomaston, Maine, a shallow pond just behind the stores on Main Street (Route 1) would become a communal gathering place. Everyone in town seemed to know how to skate and would come down to the pond in the evenings and on weekends. Fire barrels were placed on either side of the pond, and some kind citizens (invisible to us kids) would provide a constant supply of firewood. Neighborly conversation flowed around those glowing barrels. When it snowed, volunteers would show up with shovels and form teams to push the heavy stuff off the ice. When the ice got rough, the fire department would flood the pond, leaving a mirror of fresh ice.

Among us were several skaters who could cut an elegant figure on the ice, and who left the rest of us in awe of their grace and skill. The pond was a courting place, and the figures were cut as part of a kind of winter mating dance. There were pick-up hockey games in the afternoon after school, and we would organize contests to see who could jump over the most orange crates. After gathering crates from behind the grocery store, we'd begin by setting out one, then take turns flying down the ice and leaping over it. After everyone had cleared the first crate we would add another, then another, until some jumper stuck both skates through the flimsy wood and skidded down the ice wearing the crate up around his knees.

In the fall we'd have a hard time waiting for the ice to get thick enough, so eager were we for the skating season to begin. One year three of us went to the pond and stared at the still thin, transparent pane of ice. We could see the weeds on the bottom of the pond, which was only about four feet deep. Without saying much, we laced on our skates and ventured out on ice we knew we should not be on. White lines streaked off across the ice from beneath our skates with that hollow, almost electric sound ice makes when it cracks.

We skated back and forth until the ice was almost entirely white with the web of fractures. At one point near the middle of the pond, the ice actually began to undulate as we skated across it. The three of us joined arms, laughing, fully expecting, even wanting in the perverse way of small boys, the plunge we knew was coming. A few more runs across the wavy ice, and we were suddenly up to our chests in the breathtaking ice water. Somehow we clambered out after breaking a lot more ice in the process. We weren't laughing anymore. Our skate laces froze immediately when we got out, and our hands were so cold we probably wouldn't have been able to untie them anyway. We got on our bikes with our skates on, no mean feat that, to ride a bike with ice skates on. By the time I got home, my gloves and jeans were frozen stiff as well. The story I told my mother was quite different from the truth. How could I explain something that even today I don't fully understand.

What I do understand is that the bustling life on that Thomaston ice pond is as fresh in my memory as if I had just been there. For me, it has become a metaphor, utopian perhaps, for the kind of convivial community that has largely disappeared from American life—at least the kind I am familiar with in our cities. I hope people still skate there in Thomaston, behind the stores on Highway 1.

—John McChesney, correspondent for National Public Radio, 1994

NORDIC SKIING

Most of the ski resorts listed above also offer cross-country skiing trails, as do many of the state parks and public reserved lands. For a listing of the public ones, write to the Bureau of Parks and Recreation, State House Station, Augusta, ME 04333. Here are a few especially popular sites, public and commercial.

Abnaki Ski Touring Trails. Pine Tree State Arboretum, Augusta 04330 (on east side of Hospital St.).

Acadia National Park. Box 177, Bar Harbor 04609; 288-3338.

Aroostook State Park. 87 State Park Rd., Presque Isle 04769; 289-3821.

Baxter State Park. 64 Balsam Dr., Millinocket 04462; 723-5140.

The Bethel Inn Ski Touring Center. Box 49, Broad St., Bethel 04217; 824-2175.

The Birches Cross Country Ski Area. On Moosehead Lake. Box 81, Rockwood 04478; 534-7305.

Bradbury Mountain State Park. Hallowell Rd. (Route 9), Pownal 04069; 688-4712.

Carrabassett Valley Ski Touring Center. Route 27, Carrabassett Valley 04947; 237-2205.

Carter's Farm Market Cross Country Ski Center. Route 26, Box 710, Oxford 04270; 539-4848.

Carter's X-C Ski Center. Middle Intervale Rd., Bethel 04217; 824-3880.

Cobscook Bay State Park. Dennysville 04628; 726-4412.

Gould Academy. Bethel 04217; 824-2161.

Katahdin Lake Wilderness Camps. T3R8 east of the park; P.O. Box 398, Millinocket 04462.

Lake St. George State Park. Liberty 04949; 589-4255.

Mt. Abram Ski Touring Center. Box 189, Locke Mills 04255; 875-2601.

Mt. Blue State Park. RR 1, Box 610, Center Hill Rd., Weld 04285; 585-2261.

North Woods Arts Center. P.O. Box 187, Dover-Foxcroft 04426; 564-3423.

Saddleback Ski Nordic Cross Country Center. P.O. Box 490, Rangeley 04970; 864-5671.

Samoset Ski Touring Center. P.O. Box 78, Rockport 04856; 594-2511.

Sebago Lake State Park. Off Route 302, Naples 04055; 693-6231.

Sunday River Cross Country Ski Center. Sunday River Skiway Rd., RFD 2, Box 1688, Bethel 04217; 824-2410.

Titcomb Mountain. Routes 4 and 27, Farmington 04938; 778-9031.

White Mountain National Forest. Evans Notch Ranger District, RFD 2, Box 2270, Bethel 04217; 824-2134.

Wolf Neck Woods State Park. Wolf Neck Rd., Freeport 04032. No phone in winter.

■ GOLF COURSES

Bangor: Bangor Municipal Golf Course. 27 holes. 278 Webster Ave.; 942-0232.

Bar Harbor: Bar Harbor Golf Course. 18 holes. Routes 3 and 204, Trenton; 667-7505.

Brunswick: Brunswick Golf Club. 18 holes. River Rd.; 725-8224.

Calais: St. Croix Golf Club. 9 holes. St. Croix River; 454-8875.

Kennebunkport: Cape Arundel Golf Club. 18 holes. Old River Rd.; 967-2125.

Old Orchard Beach: Old Orchard Beach Country Club. 9 holes. Route 98; 934-2188.

Orono: Penboscot Valley Country Club. 18 holes. 366 Main Rd.; 866-2060.

Portland: Riverside Municipal Courses. 2 Courses, 18 and 9 holes. 1158 Riverside (off exit 8); 797-3524/5588.

Rangeley: Mingo Springs Golf Course. 18 holes. Proctor Rd. off Route 4; 864-5021.

Rockport: Samoset Golf Course. 18 holes. Samoset Resort; 594-1431 or 594-2511.
Sugarloaf USA: Sugarloaf Golf Course. 18 holes. 237-2000.

■ SUMMER THEATERS

In summer, Maine offers a great variety of performances, from light musicals to experimental theater. Out of season, theaters in Portland and the college towns try to keep the flame alight. Here is a partial listing. Those starred are the ones that have proved consistently best.

Bangor: Penobscot Theatre Company. 942-3333.
Belfast: Iron Horse Dinner Theater. 525-0927.
Berwick: Hackmatack Playhouse. 698-1807.
Biddeford: Biddeford City Theater. 282-0849.
Blue Hill: The New Surry Theatre. 374-5057.
Brunswick: Maine State Music Theatre. Bowdoin College. 725-8769.
Brunswick:* The Theater Project. 729-8584.
Camden: Camden Opera House. 236-4866.
Castine: Cold Comfort Summer Theater. Maine Maritime Academy. 326-8830.
Damariscotta: Round Top Center for the Arts. 563-1507.
Eastport: Eastport Arts Center. 853-4166.
Ellsworth: Gilbert & Sullivan Society of Hancock County. 359-8935.
Hallowell: Gaslight Theater. 626-3698.
Leeds: Actor's Theater of Maine. 946-5049.
Monmouth:* The Theater at Monmouth. 939-9999.
Mount Desert Island: Acadia Repertory Theater. Somesville. 244-7260.
Ogunquit:* Ogunquit Playhouse. 646-5511.
Old Orchard Beach: Vintage Repertory Company. 828-4654.
Orono: Theatre of the Enchanted Forest. University of Maine. 581-1755.
Portland: Mad Horse Theatre. 797-3338.
Portland:* Portland Stage Company. 774-0465.
Presque Isle: Pioneer Playhouse. University of Maine at Presque Isle. 764-0311.
Rangeley: Rangeley Friends of the Performing Arts. 864-3311.
Skowhegan: Skowhegan Regional Theatre. 474-6710.
South Paris: Celebration Barn Theater. 743-8452.

■ TOURIST INFORMATION

STATEWIDE

Maine Publicity Bureau. Box 2300, Hallowell, 04347; 623-0363 or (800) 533-9595.

Maine Innkeepers Association. 305 Commercial St., Portland, 04101; 773-7670.

Department of Inland Fisheries and Wildlife. 284 State St., Augusta 04333; 289-2043.

REGIONAL

Androscoggin Country Chamber of Commerce. 179 Lisbon St., 04240; 783-2249.

Bar Harbor Chamber of Commerce. P.O. Box 158 (93 Cottage St.), 04609; 288-5103.

Bath Area Chamber of Commerce. 45 Front St., 04530; 443-9791.

Boothbay Harbor Region Chamber of Commerce. P.O. Box 356 (Route 27), 04538; 633-2353/4232.

Caribou Chamber of Commerce. P.O. Box 357 (111 High St.), 04736; 498-6156.

Carrabassett Valley. (see Sugarloaf)

Freeport Merchants Association. P.O. Box 452, 04032; 865-1212.

Greenville (see Moosehead Lake Region)

Kennebec Valley Chamber of Commerce. P.O. Box E (University Dr.), 04330; 623-4559.

Kennebunk-Kennebunkport Chamber of Commerce. P.O. Box 740 (Coopers Corner, Routes 35 & 9), 04043; 967-0857.

Machias Bay Area Chamber of Commerce. P.O. Box 606, 04654; 255-4402.

Moosehead Lake Region Chamber of Commerce. P.O. Box 581, 04441; 695-2702.

Mount Desert Island Chamber of Commerce. P.O. Box 675, 04662; 276-5040.

Northeast Harbor. (see Mount Desert)

Old Orchard Beach Chamber of Commerce. P.O. Box 600, (First St.), 04064; 934-2500.

Portland Convention and Visitors Bureau. 305 Commercial St., 04101; 772-5800.

Rangeley Lakes Region Chamber of Commerce. P.O. Box 317 (Main St.), 04970; 864-5571.

Sugarloaf Area Chamber of Commerce. P.O. Box 2151, 04947; 235-2100.

■ ANTIQUARIAN BOOKSELLERS

Maine is a good place for readers; the long winters and damp summers encourage people to stay near the woodstove with a good book. And Maine is a particularly good place for second-hand and antiquarian book dealers. Rents are low, large empty buildings abound, and each summer brings new customers. Here is a partial list of the members of the Maine Antiquarian Booksellers Association with shops on or near the U.S. 1 corridor. Call ahead for hours.

ACADIA AND DOWNEAST
Big Chicken Barn Books. Route 3, Ellsworth; 667-7308.
Dunn and Powell Books. The Hideaway, Bar Harbor; 288-4665.
Wikhegan Books. Main St., Northeast Harbor. Mount Desert; 276-5079/244-7060.

BELFAST AND ENVIRONS
The Booklover's Attic. Belfast; 338-2450.
Frederica de Beurs-Books. 42 Cedar St., Belfast; 338-4122.
Prescott Hill Books. Off Route 52, Belfast; 338-6346.
Victorian House/Book Barn. East Main St., Stockton Springs; 567-3351.

BRUNSWICK/BATH
Arrowsic Island Books & Prints. Old Stage Rd., Arrowsic; 443-1510.
The Book Exchange. Woolwich; 442-8188.
Edgecomb Book Barn. Cross Point Rd., North Edgecomb; 882-7278.
Elliott Healy. Middle St., Wiscasset; 882-5446.
F. Barrie Freeman-Rare Books. Quaker Point Farm, West Bath; 442-8452.
Gordon's Book Shop. 14 Center St., Brunswick; 725-2500.
Old Books. 136 Maine St., Brunswick; 725-4524.

CAMDEN
ABCDEF Bookstore. 23 Bay View St.; 236-3903.
The Dolphin Bookstore. 78 Elm St.; 236-3283.
Stone Soup Books. 35 Main St. No phone.

DEER ISLE AND ENVIRONS
Barbara Falk-Bookseller. Route 166A, Castine; 236-4036.

George and Patricia Fowler, Books. Reach Rd., HCR 64, Brooklin; 359-2070.
Bliss House Books. Pleasant St., Blue Hill; 374-2259.
Skeans & Clifford, Books. Main St., Deer Isle; 348-2660.
Wayward Books. Route 15, RFD 26B, Sargentville; 359-2397.
Stonington Book Store. 6 Main St., Stonington; 367-5821.

GARDINER/HALLOWELL
Bunkhouse Books. Route 5A, Gardiner; 582-2808.
Leon Tebbetts Bookstore. 164 Water St., Hallowell; 623-4670/626-5811.
Merrill's Bookshop. 108 Water St., Hallowell; 623-2055.

PORTLAND AND ENVIRONS
Allen Scott, Books. 89 Exchange St., Portland; 774-2190.
Lombard Antiquarian Maps and Prints. Cape Elizabeth; 799-1889.
Carlson and Turner Books. 241 Congress St., Portland; 773-4200.
Cunningham Books. Longfellow Square, 188 State St., Portland; 775-2246.
Emerson Booksellers. 420 Fore St., Portland; 874-2665.
Flynn Books. 466 Ocean Ave., Portland; 772-2685.
F. M. O'Brien, Antiquarian Bookseller. 38 High St., Portland; 774-0931.
Harding's Bookshop. 538 Congress St., Portland; 761-2150.
J. Glatter Books. 20 Danforth St., Portland; 773-4033.
Sumner & Stillman. Yarmouth; 846-6070.
YES Books. 20 Danforth St., Portland; 775-3233.

SACO/WELLS
A. David Paulhus, Books. Burnt Mill Rd., Wells; 646-7022.
The Arringtons. U.S. 1, Wells; 646-4124.
Austin's Antiquarian Books. Route 1, Wells; 646-4883.
The Book Barn. U.S. 1, Wells; 646-4926.
East Coast Books. Depot St., Wells; 646-3584.
F. P. Wood Books. 48 Ferry Rd., Saco; 282-2278.
Harding's Book Shop. U.S. 1, Wells; 646-8785.

YORK BEACH AND ENVIRONS
Books and Autographs. 287 Goodwin Rd., Eliot; 439-4739.
Samuel Weiser Books. York Beach; 363-7253.

RECOMMENDED READING

■ THE NATURAL WORLD

AMC Guide to Mount Desert and Acadia National Park. 5th ed. Boston: Appalachian Mountain Club Books, 1993. Essential for anyone hiking or canoeing on Mount Desert Island. Detailed trail descriptions, much nature lore, excellent map.

AMC River Guide: Maine. 2nd ed. Boston: Appalachian Mountain Club Books, 1991. Essential for anyone canoeing or kayaking on the state's rivers and lakes.

Clark, Stephen. *Katahdin: A Guide to Baxter State Park & Katahdin.* Unity, ME: North Country Press, 1985. Definitive guide to the wild Katahdin region.

Kendall, David L. *Glaciers & Granite: A Guide to Maine's Landscape and Geology.* Unity, ME: North Country Press, 1987. Detailed explanation for the non-specialist of why Maine looks the way it does.

Pierson, Elizabeth Cary and Jan Erik Pierson. *A Birder's Guide to the Coast of Maine.* Camden, ME: Down East Books, 1981. Definitive work on enjoying the state's coastal birdlife.

■ HISTORY

Brault, Gerard J. *The French-Canadian Heritage in New England.* Hanover, NH: University Press of New England, 1986. First comprehensive account of New England's third largest ancestry group.

Calhoun, Charles C., *A Small College in Maine: Two Hundred Years of Bowdoin.* Brunswick, ME: Bowdoin College Press, 1993. Almost as much about Maine as about its oldest college.

Calloway, Colin G. *Dawnland Encounters: Indians and Europeans in Northern New England.* Hanover, NH: University Press of New England, 1991. New scholarship presents the Native Americans, including the Abnaki, not as victims of colonization but as resourceful peoples quickly adapting to change.

Clark, Charles E. et al., (eds.). *Maine in the Early Republic: From Revolution to Statehood.* Hanover, NH: University Press of New England, 1988. Important collection of essays on Maine from the Revolution to 1820.

Duncan, Roger F. *Coastal Maine: A Maritime History.* New York: Norton, 1992. A popular history of how and why Mainers went to sea.

Giffen, Sarah L. and Kevin D. Murphy. (eds.), *"A Noble and Dignified Stream"*: *The Piscataqua Region in the Colonial Revival, 1860–1930*. York, ME: Old York Historical Society, 1992. Essays on the "invention" of traditional New England in the York and Portsmouth region.

Goldstein, Judith S. *Crossing Lines: Histories of Jews and Gentiles in Three Communities*. New York: William Morrow and Company, Inc., 1992. Comparative account of Jewish communities in Bangor, Calais, and Mount Desert Island.

Leamon, James S. *Revolution Down East: The War for American Independence in Maine*. Amherst, MA: University of Massachusetts Press, 1993. British raids, economic disruption, and near-civil war between loyalists and rebels in the District of Maine.

Morison, Samuel Eliot. *The Story of Mount Desert Island*. Boston: Little, Brown, 1960. Brief, charmingly written history by a longtime summer resident of Northeast Harbor.

Mundy, James H. *Hard Times, Hard Men: Maine and the Irish, 1830–1860*. Scarborough, ME: Harp Publications, 1990. Fleeing famine, Maine's Irish immigrants found jobs but had to fight religious and nativist prejudice.

Rolde, Neil. *Maine: A Narrative History*. Gardiner, ME: Tilbury House, 1990. Best popular history of the state in print.

Taylor, Alan. *Liberty Men and Great Proprietors*. Chapel Hill, NC: University of North Carolina Press, 1990. Backcountry civil war simmered from the 1780s until statehood in 1820 between absentee landowners and farmers squatting on what both claimed as their property.

Trulock, Alice Rains. *In the Hands of Providence: Joshua Lawrence Chamberlain and the American Civil War*. Chapel Hill, NC: University of North Carolina Press, 1991. Definitive biography of Maine's greatest Civil War hero and four-time governor.

Ulrich, Laurel Thatcher. *A Midwife's Tale: The Life of Martha Ballard, Based on Her Diary, 1785-1812*. New York: Alfred A. Knopf, Inc., 1990. Brilliant recreation of the world of a small Maine community (Hallowell-Augusta), based on a diary kept by its highly skilled midwife.

■ CLASSICS

Beston, Henry. *Northern Farm, A Chronicle of Maine.* Camden, ME: Down East Books, 1948. Lyrical record of a year on the farm near Nobleboro where the author and his wife Elizabeth Cotesworth lived.

Jewett, Sarah Orne. *The Country of the Pointed Firs and Other Stories.* New York: W. W. Norton, 1981. Available in many editions since its appearance in 1896. Quietly lyrical account of the "lost" world of pre-modern Maine, set on the coast near Tenants Harbor and Martinsville.

McCloskey, Robert. *Blueberries for Sal.* 1948. *One Morning in Maine.* 1952. New York: Viking Children's Books. Two classics for young readers, and their parents.

Moore, Ruth. *The Weir.* New York: William Morrow and Co., 1943. The story of a fishing family on Gott's Island, by the novelist (now unjustly neglected) who came the closest to capturing the reality of coastal life in the twentieth century.

Rich, Louise Dickinson. *We Took to the Woods.* New York: J. B. Lippincott Co., 1942. *My Neck of the Woods.* New York: J. B. Lippincott Co., 1942. A generation ahead of the counter-culture, the author went to live in Maine's northwestern forest.

Stowe, Harriet Beecher. *The Pearl of Orr's Island.* Hartford, CT: Stowe-Day Foundation 1979. An early attempt (1862) to convey Maine folkways (and Maine accents) in fiction.

Thoreau, Henry David. *The Maine Woods.* New York: Penguin Books, 1988. Many editions since its first, posthumous publication in 1864. This one from the Penguin Nature Library has a notable introduction by Edward Hoagland.

White, E. B. *Stuart Little.* New York: Harper & Brothers, 1945. *Charlotte's Web.* New York: Harper, 1952. *The Trumpet of the Swan.* New York: Harper & Row, 1970. Probably the most famous stories to have been written in Maine.

■ RECENT MAINE WRITING

A number of well-known writers today live or at least summer in Maine—Stephen King, James Michener, May Sarton, Elizabeth Hardwick, Philip Booth, Frances Fitzgerald—but the authors who follow have written perceptively about Maine and Mainers. For a more complete listing of Maine fiction in print, contact the Maine Writers & Publishers Alliance, 12 Pleasant St., Brunswick 04011; (207) 729-6333.

Chute, Carolyn. *The Beans of Egypt, Maine.* New York: Ticknor & Fields, 1985. Chute is to Maine's rural poor what Erskine Caldwell was to the South's earlier in the century. Incidentally, there is an Egypt, Maine—near Hancock—but Chute's is invented. More recent novels are *Letourneau's Used Auto Parts* (1988) and the well-regarded *Merry Men* (1994).

Grumbach, Doris. *Coming into the End Zone.* New York: W. W. Norton, 1991. An urbanite reflects on rural living in Maine's East Penobscot Bay region.

Johnston, Willis. *The Girl Who Would Be Russian and Other Stories.* San Diego: Harcourt Brace Jovanovich, 1986. Short stories about life in the Russian Orthodox community in and around Richmond, Maine.

McPhee, John. *The Survival of the Bark Canoe.* New York: Farrar, Straus, 1975. A twentieth-century writer takes to Maine's North Woods, traveling along its rivers and lakes with a canoe and the man who wrote it.

Melnicove, Mark. *Inside Vacationland: New Fiction from the Real Maine.* South Harpswell, ME: Dog Ear Press, 1985. A collection of stories designed to show how far the "real" Maine is from the "ideal" one of Robert P. T. Coffin and E. B. White.

Pelletier, Cathie. *The Bubble Reputation.* New York: Crown Publishers, 1993. The Carolyn Chute of far northern Maine, but with a much more manic sense of humor. Also, *The Funeral Makers* (1987) and *The Weight of Winter* (1991).

Phippen, Sanford. *The Police Know Everything: Downeast Stories.* Orono, ME: Puckerbrush Press, 1982. Wry, amusing, affectionate sketches of life in and around Hancock, Maine.

Snow, Wilbert. *Codline's Child: The Autobiography of Wilbert Snow.* Middletown, CT: Wesleyan Univ. Press, 1968. An honest and humorous portrait of a childhood in Maine.

■ THE VISUAL ARTS

Beem, Edgar Allen. *Maine Art Now.* Gardiner, ME: Dog Ear Press, 1990. Short essays on contemporary art in Maine by one of the state's leading cultural commentators. A worthy successor to Gertrude Mellon (ed.), *Maine and Its Role in American Art, 1740-1963.* New York: Viking Press, 1963.

Docherty, Linda J., et al. *The Legacy of James Bowdoin III.* Bowdoin College Museum of Art, 1994. Essays on Maine's early cultural history based on the collections of one of America's first great art patrons.

Skolnick, Arnold (ed.). *Paintings of Maine*. New York: Clarkson Potter, 1991. Best recent anthology of Maine landscape painting. Introduction by Carl Little.

■ OTHER USEFUL GUIDES

Acheson, James M. *The Lobster Gangs of Maine*. Hanover, NH: University Press of New England, 1988. An anthropologist's close study of the complex social and economic world of a very territorial trade.

Anderson, Will. *Was Baseball Really Invented in Maine?* Portland, ME: Will Anderson, Publisher, 1992. No, but there were an awful lot of Mainers who played in the majors.

Cross, Amy Willard. *The Summer House: A Tradition of Leisure*. New York: Harper Collins, 1992. Why do people go to such trouble and expense to summer in places like Maine? It all goes back to the Romans.

Duncan, Roger F. and John P. Ware. *A Cruising Guide to the New England Coast*. New York: G. P. Putnam's Sons, 1987. A classic. Intensely practical, but with lots of local lore. Wonderful bedtime reading in winter.

Fodor's Maine, Vermont, New Hampshire. Fodor's, New York: 1994.

Gould, John. *There Goes Maine!* New York: Norton, 1990.

Henderson, James S. (ed.). *The Maine Almanac*. Maine Times, 1994. Much data on the state, some useful, some quirky.

Isaacson, Dorris A. (ed.). *Maine: A Guide 'Down East'*. Courier-Gazette, Inc., Rockland, ME., 2nd ed., 1970. Updating of the 1937 edition published by the WPA's Federal Writers Project. Still the most comprehensive book on the state, though some of it is based more on local tradition than research.

Shain, Charles and Samuella. *The Maine Reader*. Boston: Houghton Mifflin Co., 1991. An anthology of writing about the state.

Steadman, Mimi, and Christina Tree. *Maine: An Explorer's Guide*. Woodstock, VT: Countrymen Press, 1993. There is simply no more useful and encyclopedic travel guide to the state than this one. A personal favorite.

The Maine Atlas and Gazetteer. Freeport, ME: DeLorme Publishing Co., 1993. Don't go anywhere without it.

Uhl, Michael. *Exploring Maine on Country Roads and Byways*. New York: Clarkson Potter, 1991. A personal account of touring Maine. Good for armchair traveling.

I N D E X

COMPASS AMERICAN GUIDES

Comprehensive, literate, and beautifully illustrated guides to the individual cities and states of the United States and Canada, Compass American Guides are unparalleled in their cultural, historical, and informational scope. They are to the 1990s what the WPA guidebook series was to the 1930s — insightful, resourceful, and entertaining.

"Each [Compass American Guide] pairs an accomplished photographer with a writer native to the state. The resulting pictures and words have such an impact I constantly had to remind myself I was reading a travel guide." — National Geographic Traveler

"Entertaining and well-illustrated with maps and photographs, in color and vintage black and white...good to read ahead of time, then take along so you don't miss anything." —San Diego Magazine

"You can read [a Compass American Guide] for information and come away entertained. Or you can read it for entertainment and come away informed . . . an informational jackpot." —Houston Chronicle

"Wickedly stylish writing!" —Chicago Sun-Times

Compass American Guides are available in general and travel bookstores, or may be ordered directly by calling 1-800-733-3000; or by sending a check or money order, including the cost of shipping and handling, payable to: Random House, Inc. 400 Hahn Road, Westminster, Maryland 21157. Books are shipped by USPS Book Rate (allow 30 days for delivery): $2.00 for the 1st book, $0.50 for each additional book. Applicable sales tax will be charged. All prices are subject to change. Or ask your bookseller to order for you.

"Books can make thoughtful (and sometimes even thought-provoking) gifts for incentive travel winners or convention attendees. A new series of guidebooks published by Compass American Guides is right on the mark." —Successful Meetings magazine

Consider Compass American Guides as gifts or incentives for VIP's, employees, clients, customers, convention and meeting attendees, friends and others. Compass American Guides are available at special discounts for bulk purchases (100 copies or more) for sales promotions or premiums. Special editions, including personalized covers, excerpts of existing guides, and corporate imprints, can be created in large quantities for special needs. For more information, write to Special Marketing, Fodor's Travel Publications, 201 E. 50th St., New York, NY 10022; or call 800/800-3246. Inquiries from the United Kingdom should be sent to Fodor's Travel Publications, 20 Vauxhall Bridge Rd., London, England SW1V 2SA.

CHICAGO
1st Edition
Author
Jack Schnedler
Photographer
Zbigniew Bzdak
1-878-86728-8

$16.95 Paper 288 pp.
($22.50 Canada)

Also available in a hardcover
edition:
1-878-86729-6
$24.95 ($31.50 Canada)

"Great to send to anyone coming to Chicago for the first time, or anyone who left town before Wrigley Field got lights." —*Chicago Sun-Times*

LAS VEGAS
3rd Edition
Author
Deke Castleman
Photographer
Michael Yamashita
1-878-86736-9

$16.95 Paper 304 pp.
($22.50 Canada)

"Visiting this neon oasis has been made much more interesting thanks to Deke Castleman's *Las Vegas*." —*Travel & Leisure*

LOS ANGELES
1st Edition
Author
Gil Reavill
Photographer
Mark S. Wexler
1-878-86717-2

$14.95 Paper 324 pp.
($19.95 Canada)

Also available in a hardcover
edition:
1-878-86725-3
$22.95 ($29.00 Canada)

"No cinephile should head out L.A. way without a copy of *Los Angeles*." —*New York Daily News*

NEW ORLEANS
1st Edition
Author
Bethany Ewald Bultman
Photographer
Richard Sexton
1-878-86739-3

$16.95 Paper 304 pp.
($21.95 Canada)

Also available in a hardcover
edition:
1-878-86740-7
$24.95 ($31.50 Canada)

Vibrant photography and jaunty commentary guide travelers through the heart and soul of sizzling New Orleans.

SAN FRANCISCO & THE BAY AREA
2nd Edition
Author
Barry Parr
Photographer
Michael Yamashita
1-878-86716-4

$14.95 Paper 396 pp.
($19.95 Canada)

"*San Francisco* tackles the 'why' of travel to that city as well as the nitty gritty details." — *Travel Weekly*

CANADA
1st Edition
Author
Garry Marchant
Photographer
Ken Straiton
1-878-86712-1

$14.95 Paper 320 pp.
($19.95 Canada)

"*Canada* goes a long way in presenting this country in all its complex, beautiful glory." — *Toronto Sun*

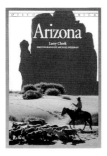

ARIZONA
2nd Edition
Author
Lawrence Cheek
Photographer
Michael Freeman
1-878-86732-6

$16.95 Paper 288 pp.
($22.50 Canada)

"This is my kind of guidebook."
—David Laird, *Books of the Southwest*

COLORADO
2nd Edition
Author
Jon Klusmire
Photographer
Paul Chesley
1-878-86735-0

$16.95 Paper 320 pp.
($22.50 Canada)

"A literary, historical and near-sensory excursion across the state."   —*Denver Post*

MONTANA
1st Edition
Author
Norma Tirrell
Photographer
John Reddy
1-878-86710-5

$14.95 Paper 304 pp.
($19.95 Canada)

Also available in a hardcover edition:
1-878-86713-X
$22.95   ($29.00 Canada)

"The most comprehensive guide to the state...will have you ready and rarin' to go." — *Travel & Leisure*

NEW MEXICO
1st Edition
Author
Nancy Harbert
Photographer
Michael Freeman
1-878-86706-7

$15.95 Paper 288 pp.
($19.95 Canada)

Also available in a hardcover edition:
1-878-86722-9 $22.95
($29.00 Canada)

"Bold yet artful in its photography. "

— *Albuquerque Journal*

UTAH
2nd Edition
Authors
Tom & Gayen Wharton
Photographer
Tom Till
1-878-86731-8

$16.95 Paper 352 pp.
($22.50 Canada)

"The jaunty text and eye-popping photos make this a keeper."   —*Deseret News*

Winner of the Rocky Mountain Book Publishers' Award for Best Guidebook

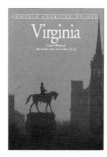

VIRGINIA
1st Edition
Author
K.M. Kostyal
Photographer
Medford Taylor
1-878-86741-5

$16.95 Paper 320 pp.
($21.50 Canada)

Also available in a hardcover edition:
1-878-86742-3 $24.95
($31.50 Canada)

"History haunts Virginia like a lost lover," writes author Kostyal in this fascinating guide to the history and culture of Virginia.

HAWAI'I
1st Edition
Author
Moana Tregaskis
Photographers
Wayne Levin & Paul Chesley
1-878-86723-7

$15.95 Paper 364 pp.
($19.95 Canada)

Also available in a hardcover
edition:
1-878-86724-5
$22.95 ($29.00 Canada)

"A fine guide and a welcome addition to travel
collections."   *—Library Journal*

1993 Award of Merit—Hawai'i Visitors Bureau

MAINE
1st Edition
Author
Charles Calhoun
Photographer
Thomas Szelog
1-878-86751-2

$16.95 Paper 304 pp.
($21.50 Canada)

Also available in a hardcover
edition:
1-878-86752-0 $24.95
($31.50 Canada)

The leaves of this book display photographs as colorful
as Fall in Maine, and the narrative is entertaining and
informative to travelers and natives alike.

OREGON
1st Edition
Author
Judy Jewell
Photographer
Greg Vaughn
1-878-86733-4

$16.95 Paper 320 pp.
($21.50 Canada)

Also available in a hardcover
edition:
1-878-86734-2
$24.95 ($31.50 Canada)

Special emphasis on outdoor recreation and natural
resources highlights this first edition celebrating
Oregon's magnificent landscape.

SOUTH DAKOTA
1st Edition
Author
Tom Griffith
Photographer
Paul Horsted
1-878-86726-1

$16.95 Paper 304 pp.
($21.50 Canada)

Also available in a hardcover
edition:
1-878-86727-X
$24.95 ($31.50 Canada)

The first illustrated guide to explore the hidden
wonders, colorful characters, and legends of the Land
of Infinite Variety—South Dakota.

WISCONSIN
1st Edition
Author
Tracy Will
Photographer
Zane Williams
1-878-86744-X

$16.95 Paper 304 pp.
($21.50 Canada)

Also available in a hardcover
edition:
1-878-86745-8
$24.95 ($31.50 Canada)

Wisconsinite Tracy Will recounts the history and the
peopling of the state from its first inhabitants, the
Chippewa and Dakota Sioux, to the Scandinavian
pioneers of the 19th century.

WYOMING
1st Edition
Author
Nathaniel Burt
Photographer
Don Pitcher
1-878-86704-1

$14.95 Paper 396 pp.
($19.95 Canada)

Also available in a hardcover
edition:
1-878-86703-2
$22.95 ($29.00 Canada)

"Their mixture of anecdotes, history, and beautiful
photographs provide a genuine taste of the 'Wild
West.'"   *— Library Journal*

■ ABOUT THE AUTHOR

Charles Calhoun grew up in Monroe, Louisiana, studied history at the University of Virginia, and went on to study law as a Rhodes Scholar at Christ Church, Oxford. After a newspaper career in South Florida, he moved in 1981 to Maine, where he has written and lectured on Civil War history and other topics. He edited *Bowdoin* magazine for seven years, and in 1993 published *A Small College in Maine: Two Hundred Years of Bowdoin.* He now works in the field of education reform in Portland, and reports that he lives in "genteel shabbiness" in his 200-year-old house in Topsham, a link between his Southern roots and his New England domicile.

■ ABOUT THE PHOTOGRAPHER

Thomas Mark Szelog specializes in photojournalism. His images have been widely exhibited in museums and galleries and have been published both in the United States and abroad. He has also won numerous awards for his work. Szelog with the assistance of his wife, Lee Ann, is developing a major body of color work exploring the beauty, romance, and adventure of living in a lighthouse. He resides at Marshall Point Lighthouse in Port Clyde, Maine, which allows him a thorough photographic understanding of these quintessential symbols of Maine.